AFRICAN-
AMERICAN
SCREEN-
WRITERS
NOW

AFRICAN-AMERICAN SCREEN-WRITERS NOW

Conversations with Hollywood's Black Pack

by ERICH LEON HARRIS

SILMAN-JAMES PRESS
Los Angeles

2/97

34283986

First Edition
10 9 8 7 6 5 4 3 2 1

Library of Congress Cataloging-in-Publication Data

ISBN: 1-879505-28-2

Cover design by Heidi Frieder

Printed and bound in the United States of America

Silman-James Press
1181 Angelo Drive
Beverly Hills, CA 90210

*In loving memory of Delma Lillie Gates,
whose legacy and laughter live within me.*

Contents

Acknowledgments

I must first thank God, who makes all things possible. Heartfelt appreciation to my family and extended family who have always nurtured my dreams. To Gwen Feldman, the Godmother of this project, whose support and enthusiasm have been constant. To Jim Fox, a brilliant and patient editor. Much love to Kevin Davey for his extensive red-pen work. Thanks to Gregory Zabilski Photography. Lowell Steiger, friend and advisor. Audrey Wells, my heroine, my mentor, *mon amie*. To Guy Chateau, Randall K. Skolnik, and David Colden for being there from the very beginning.

And finally, to the writers. It is my hope that your words will serve as a source of pride and empowerment for all who read them.

Introduction

Ever since D.W. Griffith made *Birth of a Nation* in 1915, blacks have been represented in American films in one form or another. Unfortunately, we have had very little creative input into the way our culture has been represented on the screen until recently. Even less has been written about the African-American experience in American filmmaking. It is in this spirit that I feel compelled to expand the scope of this literature by creating *African-American Screenwriters Now*.

The genesis of this project came after I had the opportunity to read William Froug's *The Screenwriter Looks at the Screen Writer* and *The New Screenwriter Looks at the New Screenwriter*. These books inspire young writers through personal interviews with established screenwriters. Both works, published by Silman-James Press, stand head and shoulders above similar books. Mr. Froug has presented engaging and compelling interviews that spend a good deal of time exploring each writer's process. My only critique was that there were no writers of color included. I wished that there was someone whom I could identify with in more than just general terms.

Not being the type of person who sits around wishing, I submitted a proposal and was fortunate to have been commissioned by the good folk at Silman-James Press to create this collection of full-length interviews with some of the hottest emerging screenwriters of color. Using Mr. Froug's work as a paradigm, *African-American Screenwriters Now* explores the art, craft, and commerce of professional screenwriting today.

The selected writers represent a broad cross-section of the African-American film and television community. They encompass independent and studio feature writers, men and women, established and emerging talent. Not surprisingly, many of these writers also act, direct, and produce their own work.

In addition to discussing breaking into and surviving inside the screen trade, each writer's specific body of work and screenwriting techniques are explored. I have given special consideration to the discussion of the collaborative nature of film and television production.

To gain a greater perspective on the business aspects of this business, I have also included interviews with Jeanne Williams, a literary agent with International Creative Management, and Carol Munday Lawrence, Chairperson of the Black Writers Committee at the WGA, west.

The forum was candid, face-to-face discussions held either in the screenwriter's office, the studio, or a place of the writer's choosing. Hence, the tone of the interviews is relaxed and conversational.

You will find photographs of most of the writers taken in their workspace. My intention was twofold. First, I think that when a young writer can look upon another writer and say, "She wears glasses, just like I do," or "He has nappy hair, just like I do," or "She works on a Macintosh, just like I do," he or she can then personalize their experience of these interviews. My idea was to provide young writers with what I am calling a "vicarious mentor," someone whose career they can emulate and be inspired by. Second, I wanted to learn how to operate an antique Eastar camera that I only recently had acquired. I owe a real debt of gratitude to the writers who were more than patient with my questions, my extensive lightmeter readings, and my fumbling with the focus and f-stops of my completely manual two-and-a-quarter format camera.

As a young African-American screenwriter, I feel uniquely qualified to bring the experiences of my often forgotten peers to other young writers who hunger to find role models in the field. This work also offers a chance for the established writers to return advice to the community from which they emerged.

This, in essence, is the book that I wished I had when I was studying film in college. I hope it serves you well.

Erich Leon Harris
Los Angeles, CA
18 December 1995

DWAYNE JOHNSON-COCHRAN

*"If you're interested in cinema,
you'll write what you like."*

M ore prolific than a prison poet, Dwayne Johnson-Cochran
writes in a tiny alcove in his otherwise spacious Beverly
Hills apartment. A Nike poster hangs above his desk remind-
ing him to "Just Do It." It's a slogan he has apparently taken to
heart.

Of all the writers interviewed for this project, Dwayne
seems to be the busiest. He boasts of completing six full-
length features in a single year, three of which sold for six
figures. His spec script *My Tribe Is Lost* was one of the first
acquisitions of the newly formed multimedia company
Dreamworks.

Dwayne's hazel eyes shine with a steely determination.
You will find him to be an intelligent, articulate man with a
strong, clear voice, focus, and a high level of motivation.

HARRIS: I have been looking forward to meeting you because so many people already know and like your work.

JOHNSON-COCHRAN: I think my writing speaks for itself. A lot of people know my work from scripts I've written. I've only worked on one TV show that was produced, *Angel Street*, for Warner Bros. and CBS. I also co-created a sitcom, *Minor Adjustments*, for NBC. I'm not sure whether it's still on the air because I don't work on it.

HARRIS: What was the show about?

JOHNSON-COCHRAN: It was on in 1992-93 and starred Robin Givens. She was a detective. John Wells, who now produces *ER,* was the executive producer. I was very happy that I did it because I had never before written anything for TV.

HARRIS: Was it a sixty-minute format?

JOHNSON-COCHRAN: Yes, a sixty-minute drama.

HARRIS: I've always liked that format. Structuring the story around the commercials.

JOHNSON-COCHRAN: Yes, you write for that break. That thirty-minute break and that fifteen-minute kicker. That forty-five-minute kicker and that ten-minute dénouement. All of the scripts are like that. The thing that I learned was that John Wells is an expert at that type of writing. He tried to make everybody else on the show an expert at it. He'd say, "I'll give you ten days to write this script." The real surprise is how good the writing can be.

HARRIS: You really hear the clock ticking.

JOHNSON-COCHRAN: It's good because you're working all night. You pitch your show, you write your treatment in a day or two. It's approved. You write your script in a few days. It's approved with notes. You redo it. It's approved again. That show had to be written in ten days. Sixty pages in ten days.

HARRIS: That's a wonderful discipline. It sounds frightening, but the best thing about writing in film school was that sense of urgency. It's so easy to do anything but write.

JOHNSON-COCHRAN: Tell me about it. Last year I literally wrote six full-length feature films because I had that training from television. The year before that, I wrote three. Every year I said that I would write two or three. But last year I wrote six, and three of them sold. So it really worked for me. It was tough. I would disconnect the phone. I would be up all night. I was determined to get it done, and at the end of the day I had something.

HARRIS: You must not be married.

JOHNSON-COCHRAN: No, I'm not married. And last year, I didn't have a girlfriend, so I did what I had to do. This year the writing has gotten better.

HARRIS: Who are some of your favorite filmmakers?

JOHNSON-COCHRAN: Truffaut particularly, Kurosawa, also Sidney Lumet. I am a big fan of Carl Franklin, a big fan of Stephen Frears. I like a dynamic visual style. Milos Forman. I can't identify anybody in Hollywood right now, except maybe Gus Van Sant. I think he has an incredible vision as a writer-director. He's out there. Those are the people I like. They push the envelope. They tell stories that they want to tell. Even if they adapt a novel, they make it their own. They mine the work.

HARRIS: What do you think about the black pack?

JOHNSON-COCHRAN: I think the black pack, if you want to call it that, is a good thing. We have to have our niche, where a bunch of people are making our movies right now. In 1986, *She's Gotta Have It* came out. Before that, there was nothing really going on. I think Spike was and still is the hero of modern-day African-American cinema.

HARRIS: You've sold a spec script to Dreamworks. Tell us how that came about.

JOHNSON-COCHRAN: It's called *My Tribe Is Lost*. It's mostly based on events that happened to myself, my parents, and my best friend. It's set in 1969 Chicago and is essentially a coming-of-age story. I think that black films in America haven't told too many stories that black kids can attach themselves to. The surprise, I believe, will be that white kids will see this film and say, "Hey, this story speaks to me, too."

HARRIS: Isn't a good story universal?

JOHNSON-COCHRAN: Exactly. When Steven Spielberg read it, I'm sure there were a couple of things that were in his mind. I heard that he adopted a son who is black. I had heard, and who knows if this is true, that Steven said that he couldn't find any movies that his son, who is eight years old now, would want to see. He said that this movie is one that his son would want to see. That might have something to do with why he bought it. It sounds selfish, but it's to his advantage and maybe to the world's advantage.

HARRIS: I think that a good story will transcend all of the politics of race. How else can you explain why black people go to the movies twice as much per capita, yet the representation of people of color on the screen is so poor?

JOHNSON-COCHRAN: The thing about films in general is that they attract everybody, and black folks love them. We go see those images, and we love to see ourselves in them. Filmmakers like Spike and Carl want to do something that reflects how they were raised and have people connect to that experience. I think people want to find a way to connect, so I wrote a film that makes them connect—connect to the community in a story that's universal. Spielberg bought it in 1994, and in May of 1995 I did the rewrites. And two weeks ago, they green-lit the film, based on the rewrites. I got help from director Rusty Cundieff.

HARRIS: You're working with Rusty? Excellent.

JOHNSON-COCHRAN: Yes, Rusty is attached as a director and Tammy Hoffs is a producer. Actually, her nephew Jason Hoffs took it to Steven. It was weird. Jason had the script in his hand the day *Schindler's List* opened. He told me, "I read the script and I love it, but Steven's mind is on this movie. He cannot hear a pitch, he cannot read a script." From that point in November until the Academy Awards, all I would say to Jason was, "Let Steven read it. Let Steven read it." That went on until the Friday after the Academy Awards. He read the script at twelve o'clock, and by four o'clock he had bought it. He had to get everything off his plate before he could focus on something new. I think that the sensitivity that he has, having made films about young people growing up in America, made him a perfect candidate for a film like this. So I'm very happy he bought it, and we'll see what happens.

HARRIS: What's the premise of the film?

JOHNSON-COCHRAN: It's about what happens when this kid from a black community, me, moves into a predominantly white community. In 1969 in Chicago, there was neighborhood busting, panic buying, and white flight was just starting up. All these things were going on. I meet this kid who is the baddest kid I had ever met, who did some shit you wouldn't believe. And I loved him. I was in awe. It was like the Green Lantern meets Flash. He was like a super-hero to me. He was the same height as I was, but he was fearless and he was always saying, "I'm a black man, I'm a black man." A young kid, twelve years old in 1969, saying all of this. My parents would always say "colored people" this and "colored people" that, and he would always correct them. "Don't say colored, say black!"

HARRIS: He put you right back in touch with your identity.

JOHNSON-COCHRAN: He did! And he opened the eyes of my mother, my father, my sisters, and my brothers. I was twelve years old at that time. I could be influenced by almost anything.

HARRIS: What do you say to people who think that they can conduct film business outside of Hollywood?

JOHNSON-COCHRAN: I do not think that you can conduct film business living anywhere else. You have to be here to do that. You have to pitch your movies and you have to write your movies here. Conducting business takes personal contact. People have to see you, they have to know you, they have to like you. They have to like that you have a point of view. They have to see the work. You cannot be a phantom in the dark—you can't be J.D. Salinger, who wrote a few books and then no one saw him anymore. If you want to be a writer in Hollywood, you have to be there so they can talk to you about it. If you're not writing in Hollywood, your name has to be big enough that you can be asked back: "Please come here and take another pitch meeting," or "Please come here so we can pitch something to you." That means that you have achieved a level of writing ability that is wanted, as opposed to you just wanting.

HARRIS: How long have you been here?

JOHNSON-COCHRAN: I'll have been here four years as of March third. The reason I remember that date is because I drove into town on the day Rodney King was beaten.

HARRIS: Welcome to L.A. Please drive carefully, or we'll beat your ass.

JOHNSON-COCHRAN: No doubt.

HARRIS: Was yours the classic story of rolling into town with a duffel bag full of dreams and a Remington typewriter?

JOHNSON-COCHRAN: No, mine was a very different story than that. There was a time in 1990 when I was a producer for WTTW in Chicago. I produced documentaries and public-interest shows for the PBS station. I produced, directed, and wrote. I always wanted to be here, but I never wanted to come here unless I was asked, because everyone in Hollywood has a script in their desk or in the trunk of their car. Cab drivers have one. I never wanted to be a guy who is out here suffering and trying to find an agent. So I said, "I'll never go unless I am asked."

HARRIS: That's a smart move.

JOHNSON-COCHRAN: It's been my move since I started working in film back in Chicago. I had been in advertising, and I had made documentary films. People would say, "Dwayne, you have all of these ideas, why don't you go to L.A.?" I had applied to Sundance and had never gotten in, but I knew I could make it here. While I was working for PBS, I wrote a script called *The Car Thief*, which was a remake of *The Bicycle Thief*, the Italian classic. I loved the film and wrote it as basically an urban drama about a black man who returns to his family after having left them. The family didn't want him back. So, to prove that he was a good man, he gets a job as a car messenger. They love him, but the son, who belongs to a gang and has lost some drugs or money, undermines him by getting the car stolen. The father has to go out with his son to find the car. The son misdirects him because he knows that it was his gang that took the car. It destroys the family, and right when the father is about to leave, just like in the original film, the son admits that he had the car stolen. So father and son go off to get the car. That was my first script.

HARRIS: A beautiful story.

JOHNSON-COCHRAN: It's written in the way we speak. Especially the people on the west side of Chicago. It's a desperate script. The father wants his family to love him, he wants his car returned, and he wants his son to talk to him. I sent the script to a couple of producers in New York, but we didn't see eye-to-eye on how to make the film and things moved slowly. I had friend who said, "Why don't you send your scripts to a few agents whom I know?" Well, they weren't friends, they weren't people he knew, they were names he had heard. I sent the scripts anyway. Well, Jennifer Billings at CAA read the script and gave it to some other assistants, who all read it. They called me up and said, "We read your script, we love it. Who else in town has read it?" I said, "About thirty or forty people in Chicago." She said "No, no, no, no, no. In this town? This is the only town that counts! Can you come out to L.A.?" I said, sure.

HARRIS: Right away.

JOHNSON-COCHRAN: Well, it took about three or four weeks for the senior agent to read it. But I didn't antagonize them or get them mad, because if you get someone like an assistant mad, they cut you off. They'll say, "We don't want you over here." This was CAA, a big agency. So I played the game. Their game was: "We don't know if we want to represent you. Yeah, we're going to read the script. Yeah, blah, blah, blah. We're just not sure." I said, "Well, Triad read the script and they loved it. They want me to come out tomorrow." "Oh really? Okay." They read it overnight. Then I told Triad the same thing and they read it overnight. All of a sudden, three agencies were vying for me because I had said the magic words: "Somebody else wants to represent me." That makes agents go ga-ga. So I came out, I met with CAA, and I signed with them. They got me about thirty meetings in five days.

HARRIS: Thirty meetings?

JOHNSON-COCHRAN: I was getting lost all over L.A. I didn't know where I was going. But I got two writing assignments out of those thirty meetings. That's how I started.

HARRIS: Not small victories.

JOHNSON-COCHRAN: Yeah. I quit my job at PBS because I had a movie to write at Fox and a movie to write at Warner Bros. in about a week.

HARRIS: But you were already seasoned in terms of taking care of business and the discipline of writing. I don't want the kids at home to think that Dwayne just showed up and got paid.

JOHNSON-COCHRAN: Absolutely. I had been working in the film business, writing commercials and documentary films for at least eight years before I came out here. So I had a seasoned ability to get things done and a discipline for writing. What also helped me was college. The things you do there teach you how to do it, how to get it done on time.

HARRIS: Do you think young writers should go to film school?

JOHNSON-COCHRAN: No, I don't think so, not writers.

HARRIS: I disagree. If only for things like learning structure and discipline.

JOHNSON-COCHRAN: I think school gives you discipline. Not film school. I got discipline because I went to a university. Just the idea of somebody saying, "I need a paper by Friday. I want it concise, I want it about something, I want it to make sense, and I want your ideas in it." That can be translated to poetry or songwriting or short-story writing or film. I do think that you are right about film school. They put you in a place where you are completely immersed in film. You are seeing films all of the time. You're talking film all of the time. If someone's not into movies, they're not going to do that. They'll be writing short stories, writing poetry, or writing songs. Film school captivates you with the world of film. I was so captivated by films that I saw 2,500 movies between the ages of twenty-one and twenty-four. That was my film school, just watching films that I paid to see.

HARRIS: How did you come to that number?

JOHNSON-COCHRAN: I counted. I sometimes saw three films a day. From Kurosawa to Ozu to Goddard to Truffaut to Bergman to Tarkovsky to Ray, Nicholas and Satyajit, to Wenders to Ford. Everybody, anybody, all the time. So I had my language down to put on the page by the time I started writing.

HARRIS: I want to ask you some craft questions. When you're working, do you work from a paradigm, with clear act breaks?

JOHNSON-COCHRAN: Well, there is that paradigm that Hollywood sets upon you. That thirty-page act-break thing and that mid-second-act thing.

HARRIS: Do you work like that?

JOHNSON-COCHRAN: Sometimes there are scripts where I do not work like that. I decided that I would sometimes let the story tell itself, to work organically. Those scripts have been equally successful in terms of the writing. There has been no big change on page thirty, no new character is brought in on page thirty. On page forty-five, maybe something strange happens. I just finished a project for Touchstone where I had to have a major change on page thirty. That's how most major studios want things to happen in films that are assignments. In assignment writing, you're more obliged to write from a paradigm—three acts with turning points and foreshadowing, the basic techniques that people need to see in film writing.

HARRIS: Do you set up the work from treatments and scene cards?

JOHNSON-COCHRAN: I outline and make treatments. I have part of a treatment here. [He pulls out a folded sheet of paper.] This is part of a political thriller that I'm working on now. I had to fax part of it, so I have it here. Basically, when I write a script, every plot point plays out in two or three scenes. I just check them off as I go. And add elements as I go.

HARRIS: That's an interesting tool. It's funny, I was trying to trim down a treatment to send in to the screenwriting workshop at Sundance, and I was having some trouble because I overwrite. It almost doesn't matter because they'll never pick a writer from L.A. It's worse than the lottery.

JOHNSON-COCHRAN: It's very political now. I did it for two or three years in a row, and I have some personal irony connected with it. The picks they make for the workshops are not necessarily about the work. It's just as political as Hollywood is. It used to be about the obscure writer from Nobodytown, Iowa, who gets brought in and established in Hollywood. Now it is certain writers from L.A. with certain agents. A phone call gets made to the right people at Sundance, and those selections get made.

That's how it is. I think being in L.A. has hurt my chances there. When I was in Chicago and I sent my first script, I placed in the top ten, but was cut out at seven. I stopped wasting my time. I got my own personal revenge this year after they sent me a letter saying, thanks, but no thanks on *My Tribe Is Lost*. It arrived on the same day that Amblin called and said they wanted to buy it.

HARRIS: Ha!

JOHNSON-COCHRAN: It's not that I don't think that Sundance is a fine organization, because I do. I was just tired of feeling like I was banging my head against the wall when I knew that I was doing good work.

HARRIS: I think that whenever a writer or director emerges from middle America, as opposed to the coasts, there's a lot more celebration. It's as if the kids from Iowa have no film grammar, when every town has cable TV and Block-buster video now.

JOHNSON-COCHRAN: Yes, we're all on the same page now. No one has less of a film grammar anymore. It's all wide open.

HARRIS: But to be fair, a clique is only horrible when you're standing outside of it.

JOHNSON-COCHRAN: True, and I was happy to make it to the final round. The reality is that out of thousands and thousands of entries, it all comes down to a subjective choice.

HARRIS: Do you see the character first or the story, or is it different every time out?

JOHNSON-COCHRAN: It's different every time out. I'll see a person standing on a bus stop, like I did today. I saw this woman sitting on the bus bench. Her face was imperfect, her hair was tossed, her dress was sort of frazzled, and I saw a story in her. But sometimes I'll write in terms of story first. What if? What if? What if?

HARRIS: Do you read many screenplays?

JOHNSON-COCHRAN   No. It doesn't really help me. I had to read other writers for *Angel Street*, to see who they would hire to freelance. I had a tough time reading those scripts because I had to stop writing to read. I had to absorb someone else's tone. It was hard. I've got to do my work. It's hard to read novels now, because of all the work you feel you have to get done. William Goldman's *Adventures in the Screen Trade* and *The Craft of Screenwriting* are two of my favorite books. Reading Paddy Chayefsky really made me want to be a writer. Here's a guy who got his name on top of the credits. Paddy Chayefsky's *Network.* That shows the writer is elevated to the point of being the artist. He had something to do with every facet of the production.

HARRIS: How do you decide that an idea is strong enough to justify spending months writing the screenplay?

JOHNSON-COCHRAN: That's the sixty-four-thousand-dollar question. That's a really tough one, because I have four or five treatments on the table. Specs that I can knock out in the next few months.

HARRIS: How long does it take you to write a spec script?

JOHNSON-COCHRAN: About a month and a half to two months, if I really concentrate. But that's a really good question. Take *My Tribe Is Lost,* for instance. I was working on *Angel Street,* and downtime was rare. What we would do is sit around and talk about projects. Things we wanted to write.

HARRIS: Sort of riffing, like jazz musicians?

JOHNSON-COCHRAN: Exactly. I remember that we were all sitting in the room, and I was telling them the story of my family. I would tell about people on my block, funny little things, and this and that. They said, "You better write that as a movie." I never wrote a treatment and I never wrote an outline. I just sat down when the show ended and wrote the script in twelve days. Since it was coming out of a true situation, it just flowed right out of me. That was a unique situation. Right now I have three or four treatments on the table that I know are good stories. Which one do I give the time to? Which one is worth my time? I think it has to come down to how strong your story is. The characters are one thing, but can you sit there everyday and come up with another wild story element? How many times can you turn that story over and over and over again to make it come to life? That's how I tell if I'm going to write that script on spec.

HARRIS: How many pages do you aim for in a spec?

JOHNSON-COCHRAN: I aim for 125, and then I try to come down to 115.

HARRIS: How many drafts do you do before you show the work to someone?

JOHNSON-COCHRAN: I'm nervous, so I show it immediately to people who I know are critical, but gentle. I don't give it to too many writers, because they are so busy writing that they don't want to read mine and I don't want to read theirs. Writers don't even want to talk about their work. They want to talk about who that pretty girl was you were with. And did they pay you yet? "Good job, now let's play some racquetball."

HARRIS: I'm lucky because there are a couple of people I can trust to tell me when my work is good and when it sucks.

JOHNSON-COCHRAN: Only a good friend will do that for you.

HARRIS: What advice would you give a writer choosing an agent?

JOHNSON-COCHRAN: Choosing and getting are very different. You choose your second agent, you get your first one. I'm trying to get agents for two friends of mine. It's hard as hell. Their writing is superlative, wonderful work, but the agents who I've sent the work have not read it and have not responded. It's hard for agents to read unsolicited material that other people can't say is good. Now, if I was Jeffrey Boam, the agent would say, "I'll read it tomorrow." I'm not at that level yet. I think after the Dreamworks thing happens, they'll read everything. But forget all of that for a minute. I didn't have any connections when I started. I didn't have any friends in the business. I knew a guy who had three names. I sent them a full letter with a good script. They read me and I got lucky. Actually, an assistant read it and passed it on. She felt the writing was strong enough in the first ten pages to read on. That's a very important point for new writers who want anyone to read their work. If the first ten pages aren't knocking them out, they won't go on. Jennifer Billings, who read my first work, said that she read the first ten pages and was really moved by them. That's a key thing for anybody who's starting to write in Hollywood.

HARRIS: How much did you make on your first script?

JOHNSON-COCHRAN: My first job was an assignment. I think I made scale. My first spec script sold for just under a hundred thousand.

HARRIS: And your price has gone up from there. How much did you get from the Dreamworks deal?

JOHNSON-COCHRAN: I really don't want to talk about that one, but it was sweet.

HARRIS: Fair enough. You've been purely a writer. Do you hope to direct?

JOHNSON-COCHRAN: Actually, I'm purely a director who writes. I've directed a number of commercials and documentaries. And I just directed a short film that I wrote called *The Last Set*. It's a jazz movie that takes place in Chicago. It's about two days in the life of a jazz musician who's invited to go to Paris to play a tour. I'm very excited about it. I hope to take it around to film festivals, and possibly pitch a series to Showtime.

HARRIS: It's good to see you putting your money right back into projects close to your heart.

JOHNSON-COCHRAN: Not only my own projects, but if someone I know, someone whom I respect, needs some money, I will put money into their project. I know that putting money or resources in some talented person's hands will always pay dividends back to me.

HARRIS: What words of encouragement can you offer young black writers?

JOHNSON-COCHRAN: My words of encouragement to black writers who are writing films for the American or the world market is to watch as many films about the world, including your world, as you can. That will give you the language you need. Because if someone leaves the theater laughing, or leaves the theater crying, that's the effect you want. If they leave the theater confused or not affected, that's not the thing you want. World cinema will give you that language. The other thing is to write all the time. I don't say to write every day, but as much as you can. If you don't write, you can't get better.

HARRIS: Do you see the market opening up? Is there much work for black writers today?

JOHNSON-COCHRAN: You can't really ask things like that. I'll give you an example. Only if you look across the table at me do you see a black writer. If you interviewed a white writer, that question would never be asked. I just completed a picture for Touchstone with not a single black character in it. It's set in Nebraska. I wrote this film so that I could prove to everyone that I could write as a writer, not just as a black writer. I have proven myself in that milieu. So when you ask whether there is much work for black writer, I say, "If you write, as a writer, there's enough work for you to write anything." Why couldn't a black writer have written *Dave* or *Clear and Present Danger* or *The Flintstones?* There's no reason why he shouldn't have. All he has to do is research and write. If you're interested in cinema, you'll write what you like. That's what I do. I could have written Kurosawa's *Ran*, because I love that film. A writer writes, and to distinguish a black writer, just because he's a black person, is a misnomer and disservice to a writer's rights.

HARRIS: Where do you see yourself in five years?

JOHNSON-COCHRAN: I'd like to be able to write and direct my own work. I'd also like to be able to write for other directors. I'd love to write for directors who I know get the work. Write for Carl Franklin, write for Milos Forman, write for Louis Malle. I'd like to set my own body of work out there as well, to say these fifteen films are my life's work, like Truffaut did. When he had his aneurysm, he said, "Watch my movies, think of me fondly, I am gone."

CHARLES BURNETT

"If you're a writer-director, you write differently."

Charles Burnett was the first person whom I approached to participate in this project. It was after a screening of *Killer of Sheep* and *To Sleep with Anger* at UCLA.

He listened to my awkward pitch and quickly agreed to go on the record. It was only as I was writing down his phone number that I realized that my hand was trembling slightly. I clearly recall being less nervous when I met my childhood heroes Magic Johnson and Michael Cooper at the Los Angeles Forum.

I am drawn to Mr. Burnett's work because his characters speak with a certain truth and accessibility that is more like the people I know in life than the usual movie characters. Characters in my screenplays have been directly influenced by Mr. Burnett's work.

We spoke over lunch at the World Cafe in Santa Monica. I found Mr. Burnett to be earnest and completely forthcoming, as well as thoughtful, serious, and sensitive. He's a filmmaker with integrity.

HARRIS: I saw *The Glass Shield* last night for the second time and I really noticed how spare the violence was for a film of this genre. It was almost shocking. Care to comment?

BURNETT: I never looked at it in terms of genre, even though it was story set in a police station. The story is based on Johnny Johnson's experience in this particular station, being assigned as a rookie just out of the academy. My concerns were with the theme of the story: how a man can make a wrong decision while thinking he's doing the right thing. How does he redeem himself? What is the meaning of responsibility and identity? Those were my concerns, as opposed to making a cop movie. The whole milieu was just a setting. It was more of a character study about racism and prejudice.

HARRIS: When you write a film, do you think first in terms of character and then the plot?

BURNETT: Not necessarily. It varies, it could be an image, a theme, anything. Anything can start the ball rolling, and, once it happens, it can get left behind or go someplace else.

HARRIS: In the closing credits of *The Glass Shield*, I saw that this film was based on a story called *One of Us*. Was your screenplay an adaptation?

BURNETT: No, not at all. Chet Walker had this idea . . .

HARRIS: Walker was the executive producer?

BURNETT: Yes. He had been working with Johnny Johnson, and Ned Walsh was the writer. They had this story called *One of Us* that had been turned around at Warner Bros. He said, "This could be an opportunity to make some money. Make a quick little film with this script for a hundred thousand dollars." I read it and said okay, let's make it bigger. As it went along, we decided to make it completely different. We started from a whole new premise. We ended up discarding the whole *One of Us* script.

We still used the main character of the novice cop and another real event that had taken place at the time, and I included a lot of things that were currently going on in the country. The actual event Johnny Johnson was involved in happened in the early eighties. So actually, the original script just started the whole process, and only the names of the main characters stayed in.

HARRIS: Is it common that you'll read something, take a couple of characters, and expand it into a whole different story?

BURNETT: No, it just happened on this story. I just took something that someone else had started, and I took it somewhere else.

HARRIS: I want to digress a little and talk about your credits. I know you did *Killer of Sheep, To Sleep with Anger,* and *The Glass Shield,* which is most current. What about something called *Bless Their Little Hearts*?

BURNETT: I wrote that for another guy. And I did a feature called *My Brother's Wedding,* a short called *The Horse,* and some documentaries—*America Becoming* and another film on Ted Watkins.

HARRIS: In *The Glass Shield,* you open the film with storyboards, comic-book type images. What were you trying to convey with that sequence?

BURNETT: Well, a lot actually. In a sense, it tells this guy's fantasy, and it shows dramatic irony in the fact that you see what's going to happen to the main character. You see a black guy in an all-white world. It sets the motif because most of us come to cops either from comic books or from seeing them on the streets. Most of us wanted to be cops or firemen as children, and we sort of pass through that. But he stayed in that fantasy mode. The colors are blue and yellow, which is a motif that you see in the police station

HARRIS: All of that before you even meet J.J.

BURNETT: The first time you see him is at the academy on graduation day. There's a picture of his girlfriend and there's that cartoon of the cop on his locker. The idea of the comic was as a reference so that when you see the color blue, for instance, in the police station, you would refer back to that.

HARRIS: I thought that it was very effective. How many drafts did it take to get the story where you wanted it?

BURNETT: I think that the first draft is just to find out what the story is about. The possibilities of where you can take it. The nuances and so on. Then it starts getting shaped by trying to get the finances together for it.

HARRIS: Is it like that film *In the Soup*, where everyone who comes to the process feels obliged to make some creative changes to the story?

BURNETT: Everyone feels obliged to do something or other. [Chuckles] If you're a writer-director, you write differently.

HARRIS: Could you expand on that thought?

BURNETT: Sure. One of things is that the companies here usually want a lot of exposition. They want everything in the script explained. Though I read a script that had big gaping holes in it, they thought it was all right. In minority scripts, it seems they want it really laid out. In action films, action dominates at the expense of plot. When you're trying to get financing, there's this whole thing of having parts for the right actor, and everything has to be explained.

HARRIS: There's no room for nuance, is there?

BURNETT: No, there isn't, but at the end of the day, you're the one shooting the darn thing. As the writer-director, the scripts are different, more visual, and sometimes it's harder for the producers to see it as a story. It's like an editor or a cameraman. They know what's necessary in terms of the shots or the cut, so you go right to the jugular as opposed to beating around the bush.

HARRIS: Do you have trouble finding the built-in spine of your story?

BURNETT: In a sense, it's always a struggle. One, you have to keep looking over your shoulder. That's the main problem. If you can just get the money together and make the film you want, that would certainly help to make the process easier, but you're always conscious of the tastes of the producing team or financier. You try to ignore that and write the film you want to make.

HARRIS: How much creative control did you have? Did you get final cut?

BURNETT: No, I didn't get final cut on *The Glass Shield*. SiBy 2000 refused to look at my cut, actually. It was a war dealing with SiBy 2000. That was a difficult experience because we had a run-in with one of the consultants who worked there. He had an idea, he was very hands-on, and that was one of the problems. But, at the end of the day, you manage to save something. This whole business is the art of compromise, no matter how you cut it. Somewhere along the line, someone will say, "Look, if you want us to distribute this film or if you want to get it to the next step, you need to cut this out or add this."

HARRIS: What kind of budget were you working with?

BURNETT: About three million dollars.

HARRIS: What kind of budget did you have on *To Sleep with Anger*?

BURNETT: About 1.5 million.

HARRIS: So you're bringing it in on a shoestring.

BURNETT: It's very low, let's put it that way. I wish we had a little bit more money on *The Glass Shield* because there were several scenes that would have worked more effectively if we had more money to put into them.

HARRIS: I felt the scenes were very spare and tight compared with *To Sleep with Anger*. Hardly a scene went on for more than a couple of pages.

BURNETT: I don't think that any of them were more than couple of pages long. It was one scene after another to take us from one point to another, with the exception of the night raid, which was a scene sequence. The murder sequence was one of the longer scenes.

HARRIS: Most of the violence occurs off-screen.

BURNETT: I never looked at the picture as a genre picture. I didn't look at it as an action picture. It's more of a character piece. And you get a thing in urban dramas where people depend too heavily on foul language. I think you have to get away from it. I think the community is pretty tired of it.

HARRIS: I think we're over it, completely. Personally, too much profanity in a script is usually indicative of a lack of imagination and vocabulary. Someone once told me that the studios will only spend a certain amount of money, usually under ten million, on a black film because, if it does any business at all at the box office, it can go into profits with video and ancillary markets. What are your thoughts?

BURNETT: Well, the irony of it is that black people go to the movies at a greater rate per capita than any other group, except kids under a certain age. There is this notion that keeping the budgets down low will make a film more viable. But there's more to it. You saw *The Glass Shield*. Would you characterize it as black film?

HARRIS: Yes, a black character study.

BURNETT: You're like the producers who see that I'm black and the lead character is black, which, to them, constitutes a black film.

HARRIS: Well, okay. I don't want to digress into semantics, but I have wondered if there's a white director and a white writer and a black cast, is it still a "black film"?

BURNETT: There are two things that must be made clear. First, *The Glass Shield* is an ensemble piece.

HARRIS: Absolutely. You had a great cast.

BURNETT: And when trying to get financing for it, the first

thing they say is that it's a black film. Actually, the film is about a white institution. Most of the characters were, in fact, white. But it seems that things automatically get cut. They were afraid there would be riots because of the police problems they were having in L.A. at the time.

HARRIS: Did they really think it would be that inflammatory? They said the same thing about Singleton's *Boyz N the Hood*.

BURNETT: They said it about *To Sleep with Anger*. They say it about everything. [Laughter] Those are the hidden negative connotations that come out when you try to produce a "black film." It affects the amount of money people are willing to put into a budget.

HARRIS: What, in your opinion, makes a screenplay great?

BURNETT: I think that's rather subjective in a way. People respond to different things in a movie. What one writer may find fantastic may not move me. I respond to things that are decent and character-driven, that open doors to things about human nature, reveal some insight about problems, and make the characters have to think. Therefore, so does the audience. The screenplay is only one step, and it doesn't stand on its own, like a novel.

HARRIS: Of course. Do you read screenplays generally?

BURNETT: Yes.

HARRIS: Would you consider directing a film that you didn't write?

BURNETT: Yes.

HARRIS: Have you?

BURNETT: I haven't, but I am working with a couple of writers, and we have made deals. Working with these writers is sometimes like pulling teeth. I'm almost to the point of calling the producer and telling him to bring in another writer because I'm supposed to be supervising rewrites, not writing the thing. It's becoming problematic. I don't know if it's their lack of experience or what.

HARRIS: Are these young writers?

BURNETT: No.

HARRIS: Are they black writers?

BURNETT: No, they're not. It was just a combination of things. In order to do a film successfully, the script has to work. You have to cover all of the bases in the plot. You have to know every inch of what makes it work.

HARRIS: Would you concede that most films fail based on the merit of the script?

BURNETT: No, I wouldn't, because we don't read the scripts until after the studio and everyone who's put their hands into it has already screwed it up.

HARRIS: Do you think that scripts get overdeveloped?

BURNETT: Yeah. The executives may feel that they have power, and they have something that they may want to say. They want you to be an extension of them, which doesn't work very well. So, since you have to work so quickly in a low-budget film, you have to know what to fight for. It's really important to make sure you're comfortable with the script, that the script works. You can't say, "Well, we'll fix it in the editing room." You've got to make sure you shoot the story.

HARRIS: That's a good point. Do you like to start with a treatment?

BURNETT: I like to begin with a solid image, a solid idea of theme, then a potential storyline. Then I get the treatment to work that out.

HARRIS: Are you an Aristotelian? Do you structure your work in three acts?

BURNETT: No. I never learned to write in three acts. That's similar to a stage play.

HARRIS: So, you don't think in terms of needing something to happen by page thirty that sends the action into another direction?

BURNETT: No. I don't even talk in those terms.

HARRIS: Do you use scene cards?

BURNETT: No.

HARRIS: Do you write longhand or do you use a computer?

BURNETT: I have a computer.

HARRIS: What do you think of all the screenwriting software?

BURNETT: I think things like "Scriptor" are incredible. They're very efficient. Even before I had all of that, I developed a style sheet that made things easier.

HARRIS: Your films have been made outside of the studio system. Would you be interested in making something under a studio banner?

BURNETT: Independent or studio, it's all the same.

HARRIS: The studio budgets are higher.

BURNETT: Not necessarily. There are independent films that have quite high budgets. And some people are very happy working for the studios. If they all have the same vision of the film, there's no conflict. When you have a personal vision, you'll always find conflict.

HARRIS: Do you think that writers should try to create their own form? I'm thinking of Tarantino's *Pulp Fiction* and the way it broke the classic rules of structure.

BURNETT: If you can afford to make your own movies, then you can create your own form, but when you're giving it to someone else to read, they want what's familiar. For us, being people of color, everything has to be exact. Everything counts. I don't think you have the luxury of being too experimental at the studio level. It makes practical economical sense to do it that way, but if one wants to take a gamble . . .

HARRIS: Film is often a gamble, isn't it?

BURNETT: Yeah, even if you do it the right way with proper format. To go beyond that and be experimental may be too much.

HARRIS: How many drafts do you go through before you're ready to show your work?

BURNETT: It depends. Usually I show a first draft to producers, but I've been through it several times by the time I get to what I'm calling the first draft.

HARRIS: How many pages do you aim for?

BURNETT: If I can see ninety pages, I'm happy. Anywhere from ninety to one hundred. I just write until the picture is done.

HARRIS: While you were at UCLA, you studied directing.

BURNETT: Everything. When I was there, they didn't separate the disciplines. To make your own movie you had to write your own movie. Then you had to shoot your own movie. All of these thing were one.

HARRIS: Do you think young writers should go to film school?

BURNETT: I think they should go somewhere where they can get some experience and some critique of their work. I think film school could help you out a great deal. It makes you think about film every day. You get access to equipment. You're put through the tests more frequently than if you were outside of school. I think it allows you to question where you're going, and your own form.

HARRIS: Do you have an agent who puts your name in for projects and such?

BURNETT: I have an agent.

HARRIS: What do you think a writer should look for in an agent?

BURNETT: It's hard for agents. There's a lot of people with scripts. Everybody has a screenplay.

HARRIS: Absolutely.

BURNETT: Sometimes it's a Catch-22. Get the script made, then get an agent. Go backward, as opposed to getting an agent right off. A big agency has a lot of clout, but being a small fish in it may not work well for you. A small agency that's really hustling may be better for you. Just like anything else, you have to be careful of where you are and what can be done for you, as well as what you can do for your agent. You have to give the agent something to work with. If I was starting off and I wanted to get into the business, I assume that I would try to find out what was current.

HARRIS: What's current? Could you expand on that?

BURNETT: Sometimes people write something that's not very timely. Maybe it's eight years down the line. Maybe it's eight years past.

HARRIS: Like a western?

BURNETT: Not so much that. I'm speaking in terms of themes or ideas. For example, it took a while for Oliver Stone to get his Vietnam picture off the ground. Then after that, a lot of war movies became vogue. You still see some residue, but you probably won't see any studio doing another one.

HARRIS: Didn't a movie just come out this year about the black experience in Vietnam? *Walking Dead.*

BURNETT: Yeah.

HARRIS: Is it because we've seen enough war? *Apocalypse Now* came out in 1974.

BURNETT: I don't think it's so much that. I feel that a good movie is a good movie. I mentioned that writers should do something timely, but if you have the means to do it yourself, if you can write the darn thing and get the financing, then anything can work. For example, if Kevin Costner wanted to do a Vietnam movie, he could probably get financing for it. Chuck Norris does it all the time. It all depends on a combination of things.

HARRIS: Let's talk about networking. How important is it?

BURNETT: It's very important. Yet a lot of artists in this town don't help each other. You find it a lot more in other communities where there is this fellowship or family established. I've gone to parties where the young executives make a point of supporting and promoting one another. I haven't seen much of it among black entertainers and directors, however, where they get together and meet new people and talk about what's going on in the business. It happens, but not enough.

HARRIS: Do you believe the adage that everyone in Hollywood is afraid of losing their job?

BURNETT: I don't think everybody is. It's not fear of losing the job as much as it's fear that people are going to catch up to them, and other silly nonsense. If they did it right, they wouldn't have to worry about it.

HARRIS: Do you want to talk about money?

BURNETT: Sure. What do you want to know?

HARRIS: When you write and direct a low-budget picture, do you get a flat fee for writing and directing or do you get points and money on the back end? How does that work?

BURNETT: You get things like that. You get a fee for writing and directing. In low-budget, you don't get that much up front, so you get some back-end deal, which often doesn't materialize. It's just academic.

HARRIS: How much did you make on *The Glass Shield*?

BURNETT: That was sort of a different deal because I had started the project, and it was only going to be a two-hundred- or three-hundred-thousand-dollar film. I don't think I really made anything from the writing. Maybe thirty or forty thousand, which is way below scale. The same with the directing, maybe seventy or seventy-five.

HARRIS: So you may have taken home a hundred thousand or so?

BURNETT: Maybe. But I have points on the other end to make up for that. It wasn't a mistake to do it that way because it had to be done to get the film made. We all had to do that. It was the same on *To Sleep with Anger*. We had to take almost nothing. I got very little for writing and directing, but I had points on the back end.

HARRIS: To *Sleep with Anger* is a done deal.

BURNETT: And we still owe them money, supposedly.

HARRIS: You still owe them money?

BURNETT: Supposedly. They say the film hasn't made money. So those back-end points become meaningless. But the actors made money through the royalties from television and stuff like that. They're the only ones who'll make money.

HARRIS: Do you think that you'll see anything on the back end of *The Glass Shield*?

BURNETT: I don't know. I don't get many big offers, but little things come along. Friends of mine work on these films. We all take nothing to get it off the ground, and then try to get a little more money and a little more money and a little more money. It all goes into the production. We hope it succeeds so that we'll get our money on the back end. One day it will, but right now we have to scratch to make it work.

HARRIS: To your credit, *The Glass Shield* plays like a much bigger picture. The whole look of the film was wonderful.

BURNETT: Thank you. It was a conscious decision to give the film that look, if you will. We wanted to give it some production values. Of course, on a studio picture, the director would get four to six hundred thousand, and the writer would get maybe a hundred. But when you're trying to get something going, you do these things.

HARRIS: How long have you been doing films?

BURNETT: I went to film school in '67 and after that I started working. Often, it takes a long time to raise the financing.

HARRIS: The financing, the distribution, everything. How many screens is *The Glass Shield* playing on nationwide?

BURNETT: Just over 200. It's doing fairly. It's done about three million dollars and, with all of the prints and advertising, it has to do about twice that to go into profits. I expect it will do well on video.

HARRIS: How has the trend of big-budgeted films affected black cinema?

BURNETT: You're starting to see the budgets go up. *True Identity* was about fifteen million. *The Inkwell* was about eight million. So they're up there. *Boomerang* was an expensive film. Twenty or thirty million.

HARRIS: Eddie Murphy is working on a remake of *The Nutty Professor* right now, and the budget is huge.

BURNETT: I'm sure he gets a big chunk of the budget.

HARRIS: What issues or themes can you deal with in your work that may elude more mainstream pictures?

BURNETT: Well, in *To Sleep with Anger* there are references to folklore, slavery, and segregation that work under the surface. People recognize that and grasp onto those elements. Because we live in a subculture, a lot of our experiences are unique to that perspective. For example, a white guy asked me why I was bashing the police in *The Glass Shield*. I wasn't bashing anyone. I was telling a specific story about a particular department. But a lot of times, people will be turned off before even delving into the material.

HARRIS: The depiction of the police mirrored my own experiences with the LAPD in many ways. I've experienced almost routine harassment based only on the fact that I am a young black male driving a nice car outside of South Central L.A. How did the police respond to your production?

BURNETT: The police were very cooperative. They thought it was just another Hollywood film about the police that's got it all wrong. We had some police officers acting in the movie. They had a good time with it.

HARRIS: What responsibility, if any, do you feel to dismantle negative stereotypes of African Americans?

BURNETT: I think, particularly if you have kids, you're aware of the impact of images and the lack of images. In terms of black images, no one stands up for them. If you say anything, it's censorship, but, for them, those images are reality. We can call ourselves niggers and bitches and it's "reality." Hollywood encourages those things in film. Look at Michael Jackson's record. Michael Jackson is trying to make a comment on racism in his own way. He may be right or wrong, but he brings up some words and everyone gets offended by them.

HARRIS: He's even doing a re-recording to eliminate certain references that Jewish people have found offensive.

BURNETT: We say negative things about ourselves all the time, and no one says "Let's rewrite" or "Go back and redo these films that have all of this stuff in them." We help to erode our own self worth. I think it's very problematic. I have kids and I want them to grow up in a world where they feel as though they can see themselves on the screen, see what black people have contributed, and feel a part of the human race. All you can ask for is honesty and fairness. If you don't, and you're creating this mess, then you're part of the problem, not part of the solution. I think that what we have to do is correct some of these problems while there's still a chance.

HARRIS: What words of encouragement would you give to young brothers and sisters who want to be where you are?

BURNETT: I would say that it's a long haul. Get a job that will afford you the time to learn your craft, because it may take years to get your career off the ground. The more people you know, the easier it is to reduce that time. Write something commercially oriented because the people who want to make money in this business are not necessarily the people who have a passion to make movies, or who have something to say.

HARRIS: Which one are you?

BURNETT: I'm the one who never thought about making a lot of money until I had kids. By that time, it's a little late. You get stuck in your habit. In order to change things, you have to make a sacrifice. You say, "Look, there's too much trash out there and I'm not going to do that." I think the audience has to get involved by demanding better material. The writers will respond in kind.

RUSTY CUNDIEFF

"All you have is your integrity."

Rusty and I played phone tag for about a month before finally sitting down for this interview. "You know I'm down with your book, but I've gotta make that money," he said with a hearty laugh.

It is easy to understand Rusty's steady success. His easygoing, almost breezy nature is only a mask for his intelligence and determined work ethic. A great sense of humor is usually a good indication of intelligence, and Rusty is one of the funniest people I've met, but he is also very serious and disciplined about the craft of screenwriting. One glance at his workstation will tell you that.

On the short walk from Rusty's beautiful home in Los Angeles' Silver Lake district to the Thai American Cafe, we discussed career longevity in Hollywood. Rusty concluded that "it's true that all roads lead to Hollywood, but conversely, all roads lead out of this motherfucker, too."

Rusty peppers his conversation with a fair amount of expletives, which makes for a very entertaining interview. He also peppers his conversation with a wide range of good, useful, and—occasionally—unorthodox advice on starting up and surviving in Hollywood.

HARRIS: I remember hearing you speak on a filmmakers' panel at something called the MENTOR Network. I covered the forum for the *Daily Sundial,* CSUN's paper.

CUNDIEFF: Oh, yeah, I remember that. There was a guy in the back talking about film financing, and people started hollering.

HARRIS: It was funny because I went to several panels and they were all very informative and civil, but the one you were on quickly degenerated into sort of a Hollywood gripe session. You were one of the only voices of reason. You spoke about the importance of more people of color getting involved in all aspects of the filmmaking process. Do you still feel that way, or was that just youthful idealism?

CUNDIEFF: Well, I definitely think that the more African Americans who are involved in the filmmaking process, or any media, the better chance we have of trying to influence the images that arc purported to be of us, and the better chance we have to influence the issues that we want to see in movies and the other media. So, yes, I definitely would like to see more blacks involved in all levels, not just acting, directing, and writing, but producing, financing, distributing, everything.

HARRIS: Well, this book hopefully will be a means to that end. I hope that we can help demystify the writing process, if only to the point that people realize that actors really don't make up the lines as they go along. I'm, of course, being facetious. People are more intelligent than to believe that.

CUNDIEFF: One would think so. I don't know. [Laughing] Out here I think everybody does, but I don't know how people in other areas understand or don't understand the concept of a script, the concept of rehearsal, and the concept of blocking out scenes. I think people are much more in tune to that than they used to be because of the proliferation of entertainment magazines like *Premiere* and all the glossy magazines that deal with the film industry. But sometimes people do ask some odd questions.

HARRIS: Who were some of your mentors as you were coming up?

CUNDIEFF: Actually, that list is rather short. There weren't that many people who I could look to as role models, particularly when I started writing. I looked to Spike Lee and Robert Townsend. I worked as an actor with Robert on *Hollywood Shuffle,* and I saw almost all of that process. I worked as an actor with Spike on *School Daze,* and I saw the tail end of that process. He had written the script and gone into production by the time I got onto the set. But in both cases, watching those two people gave me the confidence to pursue what I wanted to pursue. They made me say, "If they can do it, I can do it." I think that was because I knew them. I said, "Is there anything about them that I don't see in myself in terms of desire and skills? Spike knows a hell of a lot more about making a film than I do, but if he could do it, if he could learn it, I could learn it, I could achieve it, too."

HARRIS: Yours is an interesting case in that you didn't study filmmaking.

CUNDIEFF: No, I didn't. I was a Philosophy of Religion major at USC. You've got to major in something, man. I started as a Journalism major at Loyola in New Orleans. After I transferred out to USC, I wanted to shift my major and I wasn't sure what, exactly, I was going to shift it to, whether I was going to go into a different part of journalism or whether I wanted to go into television and film. But I dug philosophy, and it was easy to go into Philosophy of Religion, so that's where I ended up. Actually, the thought process in a lot of philosophy is very good for working within the film business.

HARRIS: How so?

CUNDIEFF: Well, it teaches you to stand back and analyze shit, kind of figure things out. Philosophy is all thought processes. It's looking at something and going, "Why?" There's a lot of times in this business when you say, "Why this? Why that? Why me?" It's important to be able to look at things and distance yourself from a problem and figure it out without becoming emotionally upset. That's an advantage in this business.

HARRIS: I've followed your career since we met at that film panel. I think, at that point, *Fear of a Black Hat* was in development. I don't know if you had even done the *House Party 2* script. In any event, I've come to think of you almost as a household name.

CUNDIEFF: Really? That's weird.

HARRIS: I clearly am into black cinema, and you're an emerging part of it. And I follow the writers working today. After only a few years, you have three produced films to your credit.

CUNDIEFF: As a writer, yes. Let's see, *House Party 2*, *Fear of a Black Hat*, and *Tales from the 'Hood*. I guess that's been a three- or four-year span.

HARRIS: By any standards, you're making it here.

CUNDIEFF: Well, I'm trying to move. I'm not as prolific as I'd like to be, but I'm trying. I'd like to do a little bit more.

HARRIS: How did you break through?

CUNDIEFF: A combination of luck, desire, and perseverance. I started out doing stand-up comedy and acting. At a certain point, while working on *Hollywood Shuffle*, I had some ideas of my own that I wanted to put down in script form. My logic was that if Robert can do it, I can do it. I'd seen the process and I knew that this shit is possible.

So I started to write down ideas I had for some stories. During that period of time, I did *School Daze* while I kept honing in on the story I wanted to write. And I hooked up with Darin Scott, whom a friend of mine knew from USC. He had already produced a low-budget film called *The Offspring*, which had Vincent Price and Rosalind Cash in it. I talked to Darin about what I wanted to do and he encouraged me to keep writing. That was pretty much all I did for about two or three years—write, write, write. I was still acting and doing stand-up comedy to support myself, but all of my free time I spent writing. Creatively, it was probably the happiest period in my professional life because I was writing what I wanted to write. I was writing for myself. As an actor, I'd been used to people telling me what to do. The shit is written down. "This is your role, and this is what the story is." You ain't got shit to say about that; you come in and do it, right? [Laughter] Then during the rehearsal process, the director tells you where to go, what to do, blah, blah, blah. Everybody always has something to tell you. When I started writing this project, it was just me, a typewriter (I didn't have a computer), and a room. Complete autonomy. If I wanted to kill people, I killed them. I could blow up the world, I could do what ever I wanted to do on that blank page. And still get the girl. Writing for yourself, or on spec as it is called, is the only area in the film business where you can do that. Everything else is predicated by other people. Even the director, the supposed puppeteer of the project, is still under the constraints of other people. You have actors, but you have to get the actors to do what you want them to do. You're predicated by how much money you have to spend, etc., etc., etc. So writing something on spec is the only time you have complete freedom in a creative sense.

HARRIS: What do you say to those people who only write projects in a proven genre? Sort of writing for the marketplace?

CUNDIEFF: I understand what they are trying to do, which is, I suppose, to sell their script. But at the same time, I think it depends on where you are in your career and who you are as a person. There are certain scripts that I could probably write, but not write well because they're not in me. Good writers generally write about what excites them. Either you have to know it, or you have to be excited enough about it to get to know it. What a lot of people do is watch a lot of movies and write the scenes they saw in those films. They learn life from the movies. So they don't come up with anything unique or different.

HARRIS: It's all derivative.

CUNDIEFF: Exactly. Now the unique writers, the interesting writers, the people we consider good, generally have a life or interests outside of just going and sitting in the theater, watching the images that come at them. The good writers write things that no one else has thought about, or put a new twists on old stories. The stories are all the same: boy meets girl, boy loses girl.

HARRIS: Shakespeare said that there were only about twenty-six scenarios.

CUNDIEFF: Exactly. But it's all about how you tell that story, and what you put in it. So, to someone who's just starting out, I would say that you have a much better chance of writing something good if you're writing something that's close to your heart or something that excites you. Writing is a long, hard process. If you're not doing something that interests you, you will very likely abandon it before you get ten or fifteen pages into it.

HARRIS: Do you aim for 120 pages?

CUNDIEFF: I aim for the story. Sometimes the story is over on page eighty-two. Sometimes the motherfucker goes on until 160. [Laughter] Then you start to figure out what you need to whittle back to tell that same story. I think that the first time you go through a draft, you're just trying to get it down. I write to just get it out. Just spew out all the shit, and have the format. Then I go back and hone it like a wood carver. I cut off a big hunk and say, "Well, let me define this shit with the little scalpels that I have."

But, to answer one of your first questions: How did

I get into this? I guess my first real break came with *House Party 2*. I had written maybe two or three scripts on spec, and I had sent them out to different places. Darin and I kind of did a trick to send them out, because I didn't have an agent. Darin set himself up as a producer, and we set up a fictitious business called Silent Storm Films. We had a friend design a bogus emblem and got a letterhead, which cost all of fifteen bucks. We had this letterhead run off on reams of paper, and we had envelopes made up. The shit looked official. It was Darin Scott, the producer, sending you a potential project. People will read projects from producers, even if the producer doesn't have an agent or a lawyer. They will not read a screenplay from a writer unless he has those people, because they're afraid of being sued. So, that's how I got those three scripts read. One of the people who read me was a lady at New Line named Janet Grillo. She liked the scripts, but New Line wasn't interested in doing them, even though they said they liked the writing and blah, blah, blah.

HARRIS: Which is fair. I've gotten assignments that way.

CUNDIEFF: Which is par for the course. Now I'll digress to an earlier question about the person who writes to make that sale. You should write just to have written something good. Because, if you write something good, you can use it to get other work, even if that particular project doesn't sell. For me, those three projects excited Janet enough that when the Hudlin brothers went on the fence as to whether they were going to actually write and produce *House Party 2*, Janet came to me and said, "If the Hudlin brothers don't do this project, I want you to write *House Party 2*." So I started praying for the Hudlin brothers to say no to the project. And, fortunately for me, the Hudlin brothers decided that they wanted to move on to other things. So I got to go ahead and begin writing *House Party 2*. That was my big break. Once New Line said, "Okay, we want to hire you to do this," I went out and started shopping for an agent. I just called people up and said, "Hey, some cats want to buy some shit of mine. You want ten percent?" [Laughter] "Why certainly!" I ended up with a pretty decent agent, a guy at Gersh named Ron Bernstein, who did a real good job for me and actually worked for me beyond just taking that money. Which is what you hope for.

HARRIS: I think Charles Burnett spoke about working backward, in effect, and creating some heat on your own. Agents need something to work with, and they don't know you from the last motherfucker who got off of the bus.

CUNDIEFF: Absolutely. You've got to give them something to sell. Everybody is looking for the next hot thing out here. Perhaps, in some ways, it's unfortunate. But, you've got to figure out how to make that work for you. Like you say, you try to generate some type of heat. I was just fortunate that the *House Party* thing generated some heat for me. Also, at the time, not as much was going on and there were not a lot of black writers. Perhaps there were, but people didn't know about them. I was probably one of the earlier black writers to dive in and become known. That helped me a lot when I was starting out. There's a lot more people out there now. During that period, if any project had more than five black people in it, I heard about it. People came to me and said, "Would you be interested in this?" It was almost like having a mini monopoly. I'm not saying that that's good, it just happened.

HARRIS: Yeah, and the streets were paved with gold. [Laughter] Well, let's talk about your *House Party 2* experience because that was a real education for you. And it's a cautionary tale.

CUNDIEFF: A lot of things happened over the course of that project and I very quickly grew up in a lot of ways. One was dealing with writing for someone else. Up until that point, I had been writing everything on spec. If I wanted to do something, I did it; if I didn't, I didn't. Now I had to please all of these executives. I would meet with them, I would pitch my ideas and concepts to them, and they would say, "We like this. We don't like that. What about trying it this way?" It's a very political thing. How do you tell someone who is paying you that their suggestion doesn't work? And if you have two executives, one may be pitting himself against the other. There's a lot of political things that push themselves into the creative process. That's not to say that you have to cower and say, "Okay," or sneak around and not say anything. You say what you feel. All you have is your integrity. But you do have to be careful about how you say things, depending on where you are in the project and whether you want to have a relationship with those people again. That was one thing. Another thing was dealing with directors.

The first director on the project eventually got replaced. I won't name him, but I will say that he played a lot of head games with me. He almost fucked me up, until I figured out what was going on. Some directors have a tendency to do that, depending on what kind of director they are. This particular guy, who had come from videos and commercials, was rather insecure, and this was his first feature. As I began writing the script, and began to turn in pages, he called me up and said, "They're very concerned about you at New Line. They don't think you're doing a good job. It sounds like you're talking to other people about other jobs and you're not doing this one very well. I was hoping to see something that I could just go and shoot and this is far below my expectations. I think you better watch your back and watch your step," and so on and so forth. I was like, "Damn. I never got this vibe from these people, never." I was saying to myself, "What's this all about?" He told me this on a Thursday or Friday. Now Janet, who was based in New York but also had an office out here, happened to be in New York at this time. Of course, I immediately called her. I left a message for her here, in New York, and at her home. But she did not return my calls. I was like, "Jesus, I just fucked up my first opportunity!"

I finally caught up with Janet on Monday, and I could tell in the first two to ten seconds that everything that this director had told me was bullshit because her first words were a chipper and very happy, "Hi, Rusty! How's it going? I'm sorry that I didn't get back to you. I was out of town for the weekend, I went up to the Hamptons. I'm real sorry I didn't get back to you. We got the pages and we're all really excited to see what happens next. We're really, really hyped up about this. This is going to be great!" And this fucking director had just told me that these very same pages were causing problems. I couldn't bring this up to her on the phone, but I started to watch the way he operated, which was to set everybody else up to take a fall. So, if something fucked up, he automatically had somebody to blame.

HARRIS: Much has been written about the rampant paranoia in Hollywood, and this cat gives credence to that phenomena. The important thing is that you survived that shit. You swam in the shark tank with a bloody leg and lived to tell about it.

CUNDIEFF: I swam, baby. The ironic thing is that he got fired for the exact thing he was accusing me of. He was out here taking meetings with other people on other projects and it became very apparent that he did not have the chops to direct a film. At certain points, he was trying to get me to do his work for him. He was asking me to write very detailed shot descriptions in the script. Most directors don't want to see any of that. They would rather have you write, "TRAIN GOES THROUGH TUNNEL" as opposed to "CLOSE UP OF THE WHEELS CHURNING." Most directors would be like, "Motherfucker, I'll figure that out! Just tell me if there's a train."

HARRIS: "Just tell me what they said. And did they kiss?"

CUNDIEFF: Exactly. [Laughter]

HARRIS: So, what did you learn from that particular experience?

CUNDIEFF: Well, I think that what I got out of it was a very personal thing. And I don't know how well this would translate into a lesson for someone else. It gave me an increased sense of my own talent and ability. I didn't question myself as much, and I really started to assert my opinion. Not only in meetings with him and the other producers who were on that project, but with producers and directors on other projects that I've worked on subsequently. I started to realize that they are hiring me for my skills as a writer and my understanding of how the story should work. If I don't strongly champion my own opinions about the story, they're not getting their money's worth, and I'm doing myself and the project a disservice. Now, I also believe that there's only a certain point to which I will push something. If I'm writing for someone else and I write, "THE SKY IS BLUE" and they say, "Oh no, it has to be purple," and I say, "Look" and give them all the reasons, and they say, "We still just want the sky purple," I'm like, "Okay, it's your money, motherfucker. EXT: PURPLE SKY - DAY. [Laughter] It's your cash."

HARRIS: When you look at *House Party 2* today, how do you feel about it?

CUNDIEFF: I hate it. I hate it for so many reasons. [Laughter] One, they didn't film the script that I wrote. Two, it was rewritten by another writer because, after the original director got replaced, the new directors felt like they wanted to work with somebody new. One of the actors slipped me the rewritten pages, which, the way the jokes were set up, looked like a sitcom. As it turns out, the person who rewrote me was a sitcom writer. I gave myself a pat on the back for being able to tell the difference, but it was disturbing. When I saw the movie, I almost walked out after fifteen minutes because the way they filmed the sequences ruined the jokes. In one scene, the dialogue was so bad that I couldn't even believe that the other writer had written it. I know he's a different type of writer, but he's not a bad writer. When I heard it, I sunk down in my chair. I later found out that the producers had taken out a scene and asked their assistant, or someone in the office, to write dialogue. The worst part of it was that this dialogue had exposition, which is the hardest type of dialogue to write.

HARRIS: Is your name on the credits?

CUNDIEFF: My name is on the credits. Of course, that was another lesson about Hollywood. The movie actually opened well, primarily because of the success of the first film. It dropped off quickly, but it made a decent amount of money. It was number one for a week or so, and in the top ten for a little while. I got a lot of calls because of that movie. It didn't hurt my career, and I learned that lot of these executives don't watch movies, they watch box-office scores. If they had watched the movie, they probably would not have called me. [Laughter]

HARRIS: Lets close the chapter on the *House Party 2* experience and move on to *Fear of a Black Hat*. Critics likened it to *Spinal Tap* with a murder, rap edge. Was that film a strong influence on you?

CUNDIEFF: Yeah, I had been a big *Spinal Tap* fan, and I was also a big rap fan. So I had this idea to do a rap *Spinal Tap*. I mentioned it to Darin, just as some other shit we could try to get off the ground. Then we heard that Nelson George and Chris Rock had a similar idea. So we did a quick, down-and-dirty presentation video—kind of a pitch tape—to show to potential investors.

HARRIS: That's a smart idea.

CUNDIEFF: Much smarter than our earlier process, where we spent about fifteen or twenty thousand dollars doing a short pitch-film for a sort of black *Big Chill* thing that we were trying to do. This time we said, let's not spend that kind of money. So we spent about six hundred dollars and started sending the tape around. Years later, after I thought that the project was dead, it resurfaced. Someone had seen the tape, and they called me up, saying, "Rusty, we want to do your movie at ITC!" I had never heard of ITC. In fact, I thought it was a friend calling me up and fucking with me. [Laughter] So, I never called her back. Fortunately, she called me back the following week. That's when Darin and I started to set up *Fear of a Black Hat*. We had to rush it through very quickly. The writing process was different from anything that I had ever written. We knew that *CB-4* was going to get off of the starting blocks and go that same year. We knew that we had to get these guys committed to production on our thing before they heard about this *CB-4* shit, because if they heard about that, they would cancel us. We were much lower budget and they wouldn't want to go up against Universal. The deal we made was that I would write a detailed outline of the scenes, and we would just improvise the movie from the outline. The guy who was running the company was naive enough to say okay. I said, "Bet!" We got a production date, and I wrote the outline. Then, during the rehearsals, I discovered that the actors we had in bit parts were improving themselves into more of the story. An actor who was supposed to say, "Here's your tea," would add, "Oh, by the way, I'll be at your concert tomorrow, with my dying aunt who has cancer." That kind of shit. [Laughter] I knew that this shit was not going to work. I had to have a script. These motherfuckers were gonna cost me a lot of time and cash.

So I started writing the script only a week and a half before we started shooting. I got the production boards from the production manager, who had the schedule of what scenes were shooting what day and in what order, and I wrote the script out of order, writing the scenes for each week, one week ahead. Even while I was on the set shooting the movie, I was writing next week's scenes on a laptop computer, in between set-ups. It was wild, man, but the cool thing about it was that I never had to deal with the executives on the script. They okayed an outline and we never told them that I was writing a script, so they never had any say over the actual dialogue. It will probably never happen again for me. It was very dope. The company would look at the rushes, but it was too late by then. They would say things like, "You guys have got to stop all of that Bush bashing." They made us take out some of the shit where I was fucking with Bush and fucking with the cops, really hard-core shit.

HARRIS: I thought the funniest line in the film came when the female reporter asked your character, "What is the difference between a bitch and a ho?" Do you remember your line?

CUNDIEFF: A ho fucks everybody. A bitch fucks everybody but you. [Laughter] I actually have to give credit for that line to Tim Hutchinson, who played the manager of one of the groups in the movie. I don't know if he heard that somewhere or if he came up with it. One successful tenet for being a good writer is knowing when some shit is too good to be improved upon. [Laughter] People really like that line. It's odd because we put it at the end as one of the out-takes. When we put it earlier in the body of the film, it got a laugh. But putting it where it ended up made it really explosive. It shows how pacing, and where you put something, really affects comedy. Even the change of one word can mean the difference between something working or not working.

HARRIS: The press responded well to your work.

CUNDIEFF: We got a lot of good reviews and coverage, which was very positive.

HARRIS: How did you do at the box office?

CUNDIEFF: We did okay at the box office. We didn't do great. I think we suffered from a few things. One, *CB-4* had come out in front of us. And two, to our initial target audience, *Fear of a Black Hat* appeared to be a cheaper version of an expensive film that they didn't like. It became a very hard sell to our primary market. Then, we had to try to sell to our secondary market, which was the liberals and hipsters and white people who wanted to be on the edge. That's a harder niche to target. Their initial reaction was, "Hey, I don't like rap. Why would I want to see a movie about it?" So, that was a hard sell. Basically, the movie did moderate business at the box office, but because of the reviews and the articles and the fact that people who saw it liked it, it's gained quite an audience on video. It kind of amazes me when I meet people who have seen it on video or pay-per-view, and have watched it over and over.

HARRIS: It is interesting how so many of our films do so well on home video, where people can set their alarms, lock their doors, and enjoy blackness in the relative safety of their homes.

CUNDIEFF: Set the alarm and stick it in the deck. [Laughter]

HARRIS: How much does the box office affect what you do?

CUNDIEFF: It definitely affects it. The question is, What are the other variables and how can they work for you or against you? *Fear of a Black Hat* did as much for me as a financial success might have done for another director, because it received a lot of critical acclaim and was a movie that people generally liked and ended up talking about after they saw it. It was seen by more executives than a lot of movies that actually were big hits, because it became known as a hip-cool-underground thing. Even before it was released, we had executives calling up and going, "You've gotta give me a tape of this fucking film, because everyone says they've seen it and I gotta see it." That worked very well in my favor. Even though the movie itself was not a big hit financially, the movie was a success for me and some of the people involved with it because of the perception of what it was and what it meant. A lot of the same thing happened with *Tales from the 'Hood*, which has done okay at the box office, but hasn't been a big hit either. It got a lot of good critical reviews. But it was a more polarizing film, so it also got more reviews where people just said, "Fuck you." I think that had a lot to do with the political angles that we dealt with. Still, the reviews take away a lot of the stigma of what your box office does and doesn't do, because people like to be involved with folks whom they think do good work, and work that they like. On the other hand, there are a couple of projects that I'm dealing with now that would be commercial for the sake of being commercial. If you do a project like that and it bombs, you have no safety net. People don't say, "Well, that was innovative," or "That was cool," or "That was different." They say, "The motherfucker tried to make a hundred-million-dollar grosser, and he didn't! It just sucked!"

Once again, there's another reason to write things that are important to you. If you think about actors for a minute, it might be easier to visualize what I'm saying. Look at actors like Stallone and Schwarzenegger versus Dustin Hoffman and Robert De Niro. Are Schwarzenegger and Stallone big stars because they're good actors? Maybe, maybe not. But they're likable and, more importantly, they are known as box-office champions. On the other hand, you have Hoffman and De Niro who have done movies that haven't done jack at the box office, but everybody wants to work with them because they bring an aura of prestige to a film. People aren't interested in Arnold doing a film unless it means he's going to make them some money. So where would you rather be? I would rather be in camp with the people who say, "They're just good, and we want to work with them," as opposed to being in camp with the people who expect you to write the big multi-million-dollar thing. Because if you do it once and you drop off, your value is gone. So, you should write what you love.

HARRIS: What is with this obsession with the hundred-million-dollar grossing film? Is that a real or perceived obsession?

CUNDIEFF: I think it's real to a good degree. I think that there are more options now than in the mid-eighties, when it became all about that. It all started to happen after the success of *Star Wars*. Before that, people would be happy to make four or five million dollars on a picture, and move the fuck on. In fact, that kind of mentality really killed blaxploitation. One of the studios stayed afloat on blaxploitation. They would make the movies cheaply, and they would usually make a modest profit at the box office. Nobody was buying a new Lear jet, but they were making a profit. Then came the mentality of "I've got to hit a home run every time I get to the plate. Fuck a single, fuck a double." People went away from doing the blaxploitation stuff, because they were after big, big, big money. Now I think that it's come back around to where you see both worlds coexisting. You have the independents doing things on a smaller level. You have the studios that are looking for the big hits. Look at the way people lie about the box-office results. Things have become much more about the business aspects of saying we're number one, we made the most money, as opposed to saying we made money, but look at this cool shit we've got coming out.

HARRIS: Bragging rights is currency in this town, and currency brings bragging rights. Now let's talk about *Tales from the 'Hood*. What was the genesis of those stories? I say "those stories" because of the structure of the film.

CUNDIEFF: I had written a play called *The Black Horror Show*, also called *Blackanthrophy*. It was a one-act play that was a takeoff of the disease lycanthrophy, which is the werewolf's disease. Blackanthrophy was the disease of being black. [Laughter] It was a comedy about two black businessmen, one of whom would turn into a Black Panther during Black History Month. His three-piece suit would vanish and would be replaced by a black leather jacket, he would have an Afro with a pick with a fist on it, and he would spew all of this "kill whitey" and "burn, baby, burn" shit. He just went totally radical. So I wanted to add two more one-acts and make it an evening of horror-oriented, black-themed pieces. Then I began to think that maybe I should do this as a little film—sort of like *The Twilight Zone* of black films. I mentioned it to Darin and he wanted to be involved. As we started to work on it, it became more serious. We both felt that we wanted it to have some really scary stuff going on. So I started listing some of the issues I wanted to deal with. Four of five are actually in the film, but I listed about twenty social issues and concerns that I wanted to potentially deal with: from crack babies to sell-out politicians and so on. Ultimately, we ended up with the ones that were the best stories that we could tell.

HARRIS: Did you have a hard time selling that concept to the studio?

CUNDIEFF: Darin and I were writing the script when Spike called me. Spike had finally seen *Fear of a Black Hat*. Of course, I thought that he was calling because of the little Jike Spingleton character, who was a cross between him, John, and Matty. I had heard through the grapevine that Spike was pissed off about that. So I got this call on my answering machine, and all it said was, "Rusty, this is Spike, call me. CLICK." I was like, "Oh shit, he's pissed." I called him back. He had seen the movie, liked it, and thought it was hilarious. So, he says, "What do you got? What do you want to do? What do you got? What do you got? What do you got?" I told him about what we were doing and he wanted us to send it to him. So we finished the piece and sent it to him. After we figured out and plotted out the stories, it was probably the fastest thing that I've ever done. We wrote it in a little over a month. We sent it over to Spike, and he tried to get it set up over at Universal, but they didn't want to do it. So he sent it over to Savoy. Within a month and a half from the day we sent it over to Spike, he had gotten the wheels turning toward it coming out at Savoy. He turned out to be very valuable to us. He protected us from the studio. After the film was cut, the studio wanted some changes that we thought were stupid. Spike stood behind us and said, "It's his movie." It was great having somebody stand behind us like that, and as a result, it was never a big deal to the studio. It pays to have a powerful producer like Spike. There are not too many people like that.

HARRIS: How much compromise pressure are filmmakers usually under?

CUNDIEFF: It depends on what it is, but generally, it's a lot. They take your film in and play it to a test audience of people who will say things like, "We thought the ending was kind of a downer. Maybe it would be better if the person lives at the end." So the studio comes back to you and says, "We know this is a historical piece, but why does Christ have to die?" It's almost like they don't care. They're just trying to make a movie that's acceptable to the largest number of people. I think a lot of great films would have a hard time being made today. Consider *Midnight Cowboy* and *Taxi Driver*. Today, *Midnight Cowboy* might end with Jon Voight and Dustin Hoffman driving off to Florida, where Dustin would get some cure for his gimpy-assed leg and John would meet the girlfriend he left in Texas, the one who got raped, and they would all live happily ever after.

HARRIS: Another happy ending. How much creative control do you enjoy? Do you get final cut?

CUNDIEFF: I've never gotten final cut in a contract. I suspect that I would have to get to the place that Spike has gotten to, or Quentin, where you have critical acclaim with a hit.

HARRIS: Is one hundred million the magic number?

CUNDIEFF: I don't know. Standards are different depending on who you are. For a black director, if you make sixty million or sixty-five million, they'll leave you the fuck alone. That's what I suspect.

HARRIS: Are any black films doing that kind of business?

CUNDIEFF: Not really. *Boyz N the Hood* and *New Jack* broke sixty, I think. We haven't had anything do that hundred-million-dollar thing yet. I doubt that we will. We may, but there's a lot of crossover involved in that.

HARRIS: When you're sitting around with a germ of an idea, how do you know when you're ready to write it? Do you pitch it around and wait for someone to bite?

CUNDIEFF: It depends. Generally, I keep a file on different storylines. Then, as ideas about those different stories pop into my mind, I write them down and stick them into the file, up until the point where I feel that I can write something. My computer is filled with files of abandoned projects. Three, four, five, up to ten pages of shit that I started writing, then said, "This just ain't working." I'll just play with something until it seems like it's ready to take over and have a life of its own. If I can make it past the first ten or fifteen pages of something, I just have to press on and finish it. You will always hit points in any story where you don't know where the hell it's going and you don't know what the fuck to do. That's where you just have to knuckle down and force yourself through whatever blocks are there.

HARRIS: I will usually say out loud, "Make a choice!" Then press on. Because, even if it's a bad choice, fuck it, it will reveal itself as such later.

CUNDIEFF: That's just as good as anything. You've got to move forward. You can always go back afterward.

HARRIS: Absolutely. How many drafts do you do before you go out with something?

CUNDIEFF: I don't know if there's any set number, but I wouldn't take something out until I felt comfortable with it. What I mean by comfortable is that I can read through it without wincing. You can see that in your own scripts a lot of the time. Sometimes I will write myself out of a corner or a situation, and when I go back and look at it, I know the shit ain't right. Someone else may not even think about it, but I know it's not right. So when I can get through a script and know that I'm not trying to slide one by the motherfuckers right here, that's when I can go out with it.

HARRIS: I hear you. A temporary fix is not a shortcut. There are no shortcuts.

CUNDIEFF: The main thing is to keep moving. I think the biggest problem with a lot of so-called writers is that they let things stop them. Their feeling is, "If I can't figure this out, then I cannot go on," which is bullshit; it's an excuse. It's like anything in life. When you learn how to drive, you turn the wheel from right to left until you learn how to go straight. It's the same thing in a script. You go one way, then the other, until you find your course.

HARRIS: Do you want to talk about money?

CUNDIEFF: What about it?

HARRIS: In general terms, what can a new writer realistically expect in terms of dollars for his first feature? You don't have to be specific about your own deals unless you want to.

CUNDIEFF: Well, I'll say this: The first thing that I got paid for was *House Party 2*. I think I got somewhere between eighty and ninety thousand. That was if I got complete authorship, if I wasn't rewritten. I was rewritten, so I made around sixty or seventy thousand.

HARRIS: Did you get points on the back end?

CUNDIEFF: Supposedly, but I haven't seen a Goddanged thang.

HARRIS: You're in good company.

CUNDIEFF: Realistically, anything that gets your name onto the screen as "Written by" is a good thing. Even if you get scale for it. Guild scale ain't shit to sneeze at. That's like forty thousand for a screenplay and a certain amount for revisions. Even if it's just that, that's more than most motherfuckers make in a year. Most of the guys I know who are constantly doing something or other are making between eighty-five and one-fifty, maybe two, depending on previous successes and other things, to do something original. Then you have the break-out motherfuckers who get that five and six shit. It's all possible. The cool thing about writing is that they don't see your face up there, so the audience doesn't know if the film is written by a black guy, assuming you're writing for a general audience.

HARRIS: Do you project ahead from project to project, or do you wait and see what happens?

CUNDIEFF: I try to project a bit. I try to know what I have lined up, what's getting ready to happen. From a financial standpoint, I like to plan my life. A friend of mine told me once that we're in a business that is one of the biggest gambles. We're not gambling on the weekend, we're gambling with our fucking lives. Business-wise, you may be successful, you may not be. You may sell a great script this year, next year you may not sell a goddamned thing. I try to look at it that way and plan accordingly. All I know are the deals that I have right now and the money that I've got in the bank. I'm talking about economic survival now. I have this much in the bank and I have these deals signed, and this is the minimum that I can make from them. Often, you'll see in the trades that so-and-so signed a two-million-dollar deal. Well, that's if everything goes perfectly. That's if so-and-so is the sole writer and the film gets made, etc.

HARRIS: They call those things stipulations.

CUNDIEFF: Exactly, but the up-front money may only be thirty or forty thousand dollars. So, I project from there. I say, This is what I have to work with, then I try to live in a responsible manner. Now, career-wise, I have a list of stuff that I want to do. I look at it like this: There are things that are hard to get made, there are things that I have been trying to get made forever, then there are things that are more commercial and accessible, easier to get made. Somebody said that their next project is the next thing that they get paid to do. What is it? We'll let you know.

HARRIS: You must read a lot of screenplays that get submitted for your consideration. What are your general impressions of the work that crosses your desk?

CUNDIEFF: I get a lot of comedies, primarily because of *Fear of a Black Hat.* The biggest weakness in the majority of the comedies that I read is a lack of concern about story. You can get away with a lot in a comedy. Because people are laughing, they don't notice that there are giant plot gaps. Comedies are the only type of film entertainment in which things don't always have to be moving forward. A comedy can stop its forward story progression as long as something funny is going on. Once the funny shit stops, the story must start progressing again. There seems to be a lot of comedies in which the story doesn't go anywhere and the comedy doesn't relate to the story. Maybe this is just common in bad writing. To me, the comedy should always relate to the story.

HARRIS: Do you ever worry about being pigeon-holed as the comedy writer, or the parody director?

CUNDIEFF: Oh yeah, absolutely. That's not a black thing, that's a Hollywood thing. The business finds it very easy to corner creative people into very specific tasks. And, if you have a success, they want you to have more success doing the same thing. They don't want to take a chance on you doing something else because they don't know if you could be successful at something else. They know that you can be successful at comedies or dramas or po-litical thrillers, so they want you to do that again and again. Executives are not necessarily that creative, and a lot of creative people are creative in a lot of different areas. A lot of people I know can write and play the piano. And people who play the piano will paint and do all kinds of shit. Generally, a creative person is a creative person. Granted, people have their strengths and weaknesses, but the fact of the matter is that writers and directors and even actors, to some extent, can get short-changed when it comes to the type-casting process that happens out here. It is a problem that I've tried to be aware of. But if good comedies or parodies come along, I want to do them. In fact, there are some that I'm involved with now. But at the same time, I'm struggling very hard to get other types of things, which is one of the reasons I did *Tales from the 'Hood.* I wanted to go as far away from doing another parody/satire as I could for my second film, so I decided to go to horror. What may have been the problem is that both are very specific genre films, and even though they're totally different in terms of storytelling, they're very far from mainstream filmmaking. I'm hoping to get a regular story off the ground—be it a comedy, a drama, or what-ever—to start expanding my range, or at least what people perceive as my range.

HARRIS: You've had success writing films that don't fit into the classic three-act structure. Do you encourage new writers to experiment and create their own story structure?

CUNDIEFF: I think it goes back to what excites you, and what is going to stimulate you enough to pull you through the process. Whether it's writing, directing, or producing, all three of those are very difficult, time-consuming tasks. To take on a project that doesn't give you the opportu-nity to grow as it goes along is the surest way to seal your fate of not completing the project. To me, as a di-rector, I look at projects as if they are potentially going to take a year and a half to two years of my life. Is there enough there that I can deal with this subject matter ev-ery fucking day for a year and a half and not feel like I want to kill somebody? With writing, it is the same kind of thing. I would encourage people by saying that what-ever you see as the fuel to conceptualize your story, do it that way, because you need something to push you through the bullshit and the pain and agony that you are going to have to go through to get to the end of that process. Ultimately, if you can successfully execute some-thing that is different, you will receive much more in terms of respect and critical success than you would if you ex-ecute something that everybody is doing.

HARRIS: When is it over for you? Is it after you've shot the film, edited it, or when it's in the video box?

CUNDIEFF: It's weird, it's never over. At a certain point, you put it to rest. It's like kids. Some kids turn out well, and some don't. Even if you say, "Fuck it, the kid's out on his own now," when you hear about him, you feel something. It's the same with scripts. *House Party 2* is over. There is nothing I can do about *House Party 2*. Yet, if somebody brings it up, I'm like, "Yeah, that bad motherfucker! *House Party 2*, that was a tired little brat!" [Laughter] If somebody mentions *Fear of a Black Hat*, I stick my chest out and say, "Oh yeah, that was a smart motherfucker, I knew that he would do well." The same with *Tales from the 'Hood*.

HARRIS: Any final words of encouragement?

CUNDIEFF: I don't know who said it first, but the truest quote I've ever heard concerning writing was, "What is the definition of a writer? A writer writes." He doesn't wait for someone to tell him to write, he doesn't wait for someone to tell him what to write, he doesn't wait for the contract, he doesn't wait until he knows all of the adverbs and all of the grammatical shit, he just writes. Tell your fucking story. If you do that, you'll have something at the end of the day. That is the key thing. A writer writes. Just write and you will get better.

CAROL MUNDAY LAWRENCE

Photo by Calvin Hicks

"I believe that forewarned is forearmed."

Carol Munday Lawrence is a woman with a lot on her mind. She is an acclaimed filmmaker who oversees the Committee of Black Writers within the Writers Guild of America, west. I wanted to speak with her regarding the current representation of writers of color within the film and television community.

I'm glad that she was one of the last people I spoke to because the bleak portrait that she painted of the employment prospects for young black writers coming to Hollywood would make even the most wide-eyed optimist rethink his or her position.

I left our meeting severely bummed out. It wasn't until I came home and started writing again that I began to feel better. I realized one of the tenets that she spoke of earlier: Writers write because they have to. In spite of the discouraging statistics, I would just do my best and try not to worry about things outside of my control.

I remember hearing Arthur Ashe once say that he was reluctant to encourage youngsters to pursue a career in professional sports because there were only about 3,000 athletes in all aspects of sports within any given season. Within that, children are still encouraged to "be like Mike," even though the odds are nearly a million to one. I suspect that was part of what Carol was trying to convey. After reading Carol's sobering discussion, each writer must decide for himself or herself if they want to "be like Spike."

HARRIS: You're the chairman of the Committee of Black Writers at the Writers Guild, west. What is the function of this group?

LAWRENCE: It was set up by the Guild's board of directors. The way I define its purpose is several-fold. After I define it, we can talk about how it does and doesn't work in practice, and why. We have a number of purposes. One of them is access: the inclusion of black writers, that is, black voices in the screenwriting industry. So, one of the purposes of the committee is somewhat political. We encourage, pressure, cajole, or whatever we have to do to help create access for black writers in the industry. The committee does that with the help of the Guild's Human Resources Department. We also help writers develop craft. We've done things like set up pitching workshops, where people can learn how to pitch, develop pieces, and go in and be successful. We've put together evenings with studio and production-company development directors who come in and talk with black writers about what, specifically, they are looking for and how to approach them. These development directors are required to give their names and phone numbers and agree to be approached. That helps keep people abreast of what's going on in the industry. It also allows people to know us. We've been doing that on an ongoing basis because, as you know, this is an awfully fickle industry—things change all the time. We are there for our own encouragement, because so much talent is discouraged in every area of this industry that people of color really need safe havens, wherever they can find them. Beyond that, it's really wide open. Since I have been chairman, I feel that it is up to the writers to decide for themselves what they want to do and what the committee's direction should be. We have also been active in making sure that the industry knows that black writers even exist, because they're still playing that "I can't find any black writers" game. So we petitioned the Guild's board of directors to authorize a directory of black writers, so that those writers who wish to can be listed in a particular directory for producers who are looking for black writers. Those are our official objectives.

HARRIS: Have you been successful at meeting those stated goals?

LAWRENCE: We've done what we can. All of those goals are global and huge, and the committee is made up of a handful of volunteers. So we don't have even the expectation of ushering hundreds of black writers into the industry. But I think we do make a difference, if only by our presence and that we do have access to the Guild's board of directors. We can pressure the Guild as an institution, to watch its own act and to get behind efforts to create equity for writers of color. There are so few of us. There are almost 8,000 writers in the Guild, but there are only 264 who are people of color, of whom only 112 are black. That should give you some perspective on the people in the Guild and the pool that is available to the committee. We are talking about very small numbers of people.

HARRIS: You had some criticisms of the Guild-sponsored Bielby Report, the report on equity in the industry. What are your thoughts?

LAWRENCE: The Bielby Report is on the status of the hiring practices in the industry. I look at production companies, networks, and television shows in an attempt to quantify the participation of different classes of writers. I think that the numbers are useful, but I don't think that the numbers are being used. It's not so much that it shouldn't be done, or that we shouldn't have it, it's that the money that's spent for the Doctors Bielby, to keep doing this report year after year, is not useful if we're not going to solve the problems. What are we going to do? This is a problem, like many others, that has been studied to death. The idea is: If we're studying, then something's happening. My position is: We know that it is bad, we know that it has been bad since the days of Oscar Micheaux. When is something going to be done? There is no mechanism for addressing the issues. We continue to describe them. The Bielbys are not without merit. I do not mean to imply that, but I would like to see the money spent on coming up with a means of correcting the situation. I'm weary of talk; I think a lot of people are.

HARRIS: I think that we have come to understand and almost expect a certain amount of bias in the industry at large, but how do you feel when you see that same under-representation on so-called black projects?

LAWRENCE: It makes me sad. I wonder if some of it has to do with the self-esteem of those people of color. There are black people in every area of this industry. You can find people for your crew or your team who do everything at such a high level that they do not have to apologize for being black. That's a fact. So, it's not a matter of "We can't find any" or "They don't exist." It's choices that are being made. I believe that the amount of money and the amount of perceived power to be had in this industry is incredible. There is nothing else that promises that kind of money and that kind of sway over people's minds, and that's extremely seductive. I think that on a certain level it is made very clear to black people in certain positions that they are exceptions and they are to function as exceptions. I think a lot of people can see the handwriting on the wall. I also think that there are issues for people whose hearts are in the right place, because during production, everything becomes a battle, and when you're in the middle of production and you have those kinds of inhumane pressures upon you, you are very susceptible to the feeling that, at some point, you have to stop the battling and get to work. If you have to fight over every individual you want on the crew, over every word in the script that has to be okayed beforehand, that's very difficult. You have to choose your battles.

HARRIS: I'll agree with that. I think it was Truffaut who said something like, "At the beginning of a film, the director has all of these high ideas and expectations, but by the end he just wants the damned thing to be over with." Of course I'm paraphrasing.

LAWRENCE: Shooting a film is like taking an army into a war. You don't have enough time. I don't care how much you have, it's not enough. If you have a hundred million dollars, you need one hundred and twenty. You are at the mercy of human beings, the actors in particular. The equipment, the weather, everything. Your script is only on paper. You may find as you go that certain things are not working. You're exhausted. If you're the director or on the production staff, you're working insane hours. If you're on location, you don't have any of your support system with you. It really is very difficult. I think that the people who don't do this look at the finished film, see us all dressed up and having cocktails, and think it's all wonderful—there it is up on the screen. They think that the process and the product have something to do with each other, but they don't.

HARRIS: I've often said that the best part about the movie business is going to watch one. Most of the people who read these words will probably not live in the Los Angeles area, so what would you tell them to expect in terms of getting their careers started?

LAWRENCE: I have been teaching at USC, in the film school, and I have taught at the last session of the Guy Alexander Hanks & Marvin Miller Screenwriting Program, which was set up by Bill Cosby, and I find it really difficult each time I talk to people just getting started to decide what to say and how much to say and how to slant it. But I think that the only way to do it is to give it to people from both barrels—tell them the truth. Number one, you have to go in with craft. You have to know what you're doing. Just writing FADE IN: and putting some stuff down is not going to get it. You have to have some sense of structure. I'm not talking about the structure that your computer will do for you, I'm talking about story structure. One must have some sense of what the market is. You hear so many people say, "Well, I want to tell my story" or "I have a grandmother who was great." This is a business of sales. Once it's written, you're in sales. Overall, it is political. There is no way around the politics. The bias in this industry is incredible. If you don't believe me, let me remind you that only 264 of the 8,000 Guild members are people of color. Of all of those who are employed, we are a tiny percentage of the people who get paid for their work. That tells you something. I have people who have said to me, "Well, Spike Lee did it." I say how many Spike Lees are there? There's one, and that's Spike Lee. While I am not going to discourage anyone, I do think that people should come in with all of their armor in place, and with some kind of knowledge and understanding of what they're getting into. Going to movies is not the same as writing one. The process is not fun. Facing that blank page is not fun. I think that new writers need to understand about agents. About how this industry works. One must be represented because, for the most part, you can't get anyone to even say no to you unless you're represented. I think they should be prepared for the realities, because a very small percentage of people run and own the resources that make it possible to make a film. It is such a small city, and there is no accountability. By that I mean that there is no institution to go to with a grievance. If you work for IBM, you can go into the manager or the president or whomever. There is some kind of hierarchy that you can appeal to. That doesn't exist in this industry, and the stakes are very high. A writer has to be prepared for the attitudes of those who feel that black people can't write because they're black. People will not read your stuff because of that. Many times, you will be told no for no particular reason. I think that this book is a great resource because I believe that forewarned is forearmed. Which is not to say, don't go into battle, but don't go into battle wearing chain mail when they're shooting Uzis. [Laughter]

HARRIS: What are some of the myths and misconceptions that you see new writers operating under?

LAWRENCE: I think people don't really think about what's a good story. One of the myths is, "Well, since they're buying guys-in-the-'hood-type movies today, I'll just write up a quickie one of those and sell it.

HARRIS: But you're already five years too late.

LAWRENCE: Exactly. Then there are the people who want to make the Sojourner Truth movies—people who are really committed to telling the historical stories, which need to be told, but one must know the market. And there's also the myth that your phone call will be returned.

HARRIS: Indeed. I'm considering changing my name to Erich Who. [Laughter] "Erich Who is holding on line three."

LAWRENCE: I would advise people to buy one of those headsets, or a speaker phone, so that they can continue writing while they're sitting there on hold. I think that the biggest factor in those myths is just naiveté. It's the way that we have been taught in school. We teach people to fill slots that exist in a certain system. If you want to be an accountant, there are people who put ads in the paper for accountants. There are no ads in the paper for television writers. It doesn't work that way. This is a freelance craft: you create your own career, and you are your career. You work from gig to gig. The notion of going in and getting a job with some security does not hold true in an industry where you learn by doing, and you gain credits as you go. That's why I have mixed feelings about the schools. With certain crafts like photography, you can learn how to operate a camera, and then the question becomes: Do you have a gift? Do you have an eye? With others, I am not sure that the place to be is in a university or out there doing it. I am not talking about an either/or situation; I am saying, have a real sense of craft. I am not sure that people are aware that one sells oneself. Your demeanor is extremely important.

HARRIS: Expand on that, because that is important.

LAWRENCE: If you're lucky enough to be able to sit down and talk with someone, no matter where it is, they are watching you very closely. It's a very casual business, almost pretend casual. There are certain dress codes. One must behave as if they are relaxed, yet cordial. I think that there is a great deal of acting involved at times. One must present oneself as exquisitely prepared because of the pervasive attitude that a black person has come in the back door and is not going to be able to perform. There are people who practice for meetings. You definitely practice if you are going in to pitch. No question about that. You have to practice this with someone playing the devil's advocate for you. That's very important. Nobody knows everything. It's a huge mistake to be unwilling to listen or learn.

HARRIS: Speak to the importance of being flexible and open to creative input and criticism.

LAWRENCE: You're going in to sell something to somebody. Because writing is hard, we end up feeling that our script is our baby. There's also the attitude that the script is the finished product, when, in fact, it is just the road map for a film to be made. That is very painful to hear when someone has poured their heart into the work. The screenplay is not up there on the screen. It has to be interpreted by all kinds of people before it's a movie. There are those who feel very protective of their work, but the fact is, it's going to be changed, legitimately and politically, and you just have to be prepared for that. Legitimate changes have to do with those changes that technical people feel are necessary to get it done. And there's the political input of those who feel that they should change something just to say that they did it. Again, if you're selling and you have a buyer and a market that doesn't really need you, you're going to have to be flexible. If you're not flexible, you're going to go home with your screenplay, and it's going to be sitting on the coffee table being dusted every Thursday. [Laughter]

HARRIS: Let's talk about gaining entrée into the Guild. What does one need to get Guild membership?

LAWRENCE: In order to join the Guild, a writer has to have an aggregate of twenty-four units of credit, based on work completed under contract. That is, twenty-four units of work if you are employed as a writer, such as on a television show, or you sell a script. The script doesn't necessarily have to be produced, but you have to have been paid money. Or you have to be employed by a company that is a signatory to the Guild. In short, you have to have either sold work or have been employed as a staff writer for a certain period of time to be able to join the Guild.

HARRIS: What are some of the privileges that come with membership?

LAWRENCE: The Guild does not find work for you, but what it does do is set minimums for payment. As a Guild member, you can only work for companies that are signatories to the Guild. In television, all of the companies are signatories to the Guild—they have to be. As a Guild writer, you cannot be hired for less than minimum. Of course, you can go up as high as someone is willing to pay, but there are certain set bases that cover a very wide range of writing. Screenplays, treatments, and week-to-week assignments, all of that is covered. The Guild also sends a message to employers that there are certain ways that Guild writers cannot be used. For example, I can't ask you to write a spec script for me, based on my approval, without paying you. There are a lot of writers getting burned

like that, even today. The Guild will also track down re-
siduals for you. That is wonderful: If you have written a
television episode, they make sure you get paid. No matter where it is distributed in the world, they'll get you
your money. If there is a credit-arbitration problem, you
can take that to the Guild. There was a time when someone could take your work, make small changes, and then
get screen credit as co-writer. There were also ways your
name could be omitted completely. Those are the kind of
things that the Guild protects you from.

HARRIS: What are you most proud of in your career as a
filmmaker?

LAWRENCE: I am most proud of the work that is in the area
of celebrating black folk. In other words, the work where
we see ourselves on-screen, get to tell our stories, and be
who we are. The medium that works best for that is the
documentary and the docu-drama. I have worked for a
long time on a documentary form that is very dramatic.

HARRIS: You're creating a new form?

LAWRENCE: Yeah, where it's not all talking heads. Or it's
combinations of that where one moves into the other.
The bias, of course, is in favor of the dramatic film. But, I
think that the reality is that it's going to be a very long
time before we can use that medium to express ourselves
in the way we want to express ourselves. Just because of
the way that the industry is set up. There are so many
different levels to which we have to have access. You
have to get your screenplay sold, you have to get it made
the way you want to get it made. It has to get distribution, exhibition, financing. All of those resources are in
the hands of people who are thinking of the blockbuster,
and who are quite likely to harbor certain attitudes about
black people and the value of the things they want to
see. I personally find myself, in a lot of excellent company, very discouraged now. I see the industry getting
smaller and smaller in terms of larger companies buying
up more and more smaller production entities. Book pub-

lishing also is owned by big production entities. It affects whether you can say what you want to say in print, because they're going to the blockbuster novel to make the blockbuster movie. As the news is owned by entertainment entities, as the networks are owned by individuals, they have final say in what people get to see and hear.

HARRIS: Do you feel that it's all working against the diversity of voices?

LAWRENCE: Absolutely. It's happening in the economy on a global scale. The big fish are doing a lot more swallowing these days. It means that smaller entities can't get started, and many of those that exist are getting eaten. A couple of years ago, when the independent films were running away with the Oscars, the independent companies started to look attractive to the biggies. The political move to the right is also reflected in the industry. Not only in terms of what we see, but what we do not see.

HARRIS: That, in fact, may be more profound. What have you noticed in terms of the type and scope of images of people of color on television today?

LAWRENCE: Right now, it is overwhelmingly situation comedies. Since Cosby went off the air, there is nothing comparable that I have seen that shows black people in something other than the most crassly slapstick-type comedies. There is a real proliferation of slapstick-type comedies with black people, which, for me, fit into the African-American-as-entertainment category. There is no comment, there is no commentary—its a safe arena. I see nothing dramatic, and I know of producers who have had a horrible time getting a dramatic show on the air, and getting it to stay on the air. Or even situation comedy that's really situation comedy, where the humor is driven by the situation and not the wisecracking of the characters. I did a television show a number of years ago about the state of the industry, and Marla Gibbs was one of the people who appeared and said, "What we want is balance." I don't see behind-the-scenes people getting their careers built up so that they can go on and become show-runners. It's somewhat better in terms of the number of staff writers on these shows, because there was a time when there were virtually no black staff writers on these so-called black shows. In television, writers go up the ranks by starting as staff writers. That is how producers are made. So, if you don't get in as a staff writer, you can forget it, and there are very few African Americans who are working on shows that do not have a so-called black theme.

HARRIS: It seems that most of the black writers in television, to some extent, feel limited.

LAWRENCE: Exactly.

HARRIS: Then if the show is canceled?

LAWRENCE: Those writers have difficulty taking that credit and going on to something else because black writers and black shows are so devalued. They're challenged.

HARRIS: What would you like to see in terms of the diversity of television writing? Given the obstacles, should black writers pursue assignments on the more mainstream shows?

LAWRENCE: I think we need to be everywhere. An individual writer will write. You'll find that you have a talent for certain kinds of things. I'd like to see any black writer who has the craft and the gift be able to write whatever he or she wants to write, and not be saddled by the idea that everything black has to be funny, or that blacks can only write for something that has a so-called black theme. A black theme is the single-parent family with wisecracking kids in dopey situations.

HARRIS: The eight-year-old going on thirty.

LAWRENCE: Yes. We know that television is the principal source of information for people, and that it shapes opinions and attitudes. There are studies that have shown that for years. It's probably still being studied. That is why I feel it is so important and so necessary for us to have our own voice. People are killing us and it's justifiable because of what is on television. If your opinion of a group was that they were criminal, uneducated, cheating, over-sexed subhumans, then when you see a Rodney King being beaten, it's very easy to say, "Well, he must have done something to deserve that." Or look at the rush to judgment with O.J. Simpson. Black people were saying, "Well, we don't know what the brother did, but we're willing to go by the law of the land, which is, he is innocent until proven guilty. If he did it, then we'll buy that."

HARRIS: I don't know that the Simpson case is particularly relevant to this discussion.

LAWRENCE: I think that it is important in this discussion of writing and access because here you have a situation where our reality is our reality. On the other hand, you have people who choose to believe, because it is convenient for them, that we have a different reality. Therefore, when you have a case where black people can clearly see the potential for misbehavior on the part of law enforcement, because they live with it every day, the people who have total control of the media choose not to believe it. This creates tremendous anger and frustration on both sides. The short of it is, it matters that our voice is silenced. There needs to be some kind of commentary by black people, whether it is in a journalistic context, a dramatic context, or whatever. We need to express our own perceptions of our own reality. It is essential for our own well-being and for the education of others. I see this as being much more than just about entertainment.

HARRIS: What do you see happening with new talent as they enter the industry?

LAWRENCE: Someone will make a film, usually independently. It does better than they expect, and so they get a deal to make another film. They'll get no help—they're just tossed out there. Then, unless that person is really dedicated to building their craft or working with someone else, which isn't usually the case, they come up with something that is a first effort. They don't get a chance to build and develop, and they don't get a chance to call in someone who is a little more seasoned. We have not been able to build on what we know. It annoys me when I hear that we need more new, young writers. We have plenty of people with experience who are not working, and it's not their fault. A lot of people get one shot and then get discarded. That, to me, is not progress, and not a career.

HARRIS: Is there still much age discrimination?

LAWRENCE: Oh yes. There is this attitude that the voice of black people is a teenage voice. It is amazing. I think that one of the things that contributes to this attitude is the hiring of younger and younger executives who stay for very short periods of time, and while they're there are threatened by anyone who reminds them of daddy. I need not remind you that four-year-olds do not write *Sesame Street*, aliens do not come down and write science-fiction films, and historical pictures are not written by Lincoln's ghost. Somebody writes these things: somebody who is not necessarily just like the people featured in them.

HARRIS: I think that it is damaging to believe the adage that says you're a genius if you're discovered by age twenty-five and washed up at age thirty-five.

LAWRENCE: In what industry does experience not count? If you've got craft and you can spot a good story and you can work on assignment, you will do fine at any age. If you look at the efforts of some of those who didn't come in with craft, you'll see what happens. They're not making any more films, and the people who hired them are now saying that black people can't write. That's a practice that indicts all of us.

HARRIS: What solutions do you see for this problem?

LAWRENCE: What I would suggest, if it were humane at all, is that someone who is getting a shot would also get some help, and would also get a little ego adjustment. They should know that they are getting a shot, and that this is hard work and responsibility. So, learn the craft, take direction, and be ready when you come out there on your own. I'm not saying that anyone shouldn't be out there making films, but if you look at who's getting the opportunities, it really feels like a set-up to me because we have very few people who get beyond those first couple of films and go on to create a body of work, other than the independent people who work outside of the Hollywood system.

HARRIS: What encourages you? Is there anything heartening that we can wash this jagged little pill down with?

LAWRENCE: I think all of this has to do with commitment. I think that any artist has to have a reason to be an artist. Going in and trying to make a killing will not be enough to sustain you, and it's probably not going to happen. You have to have some sense of purpose. Write because you want to be a good writer. It is also important to have a support group of some kind. There are just times when you want to sit down with other like-minded individuals. Keep writing and watch your work get better. I think that to be centered spiritually, in whatever way you choose, helps a great deal. You must keep your life in perspective because it is easy to feel, after a number of rejections, that you deserve to be rejected. Having inner strength is really key. So are life experiences outside of the entertainment industry. Everything in the industry is so intensified that you can start to believe that the whole world is the film and television industry, which it's not. There are pockets of sanity in other parts of the country and the world.

ERIC
DANIEL

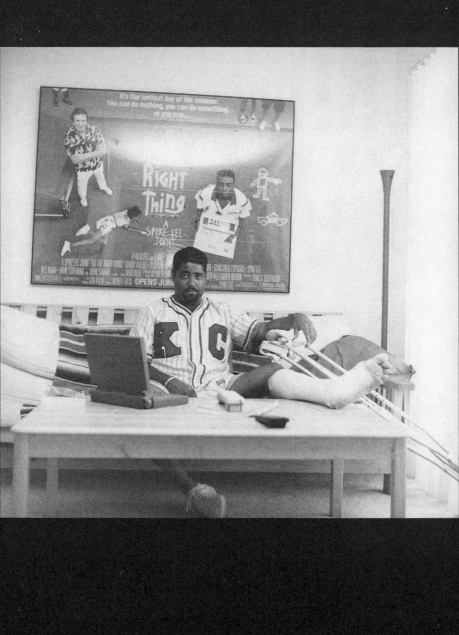

"You have to feel that yours is a story you feel passionate about."

E ric Daniel was wearing a cast on his left leg on the day we met. "It happened playing softball," he said, wincing at the memory. "It's actually been good for my writing." I didn't ask for details of the incident, but when he stood to shake my hand, I felt sorry for the catcher, if the sturdy six foot two, two hundred-plus-pound Eric injured himself in a collision at home plate. The brother is large.

Eric Daniel clearly has a passion for baseball. I am certain that his passion was a considerable factor in his success in writing *Brushback*, a comic story about a modern-day professional baseball player who gets hit on the head by an errant pitch and wakes up in 1945 as a player in the Negro Leagues. *Brushback* was developed while Eric was in the Disney Writer's Fellowship, but it has been acquired by John Singleton's New Deal Productions.

Though reluctant to give career advice, Eric recounts his rise from an unpaid production intern, to an assistant director, to an award-winning short-feature director, and finally to a Hollywood screenwriter. His learn-by-doing approach to filmmaking should serve as an example to anyone who is interested in pursuing a filmmaking career.

HARRIS: You're one of three writers from the Disney Fellowship Program who are participating in this book. How was that experience for you?

DANIEL: The program was great for me. It was a learning experience. Before the program, I was based in New York. I was writing and sending my work out here. It gave me the opportunity to come out here and learn the studio system, and have that buffer. I didn't have to worry about making that end. They provided me with that.

HARRIS: You're talking about money? The stipend?

DANIEL: Yeah, the money was cool, but I was making more than that as an assistant director in New York. The program gave me the access that I didn't have before. It was cool to have three development directors to pitch to, go over your ideas with, and, basically, pick their brains. I never had that kind of attention before. That was a benefit, as were the contacts that it set up at the studio and other places.

I learned to pitch to a room full of busy executives, realizing that they have time constraints, and how to convey and sell my ideas in a concise period of time. That was a real benefit to me. I really don't have any negatives to say. The only thing that could be improved upon is that they've never done anything with the materials that they have. I think that since it is a fellowship program, the scripts don't get the same look as those from writers who have solid deals there. I think that's unfortunate because I've read other scripts that I thought were worthy of more attention than they were getting.

HARRIS: Isn't that all subjective, because it's hard enough to get a film made anyway? We always want to say, "Mine is the film that should be made over anyone else's, damnit." But it ain't necessarily so.

DANIEL: I think that's exactly it. I think that if you happen to be fortunate enough to get into the program and you go in thinking, "I'm on easy street because they're going to make my movie—I'm set," you're going in with the wrong attitude. It is what it is: a writer's development program. You're there to learn how to work within the system and how to take feedback and incorporate it into your rewrites. I really didn't go in there with those things in mind, but when I started to get some excitement about my script, the possibility started to look attractive.

HARRIS: Talk a little about feedback, the process of rewriting, and getting something in shape.

DANIEL: Even before I was in the program, I always tried to get other perspectives, because it's real easy to get immersed in your work. After a while, if you look at it enough, you really can't judge it objectively. I was open to criticism; I think that it's helpful. I think that a writer has to learn how to accept feedback, both positive and negative. You don't have to rewrite your whole script because one person says something's not working, but I am of the opinion that if one person says it's broken, well, maybe that's just his opinion, but if ten people say it's broken, then maybe it needs to be fixed. I like getting feedback, both good and bad. I actually pay more attention to the bad than to the good, because I think that's were you can learn where you might be a little bit lacking in some aspects of your writing. If you want to be a successful writer in the Hollywood sense, you have to know how to accept feedback and know how to incorporate that feedback into your work without compromising your integrity. What I mean is, if you feel that the feedback is contradictory to what your piece is about, then don't go with it, but if you feel that there is some validity to the things being said, then you have to pay some attention to them.

HARRIS: I think there is a danger for young writers to be eager to please at the expense of the piece. A strong, clear vision of the work is probably the best defense.

DANIEL: That's the most important thing. The writer has to know what the integrity of the piece is. Everything's subjective. The executive's job is to offer contradictory opinions to the work. If they're not doing that, then they're not doing their job. I think there's a fine line between being too eager to please and not willing to bend at all. This is a collaborative process, and if you're too rigid, not many people will want to work with you.

HARRIS: That may be an indication that you need to spend a little more time doing that extra draft before you have to put it under the scrutiny of the table.

DANIEL: No question about it. Rarely, if at all, is the first draft the best draft. I think that the more time you spend with the piece, the more it will develop. You know as well as I that you're only going to get one shot at someone looking at your work. You don't want to give them something that's not in its best form. It's important that the writers know the world of their story at every level. Most executives, when they come in, may know some details and some aspects, but you're going to be the one who really knows your world. That's why, when it comes to taking feedback, you need to have a base, integrity-wise, from which you're coming. Then you'll be able to say, "Look, that may be your opinion, but I know this world. That will not work, but maybe this will."

HARRIS: Your background includes extensive production work. How important was that experience to your writing?

DANIEL: I think that it's been extremely beneficial. It was a very valuable experience to be able to work in production for as long as I did, both as a writer and as a potential director. I can't even begin to break down the amount of knowledge I gained from working hands-on in production. After my junior year at Michigan State, I got an intern position on Spike Lee's *Do the Right Thing.* I didn't really realize at the time how fortunate I was to be on that film. It was a ground-breaking film. At that time, Spike was a name, but he wasn't as big as he is now. So there was the opportunity to be involved in all facets of the production. I came in as an intern, and during the course of the film I was promoted to being a production assistant. There were only five or six PAs, so we were able to oversee all aspects of what was going on. We had many duties, but in film you do just about everything as a PA. The thing I liked about working with Spike was that he opened the door for everybody to learn the process.

HARRIS: I think that, at that particular time in his career, his stated goal was to "demystify filmmaking."

DANIEL: For those of us working on the film, he did a fantastic job of that. Dailies, the film that we shot every day, were open to the cast and crew. We were shooting for twelve weeks on one block in Bed-Stuy. At the end of every day, we would run over to Long Island University, in Brooklyn, and check out the dailies from the day before. For me, as a storyteller, writer, and director, it was amazing to get the sides, to know what we're going to shoot. To be able to think about, If I were doing this, how would I want to picture this scene, and how the dialogue flowed and all of those things. Then to go on the set and watch Spike and Ernest Dickerson, the cinematographer, construct the whole thing. Then be able to watch the dailies the next day. It was like film school right there. It was a unique situation.

HARRIS: I had a similar experience working on *The Truth About Cats & Dogs,* written by Audrey Wells. Knowing the process shapes your writing.

DANIEL: It was a special time because a lot of the crew members, PAs, and assistants were also looking to do the same thing and be creative. Spike really demystified the process. You have to be talented to do this work, but it's not brain surgery. It's possible if you're black, female, or whatever—there's nothing to prevent you from doing this. As a result, many of the people who were interns or PAs then are now writers, directors, and producers. Also, it was great to work on a production that had an all-black crew. I didn't realize it then, but that was atypical.

HARRIS: Tell us about that experience. I've experienced that rarely. For me it was completely unique.

DANIEL: For me, at the time, that was the norm. It was my first production, and there was a family atmosphere working on *Do the Right Thing*. From that experience, I expected every film to offer that same comfort zone. It was nice to see talented brothers and sisters pulling cable and hanging lights, working on camera, and doing all kinds of things. It was a job, but you also felt like you were a part of something bigger. I didn't realize how special that was. Because Spike opened those doors, and got special sanctions, he was able to utilize more black crew members and fewer union workers. As a result, more people working in those positions were able to get into the union.

   After that, I went back to school, finished up my senior year, and came back and worked on *Mo' Better Blues*, which also had that family vibe. Then I worked on *The Bonfire of the Vanities*, which was a total 180. The money was good, but the job had a totally different feel. It was definitely all business.

HARRIS: I strongly considered re-organizing my family's resources and going to New York to intern on a Spike Joint. I would have happily done it to further my working knowledge of film in that environment.

DANIEL: That's a good point: There's a lot of people who keep this high-minded attitude that they won't work unless they're being paid, but I started on *Do the Right Thing* without being paid a dime. I was looking for an opportunity to learn. You have to be willing to do what you have to do to get that knowledge and training. On the first three or four weeks of that film, I never saw the set. I was working on a barricade two blocks away, letting traffic through and blocking off pedestrians. I didn't feel like I was a part of the movie, but I knew that they needed me there, and I had a job to do. Things improved as I put in the time.

HARRIS: Indeed they will, but you're not going to come in fresh off the bus and start operating the camera.

DANIEL: There's a lot of people who want to come in and jump ahead of the line when they haven't done the leg-work. It just doesn't work that way. If you want to be a surgeon, you don't start by cutting someone open. You start in medical school. You must learn your trade. If you do start by cutting someone open, the result isn't going to be good.

HARRIS: I think it's called malpractice. [Laughter] In *Daily Variety* for Thursday, May 11, it says "*Brushback* sells for a six-figure sum." It's good to find that you have a strong production background, as opposed to just shitting a diamond, as it were.

DANIEL: That "six-figure sum" is a great thing, but that's not why I'm here. The money is a part of the work's reward, but I was writing in New York without anyone paying me any mind. The first thing I wrote was my short film. It was a learning experience. I wrote it, then I raised the money and directed it. I did it for the hands-on training. It traveled around to film festivals, won some awards, and got people's attention. Then, I wanted to apply what I had learned to a feature film. The opportunity came along when a producer at Paramount saw my work and called me in. He was looking for a project for Kris Kross, the rap group. I told him that I couldn't write a rap movie, that wasn't my background, but I could write a movie about two teenage kids. At the time, I was still assistant-directing music videos and commercials for an income, but I took the time and wrote this feature.

HARRIS: Was this a paid assignment?

DANIEL: Not at all. It was an opportunity. For this important executive to call me into his office, based on seeing my film, and take an hour of his time, was enough incentive for me to say, "Hey this is an opportunity, let me spend the next three or four months trying to get something to him." I had never written a feature before, but I thought I had a good story, so I put it on paper. While working over the next three or four months, I delivered the first draft to him. The timing didn't work out with Kris Kross, and he decided that it was something he didn't want to pursue. So I just sent it around. Through my production contacts, I gathered names and addresses and put it in the mail with a letter.

HARRIS: Did you actually send the physical script?

DANIEL: Yeah. What did I have to lose? I didn't write it for me to sit here and read—I wanted to see what I could get from it. Every day while I was an AD, I would try to get my work out and get a new contact. It paid off. That was the script that got to Walt Disney. I sent it in to their fellowship program. They saw enough in it to want to hire me. They flew me out to L.A. for an interview, and two weeks later, I found out that they were offering me a job, so I jumped on a plane with all of my stuff and moved out to L.A. I really feel that if you want to make something happen, you just have to go out and do it. Throw caution to the wind or it's not going to happen. No one is going to come knocking at your door wanting to read your stuff.

HARRIS: Let's talk about *Brushback*. What was that story's genesis?

DANIEL: *Brushback* is a story that I came up with long before the Disney Fellowship Program. I've always been a huge baseball fan, and I knew a lot about the Negro Leagues from books I had read. One of my favorite old movies was *The Bingo Long Traveling All-Stars and Motor Kings*, with Billy Dee, James Earl Jones, and Richard

Pryor. I wanted to do a modern-day telling of that story. The other thing that spurred me on was watching *Field of Dreams*, which I loved. It was about players who had been disgraced, but were able to come back and redeem themselves on this field of dreams. It just blew me away that of all of these wronged players who came back, none were Negro League players—players who were done a greater injustice than any of the white players, because they had never been allowed to play. I also remember watching an ESPN interview with Vince Coleman, who was a modern-day player with the Kansas City Royals. They were talking to players about Jackie Robinson's influence on them, and when they came to Coleman, he said something like, "Jackie Robinson? Who's Jackie Robinson? He don't mean nothing to me." I thought, how can a man making five or six million dollars a year not acknowledge the predecessors who made it possible for him to do that? That put the idea in my head. What if someone like Vince Coleman went back in time and dealt with playing in the Negro Leagues? I loved that idea. It had kind of a *Back to the Future* element to it and a *Field of Dreams* quality to it. As soon as I was hired on the Disney fellowship, I pitched them the story. I had them from the very moment I started pitching it.

HARRIS: Was *Brushback* your passion?

DANIEL: Oh yeah. It encompassed everything I wanted to tell in a story, and was the kind of movie that I wanted to see.

HARRIS: How important is it for you to write from your passion as opposed to second-guessing the market?

DANIEL: I think it's really important. If you're trying to write something because you think it's what the market wants, or you're trying to hit on something because it's hot for the moment, then you're writing with the wrong motives. I think that you have to feel that yours is a story you feel passionate about, regardless of what's hot and what's not, what has and hasn't made money, and what executives are supposedly looking for. For instance, for a while there was an influx of urban-ghetto-hood stories. At that point, these hood movies were all that was getting made. I don't want to knock the writers of that kind of stuff, because I think we need to see that, but there's a more diverse expression of our culture that needs to be on the screen. For every one or two of the hood movies, there's another movie, on a shelf somewhere, that's been written about another aspect of black culture. The people who are making the decisions are saying, "Well, we'll make this. But we haven't seen that piece be successful yet, so I'm not going to make that." For a while, the only movies that were allowed to get made were the ghetto genre movies, and there were a lot of people trying to capitalize on that. But for me, personally, that's not my background and it would be hypocritical for me to capitalize on it instead of trying to write something that I'm passionate about. I just didn't want to do that. It had a reverse effect on me, because the script I wrote for the producer at Paramount got me into the Disney Fellowship Program. It was a nice little story about these two teenage black kids, about them bonding, like a little buddy movie, and then solving a crime. It wasn't ghetto genre, there wasn't a lot of violence and guns and drugs and stuff like that. I think that a lot of executives out here didn't know how to take it because they hadn't seen teenage blacks in that way before.

HARRIS: Do you think that coming out of Spike's camp may have given you more of a sensitivity to writing to your passion as opposed to writing for the marketplace? Consider Spike Lee: He clearly writes films that are diverse, passionate, and personal, and still they all have been successful. It's a real achievement.

DANIEL: Spike is definitely in an enviable position. Not many writers or directors, white or black, are able to make the decision that this is what they are writing, write it, say, "This is what I'm making," and make it. And then say,

"I'm going to direct it and produce it, and this is how it's going to go," and be successful at putting butts in the seats. I admire that. I think he has a certain freedom in knowing that he's the one who's going to be shaping the image on the screen, so he can take certain liberties that other writers can't. Writers have to fight for their own integrity and the integrity of their material. Without writers, there is no material. They have to do what's best for their work, not just sell it out to whomever they think has the best shot at getting it made. They must try to stay true to their original vision.

HARRIS: Do you start with a strong character or a scenario, or is each script different?

DANIEL: Each script is very different. For me, the scenario probably becomes the strongest thing. The very first idea of the story should sound like an interesting movie idea. You should be able to say within a few lines, "What if?" "What if a professional baseball player, black, egotistical and arrogant, without respect for the history of black players in the game, got hit by a pitch and woke up in 1945 on the Kansas City Monarchs in the Negro Baseball Leagues?" Wow, there's a story there. What if that happened? I think that if you can do that and see a story there, you will get going. Originally, you need something like that to spark your ideas.

HARRIS: Do you work from the classic three-act paradigm? Inciting incident by page ten, first-act break at page thirty?

DANIEL: I would say that I probably work from the classic three-act structure. I learned a lot of my writing techniques while I was in the Disney program, and by taking the McKee course and things like that. What people seem to really like about my work is its story structure. The inciting incident is usually in the first fifteen pages, the first-act turn is right around page thirty. The second-act climax is fifty to sixty pages after that, and that kind of thing. As the material grows, you have to grow with it. You can't hold yourself to any constraints. You have to feel where it's taking you and go for that ride, then try to tell it in a structure that's suitable for that story, yet appealing to the viewer. Most people want to go to a movie that's going to present some dilemma that throws the protagonist's life out of balance, then watch him as he goes down this trek to try to put it back in place and resolve itself in some fashion, all in two hours. That's what I try to do. I don't think that I am a slave to structure, but I try to stick by it. I've learned that if you can write within the parameters of good story structure, then people will notice that, even if the story isn't where it could be.

HARRIS: In your process, do you work out the plot points in treatment form, or do you work organically, letting the scenes shape themselves?

DANIEL: I definitely do a lot of work before I start writing. The treatment is the first thing for me. I try to identify the inciting incident, the first-act break, the body of the second act and what leads us to the second-act break, how the second-act climax will spur us toward a crisis decision for the protagonist, what the result or climax of that decision is, and how it is all resolved. That is how I try to look at the story. But the first thing is a treatment, probably a short treatment, and I try to build from there. I like to get very detailed. I don't think that a two- or three- or even five-page treatment is enough to really express the amount of detail I need to get to the crux of the story. The more work I do at that level, the easier it is for me to begin, scene by scene, putting the pieces of the puzzle together. It helps to outline the work.

HARRIS: So, maybe you'll do a twenty-page treatment?

DANIEL: Yeah, fifteen or twenty, but I'm not saying it has to be. The last one was twelve or thirteen. Some are longer, some are shorter. Whatever suits the story I'm telling.

HARRIS: When you're plotting out your scenes, do you work them up on cards?

DANIEL: I did that for *Brushback*, and it helped to kind of keep a flow, but I try to do a scene-by-scene outline. The cards, for me, became time-consuming. But they do help to lay out the scenes and tell the story in a fashion that is sensible and unfolds at the right pace. In *Brushback*, I was dealing with some things that were based in real-life experience, so there was a lot of research that went into that. I was really trying to pull together a wealth of stories that could be told about the Negro Baseball Leagues. It was a matter of pulling out these great stories and trying to figure out how I could pull my character from the present and let him be involved in this situation and let him reflect on his own situation. Once I had an idea for what stories I wanted to use, how they best fit in combination and advanced the story, it was essential that the character have an arc.

HARRIS: Each scene must advance the story?

DANIEL: Yes, or it's not worth having. You must identify who the protagonist is, how the events are affecting the character, and what change he goes through during the course of the film. It's like putting pieces of a puzzle together.

HARRIS: With your first draft, do you aim for 120 pages?

DANIEL: I'd say 120 pages is what I go for. Both of my scripts, thus far, have been 120. I write with detail. I like to write so that the viewer can really envision what's going on. I like to pack a lot into the pages.

HARRIS: How many times do you go over that first draft before you show it to someone?

DANIEL: I've been over and over it. Usually, I know it backward and forward—I can quote the lines. The first draft usually ends up being like a second draft, because I've been over it so much. Then I show it to people close to me, but also to people whose opinions I value and trust. Not just friends, because they end up being your worst critics. They just end up telling you it's great. I really want to hear from somebody who will step up and tell me, "Hey, this is not right." I try to get a range of opinions, and then step away from it for a little bit, then look at it again. You don't want to give your script to someone whose opinion you don't value. That's not going to do you any good. [Laughter]

HARRIS: After the work was done, how did you get representation?

DANIEL: *Brushback* sort of hit a wall at Disney. I thought I gave them something that was worthy of attention. I think a lot of the executives thought that it was a strong piece of work, but because of the constraints of the fellowship program, it wasn't going to go anywhere. I moved on to my next project for them, but I felt that *Brushback* needed to find a new life elsewhere.

HARRIS: Did you do two years at Disney?

DANIEL: No, one year, but we were supposed to write two projects. So I moved on to my second project, but *Brushback* was still in my heart. I was developing my third draft while developing my second project. As soon as the year ended, I immediately submitted my letter stating that I would like to re-acquire my work through turnaround. Then it was a matter of about a month of waiting for the work to pass through every department at Disney and getting the screenplay back. Fortunately for me, it didn't take too long.

HARRIS: So Disney normally owns the work created through that program?

DANIEL: Oh yeah, they don't pay you to come in and look good. You're working for them. You know that that's the situation going in. In your contract it states that if they're not interested in pursuing it, then you have the right to re-acquire the work and try and do something else with it. So, that's what I did, I re-acquired it. I knew that there was some outside interest in my work. I had gotten my work to Sinbad, and he loved it. He really wanted to make *Brushback* as a project for himself. I developed a great relationship with him and his company, and I thought that that was how it was going to progress, with Sinbad behind it. Then John Singleton's company got hold of it, and John decided that it was something that he was interested in. Meanwhile, I had all of my production contacts. So, when I finished my third draft, I made up about forty copies and had one giant mailing. I wouldn't really suggest this to too many people, because I learned that you don't know who's going to get your script and where it's going to end up.

HARRIS: Just tracking it seems impossible.

DANIEL: I figured that this is my shot—let me get it out there. At the same time, there were a couple of people who passed it around. A director got it and was eager to be involved, but was not in a position to make it, so he passed it along to a producer who passed it along to talent, who took it with him to Sundance. He showed some people, without me knowing it, and it got into other hands.

HARRIS: That's heat, baby.

DANIEL: But it was a learning experience. You really have to stay on top of your work to know who's got it, and you can't let it slip out of your hands. It ended up working in the long run. I got people reading it, I got a few people interested, and it got to John. It also led to another job opportunity with Sinbad, whom I'm currently working with.

HARRIS: On an assignment?

DANIEL: Exactly. I was grateful because it gave me a job right after the fellowship ended.

HARRIS: Talk about building momentum! You did all of this with out an agent?

DANIEL: Most of this was happening without an agent. It happened just from the script. Sinbad believed in it. I give him all the credit in the world for that. He was, basically, the first one to step up and say, "I want to see this as a movie." A few other people followed suit after that. I was meeting agents. I had a couple of contacts from the fellowship program that felt more like obligations rather than real interest in me. Then John Singleton found a home for my script at TriStar, and they were ready to proceed through the deal while I was still seeking an agent. So things happened for me opposite of the way that they usually do for most writers.

HARRIS: A number of writers have expressed similar things. Maybe it's better to do the work and push your project, create some heat, and wait for the agents to come around?

DANIEL: Sure, nobody will do it for you. Agents don't want to take that risk. They are just like anybody else—they want a proven commodity. They want validation of some sort. I wasn't at that point. And you can't jump at the first agent you find. You've got to find somebody who really believes in your work, and feels like they are going to be able to find a market for it. That's what ended up happening. After meeting with all of these agents whom I really didn't click with, I ended up bumping into a guy at the building that my mother lives in. I had just come back from a seminar of independent filmmakers, and I was wearing the ID tag from the panel. This gentleman was talking to my mother when he saw the tag I was wearing and asked me what I did. I told him that I was a writer. We started talking and I told him I had directed a short film, that I had a script that I had some interest in, and that I was looking for an agent. He said, "That's interesting, I'm an agent."

HARRIS: Did your mother tell you?

DANIEL: No. I had no idea. My mom didn't even know. She had only recently moved into that building. The agent and I hit if off on speaking terms, and he told me his name. Coincidentally, I had his name at the top of my list of three or four agents whom I still had to get my work out to. So, I got him my work, and he enjoyed the read. He really believed in the project without knowing the extent of the interest in it. He jumped into the project without feeling it was a sure thing, and I respect that. He stepped right in and built on the work I had done and made the deal a reality. It worked for me, but I doubt that anyone else is going to bump into an agent in their building.

HARRIS: Let's talk about what happens after the sale. A favorite quote from my friend Audrey Wells goes, "If you're talented and persevere, you will sell your script. Then your troubles will begin." [Laughter] Tell us about the post-sale development. They don't buy a script and then just shoot it.

DANIEL: Very rarely, from what I'm learning. I've heard some horror stories about development, but this is my first time going through it. Basically, I've been brought on to do the re-writes of my script, to put it in shooting-script form. I'm getting notes from John Singleton's company and from TriStar. Like I said before, it's my job to maintain the integrity of the script, enhance what's there, and to work with the feedback, incorporating it into the story to hopefully bring about a better version of the script that is to everyone's liking. That's what I'm going through right now, and I have no complaints about the development process so far. I feel fortunate in that way. Things progressed so well with New Deal because we had a lot of meetings where we talked about their ideas, which weren't anything that I felt uncomfortable with, before the deal came through. It was basically enhancing what I already had there, bringing out more of the humor. Fortunately for me, John is in tune with the subject matter, which makes my job even easier. I know how fragile it is to get a picture made. That's the thing that I think a lot of writers need to realize. This is only step one of many steps that have to happen before the film can come to fruition. I know everyone is excited, and I have to do my part. I have to give them a script that everyone wants to make. There's a fine line that separates me from the outside, looking in, trying to get a deal, trying to get my script seen. I was lucky that, through the chain of events, I was able to get my script in their hands, because that's really what got it going. If I wasn't able to make that happen,

then I would be on the other side of the fence, still ped-
dling my work.

HARRIS: Any final words of encouragement for the kids at
home?

DANIEL: I don't know if I'm in any position to give advice
on how they should proceed. I can only say that you
should be true to who you are as a writer and as a person. If you are talented and you have something to say
and you have a good story and it's in good structure,
even if you don't have an agent or production contacts, if
you believe in your work and you get it out there any
way you can, good things will happen. The main thing is
that you have to be prepared. You have to know how to
accept feedback and reaction to your work, and you have
to know how to deal with it and utilize it to improve
your work.

JULIE
DASH

"I'm doing this because I like to create worlds."

I was taken off-guard when I met the Julie Dash because she was half the age that I expected the writer-director of *Daughters of the Dust* to be. Instead of a woman of sixty, I met a vivacious woman nearly half that age. I resisted the urge to ask, "Is your mommy home?"

We settled in the sitting room of her spacious Victorian home in the Hancock Park area of Los Angeles, and her daughter N'zinga treated us to a batch of oven-fresh cookies while Julie and I discussed the state of independent filmmaking today.

Julie Dash has made a career in this male-dominated field by staying true to her vision and speaking her mind. But more impressive than her words are her writings. She treated me to a copy of her latest screenplay, *Enemy of the Sun*, which is nothing short of spectacular.

I am certain that with Julie's determination and visionary nature, this film will be made and will exceed the great successes of her earlier projects.

DASH: I didn't start as a writer; that was not my intent. My intent was to be a director.

HARRIS: Is that right? Your writing is so clear, so authentic.

DASH: They said *Daughters of the Dust* was a film that was not accessible. Why should I, as an African-American female, want to write the same kind of thing that has been done, and probably will be done in the future?! We have another way of saying things, we have another way of speaking, we have another way of standing on the corner, etc.

HARRIS: My first reaction was that *Daughters of the Dust* was nothing like anything I'd ever seen before—it was a completely different world.

DASH: You disengage from what you know to be correct, because you're someone who has been educated, and learned how to tell a story using archetypes that embody western characters. A lot of people find it very disturbing. The story doesn't unfold the way a western story unfolds. Even though it did have a beginning, middle, and end, it unraveled in a totally different way.

HARRIS: When I let go of my own conventions and dogma, I was able to fall right in. It was like returning to a place that was in legend and lore, instinctively in me, but not seen for a long time. It was the most challenging film I think I've seen in terms of making me let go of some of the conventions that I held.

DASH: It's science-fiction. It's speculative fiction. It's a "what if" film. What if an old grandmother could . . . ? What if an unborn child could come out a mother's stomach and walk among them as a five-year-old? What if, what if, what if. That's speculative fiction.

HARRIS: It's important to note that if this is the type of story that you want to tell, all you have to do is research it. After all, I'm sitting across the table from a beautiful young woman, not a woman my grandmother's age.

DASH: Everyone is shocked to see that I am young. When I went to London, people always said, "We didn't know that you were going to be so young!" When I did *Illusions*, because it was film noir, set in 1942, everyone thought that I grew up in the forties. I wasn't even born in the forties.

HARRIS: A tribute to your writing.

DASH: Whenever I'm doing a story, I try to totally immerse myself in the period, in the ambiance. I've had teachers who said that if you want to write a character, you need to know the character's perfume—their fragrance. I wear male fragrances. I play Sam Cooke records to get into what someone who would be living in the sixties would be like. I really get into it. One of my favorite periods is World War II, which I learned about through the research I did on *Illusions*. That's perhaps why, when it's done, I can walk away from it. It's not mine anymore. It's familiar, I can remember the date of the engagement, but it's not mine.

HARRIS: How much time did you spend researching *Daughters*?

DASH: About fifteen years. The first writing of it was done at AFI in the seventies. At that time, I was told everything: "It's been done before, it's not interesting. Why would you want to tell this story?" The writing teachers wanted me to gear it a different way. It took me fifteen years to realize that people want to see stories that have to do with themselves, or their families, or their children, or what they fear, or what they love. When it has nothing to do with them, then they tend to disengage from the subject matter. I can't say all people, but Americans are like that. Europeans and people from other countries are more willing to embrace other cultures.

HARRIS: That's interesting, since we as Americans push that melting-pot ideology.

DASH: Yes, I've sat in theaters from Madrid to Munich, places where they don't understand English, let alone Gullah, and they could tell me what the whole story was about.

HARRIS: I know what you mean. I was lucky enough to spend some time in Paris, with a friend who's a film student there, and his video-tape library was outstanding. There were American films, French films, Italian films, Japanese films, African films, everything.

DASH: I was on a plane this past march, on my way to Milan to be on the jury for an African film festival. I was sitting next to a woman who was a university professor. I told her where I was going and what I was doing, and she told me, "Oh, no! Africans don't make films." [Laughter] Well, let me off the plane, I've been misinformed. She was convinced that she knew this, just because she was a university professor.

HARRIS: Amazing. We can be so limited and self-absorbed. This is why I feel Americans don't make the best films. We do, I believe, make the best movies. There is a difference.

DASH: Of course there is. I was very fortunate because I was trained at film school in the seventies. This was before the director became a celebrity. Everyone in film school was a nerd.

HARRIS: "Film geeks" is what we used to call ourselves.

DASH: Exactly.

HARRIS: It took years to achieve the level of cool that you see before you today. [Laughter]

DASH: Anyway, we studied Russian films, Indian films, Romanian films, British films of course, and African films, north and sub-Saharan films. And very importantly, Latin-American films. We had a well-rounded training in surveying film. Now, many kids feel that if it doesn't come out of Hollywood, it doesn't exist.

HARRIS: I noticed there were two pervasive and equally delusional schools of thought that ran rampant in film school. One was the "fuck Hollywood" group, kids who rejected the three-act structure that they had never bothered to learn. The other was made up of the kids who thought they would make a million dollars from their first spec script.

DASH: Another Hollywood fable.

HARRIS: The latest one I heard goes: Once upon a time, there was a young filmmaker who prayed to be the youngest filmmaker the world had yet seen. Unfortunately that title had been given out. Undaunted, he simply said that he was the youngest one and, to his surprise, the world believed him and gave him a crown. Unfortunately, his film was not very good and he suffered under the criticism. The moral is: Perhaps he should have prayed to be the best filmmaker.

DASH: [Laughing] That sounds like an American fable. Yes, there's so much concern about money and fame. I don't know about all of that, I only know about the work. It's like those books about how to write a screenplay in twenty-one days. I won't even have a title by then. I guess that it's good to motivate people, but really.

HARRIS: Just to get those 120 pages done. Is 120 what you aim for?

DASH: I'm from the old school. I go for 135, then cut down.

HARRIS: I like that. Do you use a paradigm?

DASH: That Syd Field paradigm? No, but you have to mention it. It does work if you have no idea how to write a screenplay. I think it's good to pick up something like that. It gives you something to grasp onto. When I was at City College in New York, I had no idea whatsoever about how to write a screenplay because everybody I knew was working in the documentary field. I wanted to write a dramatic script, and I would write long, rambling stories. I had a teacher named Rod Pitchkins who wrote on the top of my first screenplay, "Talk, talk, talk. This is film, not radio." [Laughter] I was talking about what people were doing and not showing it.

HARRIS: Do you think it's important to learn that basic structure before you venture out and try to create your own style?

DASH: Absolutely. Because of *Daughters*, people say, "Oh, you're into that non-linear stuff." That film was non-linear. But even though it was non-linear, it still had structure. It had a basic structure and a basic story. Then, from that basic structure, I went non-linear.

HARRIS: It was an artistic choice.

DASH: Sure. Someone once asked me if I made the film in the editing room, was it was free association? No.

HARRIS: I know people who think that actors make it all up as they go along.

DASH: My mother thought that, too. Yes, that's why they're so good. That's what makes a movie star: They always know exactly what to say. [Laughter]

HARRIS: In terms of the business, would you consider yourself a writer first or a filmmaker first?

DASH: I consider myself a black woman first. Because when you walk in that room, that's what people see.

HARRIS: Knowing that time is money, how important is it to you to have the script solidified before you walk onto the set?

DASH: To paraphrase Alfred Hitchcock, a film should be made in pre-production before you step out onto the set. It should be written, defined, storyboarded, and planned out. It should also be in the heads of the people working on the film. The cast and crew. You'd be surprised that not everybody is making the same film. Everyone may have their own agenda, or they may not see it the same way. It's your voice, your vision, and you have to make sure that everyone is seeing your world, which you're all painting on the same canvas. People can read things on the printed page and internalize it totally differently.

HARRIS: What steps do you take to ensure that everyone is on the same page?

DASH: I write background breakdowns for all of the characters. I give these to the actors. I also give them history lessons about the period. I give them a long and a short form. I've brought in a Gullah tutor to talk about the language, the region, and the characters as well as what was happening politically at the time. I brought the actors down early, so they could get used to the locale, feel what it was like, feel the mosquitoes biting. They said that they had never experienced anything like the region.

HARRIS: You took a very writerly approach. How many drafts did you go through before you shot the film?

DASH: I remember at least ten complete rewrites. I'm sure there were more polishes, but in terms of major changes, about ten drafts.

HARRIS: Is it as painstaking for you as it is for me?

DASH: Not since I've got a word processor. When I started writing in the seventies, I had an Admiral typewriter. You'd be so happy to finish a draft that didn't have a lot of typos, [Laughter] because you're not going to re-type a page for just one typo. Now it's a lot easier, especially for format. With "Scriptor" and all of that, there's no excuse for your script not being in the correct format. I've spoken to different producers and creative executives for the studios and, believe me, if they come across a screenplay and the first three pages are not in correct format, they are not going to read it. It gets to the point where it's hard to visualize it if it isn't formatted correctly.

HARRIS: On the rewriting process, Maya Angelou said in an interview with Tom Snyder that she rewrites and rewrites until she comes to the point where she says, "Enough." Then she releases her work out into the world, but it's never really finished in her mind.

DASH: You have to. Otherwise you'll never get anything out. Nothing is ever 100 percent perfect. Nothing should be, as in Zen. Like Japanese painters who often put flaws in their work for balance.

HARRIS: Take us into your process. Do you work from a treatment or an outline?

DASH: I work from a very detailed treatment. Sometimes, it can be up to a hundred pages. Then I do scene-by-scene treatment that's very detailed and that has a lot of background in it. Sometimes I have interior thoughts in the working subtext of the treatment. Of course, in the script program you can have script notes, and you can hide them in the screenplay. I work with cards, too. I have cork boards inside of my final-draft program.

HARRIS: You're right in the software moment, pushing the envelope of 1995 and beyond.

DASH: Get wired! You've got to get wired! If you want to be a punk, be a cyber-punk.

HARRIS: You're the high priestess of the cyber-world. I'm still listening to eight-track tapes. [Laughter]

DASH: Didn't everything just sound better on eight-track? Maybe that was just my memory. I used Memory as a character in *Daughters of the Dust*. Sometimes in film school, the instructors could be so rigid. Some things were just cardinal sins. I sinned all over in the writing in *Daughters of the Dust*. I have two people narrating in the same film. That's a cardinal sin. I have Memory as a character. I have voice-over and flashbacks. You can do anything you want to do, as long as it works.

HARRIS: That's a good point. But, it really has to work.

DASH: Sometimes it doesn't work. [Laughter] I think the important thing is to try. You have to have an underlying logic to everything that's there on the page.

HARRIS: How long does that whole process usually take?

DASH: About three or four months, but that's a first draft that I won't show anyone. That's just for me to see where I'm going.

HARRIS: Let's talk about the new work.

DASH: The new work is something that I co-wrote with

Michael Simanga called *Enemy of the Sun*. It's a psychological thriller.

HARRIS: You're returning to traditional Hollywood terrain.

DASH: Yes, but it's still very culturally specific. Most people who read the script have problems with it because it's filled with black folk whom they have never seen before.

HARRIS: That's someone else's problem isn't it?

DASH: Yes, it is. One of the characters is a teacher, trying to teach Plato's *Republic* to his so-called urban ghetto classroom. In *Enemy of the Sun*, everything is a metaphor for light and darkness. Knowledge, judgment, and usage of information. I think it may be too much for some people.

HARRIS: I enjoy the fact that your work plays on a number of different levels.

DASH: I try to put digital metaphors into everything that I do. I like being able to uncover or peel away layers of visual information to find the nuggets.

HARRIS: What's the most difficult problem that you've encountered with your scripts thus far?

DASH: The most difficult problem I've encountered has been consistent. Every time I write a new piece, there's a war to produce the damn thing. It takes several years before it is accepted or understood. This happened with *Illusions*, which was produced in 1983. Then, in 1986, people were writing that this is a must-see film. But in 1983, the press pushed it aside because it didn't seem like a black film to them.

HARRIS: Do you think that Hollywood will make *Enemy of the Sun?*

DASH: I'm shopping it, but it's going to be made regardless. Hollywood never financed a film for me before, yet I've been able to do twelve movies. Not all features, but I've been working.

HARRIS: Do you think that you've fared better financially, artistically or ideologically, if you will, by working as an independent filmmaker?

DASH: Absolutely. If *Daughters* was not an independent film, I would not have been able to have the character of Memory playing throughout. I would not have been able to keep the Unborn Child character. I would not have been able to have narrative tracks by a Great Great Grandmother and an Unborn Child. In traditional Hollywood cinema, these things are not understood, nor accepted. Someone wrote on one of the earlier drafts of the script, "How in the hell would you have an unborn child in a movie? What is an unborn child?" That was at the time when I wanted to start the movie with a storm raging inside a mother's womb, with the Unborn Child trying to decide whether to come out or not. This same person asked, "How can you shoot a scene inside a mother's womb?" I said, "With a tiny, tiny camera." [Laughter] It would have been a totally different film.

HARRIS: The money would have been different. You probably would have gotten your director's fee, your writer's fee, and that's all.

DASH: My director's fee and my writer's fee went back into the production for costumes. However, since I had a very independent distributor, he agreed that we would split, fifty-fifty, any money over one million dollars. He didn't think that the film would gross over fifty thousand dollars. It went over that the first week.

HARRIS: So you're still enjoying royalties that you may have not seen otherwise. Is your success due to your belief in yourself and your vision?

DASH: Absolutely, and good negotiation tactics. When someone thinks you're down and out, with an alien film, don't give in.

HARRIS: What are some of the disadvantages of working independent of the studios?

DASH: Working independently, everything takes so much longer. It often takes you years to raise the money and to shoot it. Then you have to raise more money to edit. Raise more money to get it to the final lab. It's just a drag. You're suffering, getting welfare cheese and serving it at the craft-service table. They were joking on the set that we couldn't afford to have a director's view finder, so we were going to cut both ends off of a Spam can and just use that.

HARRIS: There's your aspect ratio, at the bottom of the can. Spam-o-vision.

DASH: It's better than nothing. You do what you have to do.

HARRIS: Do you think that it's a good idea for young people to go to film school?

DASH: If you can, yes. If you can't, then don't let it stop you. There are different ways of getting around it. You can go to community media centers. You can go to local film workshops in your community, or those tied to the local colleges. If you can't even get into that, then get together with some like-minded friends, with your High-8, or Super-8, or your mama's VHS camcorder and make movies. Just write and direct your own stories.

HARRIS: That's a very good learning tool.

DASH: The practice will build up your confidence and flexibility. You'll know how to see a shot, have the confidence to take the shot, and trust your eye. You'll be able to work under pressure. Many people crack under pressure. Cracking is falling back into the status quo. When you take writing courses, they force you to write on a deadline, which is good training.

HARRIS: Do you think that all of the hype about the young director and the celebrity that goes with being *"l' enfant terrible"* can be damaging to a filmmaker at the student level?

DASH: Yes, it's a disservice! It's a disservice because people will think that they can just write one draft in twenty-one days, and it will be a Rusty Cundieff film. It's not going to be that easy.

HARRIS: You've traveled around, speaking to film students. What are some of the delusions they are operating under?

DASH: A lot of young or emerging filmmakers in film schools today want to be in film because of the glamor, the celebrity, the festivals, the girls, or what have you. I've had people say to me, "I want to be a filmmaker, could you give me suggestions on what I should do a film on?" Or "I want to be a writer, how do I start to write?"

HARRIS: How do you respond to that?

DASH: I ask, "Have you been keeping a journal? Do you write poetry? Do you have any thoughts down on paper?" "No, I don't have any thoughts." "Well, why do you want to be a filmmaker?" "Because, I want to be like Matty Rich." They want to be the lead guitar in a rock band. They're not interested in cinematography, or editing; they want to be the lead guitar.

HARRIS: Can you steer them away from that thinking?

DASH: What I say to them is that they must make a film, a video, or whatever. They have to go through the production process. After they go through the production process, then they will be in a better position to decide things. I think that the process eliminates a lot of people, because people have no idea what it takes—the discipline it takes—to write every day.

HARRIS: Do you write every day?

DASH: Yes, I write every day. Even if it's just a list of things. Sometimes I write random notes, journals, even if I have nothing to write. I can't sleep at night unless I have written something. I feel good about it.

HARRIS: There's nothing like the satisfaction you feel at the end of a good writing day.

DASH: It makes you feel proud when you read it.

HARRIS: You've gotten an agent only recently?

DASH: I've gotten an agent only after *Daughters of the Dust* did well at the box office. I didn't have an agent before that, and I couldn't get an agent. I was rejected from many different agencies, one of which said that they had reviewed my work and had looked at a work print of *Daughters of the Dust* and had decided that I had no future, so thank you very much. This was before the age of the black woman director. This was before Leslie Harris did

Just Another Girl on the IRT and way before Darnell Martin's *I Like It Like That.* I will never believe that, since the Gersh agency says I have no future in this industry, I'd better be a nurse. [Laughter]

HARRIS: So how exactly did you get your agent?

DASH: After *Daughters,* they just started calling. William Morris, ICM, and Intertalent Agency approached me about representation. The reason I initially went with Intertalent was because they represented John Waters. It seems strange, but I liked that fact.

HARRIS: What advice would you give to a writer seeking representation?

DASH: They should seek it, but they shouldn't be saddened when they're rejected. It has no bearing on their talent.

HARRIS: You didn't say, "if they're rejected," you said, "when." Is that rejection a given?

DASH: Yes, it's kind of a given. I know many great writers who still have no agency representing them. I'm speaking about black writers who have no agent simply because they're writing about us. They don't have a gimmick that sells them.

HARRIS: In light of this sobering discussion, you don't seem at all daunted or worried about the future.

DASH: Why should I be daunted? I didn't get into this business for the money. I didn't get into this business to be approved or for the fact that they were or were not going to finance my work. I'm doing this because I like to create worlds. I enjoy myself doing this. I'm protected. I have degrees; I could teach if I wanted to. I made this decision a long time ago. This is what I wanted to do, and I have been successful at it. Success doesn't mean you're a celebrity, success just means that you're comfortable, healthy, and happy. I love the process of making films.

HARRIS: How do you know that you have an idea that's good enough to spend the time writing it?

DASH: You know, that's interesting because you don't know if it's good enough until it's developed, until you flesh it out. Sometimes I go off on a certain thread, or an idea, and it goes nowhere, it's not strong enough. Maybe I can use that thread or idea in something later. Unless you start actually working and developing that story, you don't know. Sometimes you're sure the idea is going somewhere and it sort of falls away. Just put it in the file of story ideas and use it another time.

HARRIS: Have you ever sold a script on spec?

DASH: Never. I don't write those types of screenplays. I have stacks of those upstairs. They send them over from the agency. I don't write what Hollywood wants. My films will be made in spite of what they want to see. Everyone has their own agenda, whether it's spoken or unspoken. Our ideas do not run parallel.

HARRIS: Yet, clearly your work is something people have hungered for.

DASH: Well, that calls into question the adage that says it's not about black power or white power, it's about green power. That's not the truth. My films make money. I've been living off my films for twelve years. Even before *Daughters of the Dust* was made, my short films supported me. I have a following of people who watch my films, and that's still not enough to convince some studios to finance my films.

HARRIS: You make it sound as if it's been etched into stone. "It has been decided that Julie Dash will receive not one thin dime from Capital Pictures!" [Laughter]

DASH: Well, nothing is etched into stone because things change, trends change, people change. Sometimes it's like musical chairs up there. I see them as gatekeepers who smile and grin over lots of free lunches. They take good meetings and all of that, but nothing happens. I'm a very determined person. I have my own ideas and views and I know exactly what I want to do and exactly what I don't want to do. I'm not all starry-eyed and looking for a break.

HARRIS: In the classic Hollywood system, the writer wears a hat and the director wears a hat and the producer wears a hat and so forth. But it seems that in black Hollywood, if there is such a place, there's no such luxury. Have you found that true?

DASH: Yes, I see us as filmmakers. We write, produce, direct, make lunch, whatever. We then turn around and edit the darn thing. Cut the negative and go on about our business.

HARRIS: Is there really such a place as black Hollywood?

DASH: There's a black Hollywood. Then there's an independent-film world, which is the world that I speak of. In black Hollywood, there are a lot of truly independent filmmakers who can do it all. Then there are people who either direct or write—wear those individual hats—and they're very happy. Some of them do very good work, some of them do mediocre work, just like everywhere else. I enjoy being a filmmaker, I enjoy the film process.

HARRIS: What audience do you see yourself writing for?

DASH: Black women. It's very clear. It's not that I'm excluding other people in that wide general audience, but my focus is black women.

HARRIS: People will say that Woody Allen writes for a middle-class New York Jewish audience, but I enjoy his work, too.

DASH: There's nothing wrong with that. But who else is speaking directly to us? Why jump into that pool with the thousands of writers in the Writers Guild or directors in the Directors Guild who are speaking at us, but not to us?

HARRIS: One of my favorite novels is now in the can as a film: Terry McMillan's *Waiting To Exhale*, which has a male director. What are your thoughts on that choice?

DASH: Well, I told the producers that I loved Forrest Whitaker as an actor, and I think that he had a great directorial debut in *Strapped*. I think he has a great future as a director. I don't think that this is a film that should be directed by him. This is a woman's story, with a very specific nuance toward women. It was written by a woman and should be directed by one.

HARRIS: Who wrote the screenplay?

DASH: Terry wrote the screenplay with Ron Bass. Judith McCreary worked on it before that. The producers apparently didn't like the direction that the story was going and assigned it to Ron Bass. It's very clear that they enjoyed the story and wanted to see it on the screen, but they also wanted to see their story, or their story of Terry's story.

HARRIS: We'll have to wait until the film is out to truly comment on the work, so these are just thoughts about the process.

DASH: Absolutely, but I still think these choices must be considered. When I am producing, I'll choose my directors as well. After knowing Terry for years, I was disappointed to read in *Movieline* that she said, "There are five black women directors I know of, and I cannot imagine any of them directing this."

HARRIS: Did you take that personally?

DASH: Yeah, because I'm one of the five she knows. She's been in this house several times. I don't know if she was misquoted or not; I suppose it's possible. Let's wait and see the work.

HARRIS: When I saw *The Color Purple*, though it was not the book, it did not offend me.

DASH: I do remember that it was not the book, it was another thing with the same title. I was not offended by the movie. I felt Spielberg did the best job that he could do. It just wasn't the book that I had read.

HARRIS: I was young when that film came out, and it inspired me to read the book. In that regard, the story was effective. However, adaptations are just that.

DASH: Exactly. They're rarely up to the book. Books are magical. It's all in your head. It's like a fantasy is so much better. There are so many adaptations that I would love to do.

HARRIS: Who are some of your mentors and role models?

DASH: I have role models, but mentors in the industry just haven't been available to me. No one has ever taken me under their wing, ever. So that's why I feel it's my responsibility to do more for someone than was done for me.

HARRIS: Who are some of your contemporaries who you are most inspired by?

DASH: Charles Burnett. Neema Burnett is my buddy. Euhzan Palsey.

HARRIS: Do you believe the next film wave is going to be the women's wave?

DASH: Absolutely, so everybody buckle up your belts and get ready for the ride. It's going to be wild. It's going to be a different take of the woman. I'm really looking forward to being a part of that and helping it happen.

HARRIS: People say you're making it happen.

DASH: Whatever, I just want to be around to see it.

HARRIS: What issues do you feel you can capture in your work that eludes the mainstream cinema?

DASH: A women's point of view. A point of view of the culture of women. A point of view of the culture of African-American women. And a point of view of women of the African Diaspora. Motherhood, the whole nurturing sensibility. Women's intuition, women's wit, it's an area that's wild and rife for development. Surely it's been touched upon by male writers and directors, but stories of the specifics of being female in a male-dominant society have not been told.

HARRIS: How do you feel about networking?

DASH: I think that it's very important. I think that deals are done based on prior relationships in the industry. Someone takes you under their wing, someone becomes a role model to you.

HARRIS: Nora Ephron is a woman with a point of view who's been successful commercially. Do you model your career in any way after people like her or Penny Marshall?

DASH: No. I'm not them. I don't have the same relationships with people as they do. I'm not white, I'm not in the same crowd as they are. It's nothing against them or the work they do, but it's not the same thing.

HARRIS: The women filmmakers in Hollywood have been getting their "shit together" at a very swift clip. Do you think that female writers of color are discriminated against?

DASH: I don't think that they are discriminated against overtly. I think racism today is very subtle, very much institutionalized. Very much a matter of habit. That's why we get phrases like "at the end of the day, no one cares about a small insignificant passage of history called the Harlem Renaissance." I was at a pitch session and they asked me what was I doing now, and I said that I was working on a piece on the Harlem Renaissance for HBO and they said, "Is that going on now?" You see, we were, as a people, forced to learn their history as well as our history, but they have not been in that same situation. They don't know very much about us. It's time we started sharing some of that.

HARRIS: I believe people want to connect with, and not fear, the unfamiliar.

DASH: I do, too, but the gatekeepers don't believe that.

HARRIS: It's not what they believe. They may not be allowed to believe what they believe. Because if you believe in something, you'll stake your livelihood on it, and nobody is ready to do that at that level.

DASH: On those "green-light" levels. Nobody is ready to stake their livelihood and their mortgage on taking a chance. They maintain the status quo, just like they did fifty years ago with the cigar-chomping mogul who was sitting up there with a bald head. Now these twenty-something people are sitting in those same chairs making those same kinds of decisions. They're like clones.

HARRIS: Bill Duke in an article in the *Los Angeles Times* said that black filmmakers should be allowed to fail.

DASH: Just like white filmmakers can fail.

HARRIS: I believe he was addressing the fact that the expectations on black projects are so high, yet the resources are so much lower.

DASH: And all of the black filmmakers have to travel with their films and be held accountable for everything in their films, even though they may not have had total autonomy in the production effort.

HARRIS: Do you have that autonomy?

DASH: Oh yes. That's the great thing about being an independent.

HARRIS: Burnett didn't have final cut on *The Glass Shield*.

DASH: I can see that he did not have autonomy. I can watch the film and see decisions being made that are not Charlie's decisions.

HARRIS: The quality of the work is amazing, considering that the playing field is not level.

DASH: The playing field is sometimes full of mines. I'm not trying to win as much as be a soloist in the choir. There will be plenty of people to come after me, or during my time. I just have some things I need to say, and I have to say them the way I need to say them.

HARRIS: What responsibility do you feel we, as filmmakers, have to dismantle negative stereotypes?

DASH: I feel it's up to each individual. I cannot sit here and say every black filmmaker must come and fight the good fight. My only request is, don't dredge up old stereotypes and throw them up on the screen with a laugh track behind it and label it entertainment or some bullshit like that. Everyone has their own journey to make on this earth. Everyone is here on a different mission. I'm doing what I'm doing, but I'm not giving anyone else instructions on what he or she should be doing. If someone wants to do films with horror, or with explicit sex, or whatever they feel, then they should do the best that they can do.

HARRIS: What final words of encouragement can you offer those who will read these words?

DASH: If you want to be in this profession, and you will know soon enough after your first productions, be true to yourself and to your internal voice. Perhaps we have something to learn from those who are not trying to dismantle the existing structure. I'm not going to censor any-one else's idea. Perhaps there's something significant that will emerge from them. I do, however, turn my back on those who seek to make money on what has kept us down and what has caused us to have low self-esteem.

ROBERT TOWNSEND

"I always try to put a little message in my madness."

Robert Townsend emerged from being an actor to being a writer-director with his 1987 hit *Hollywood Shuffle.* From that auspicious beginning, Robert has established himself as one of the multi-faceted talents working in Hollywood today. His new television show, *The Parent Hood,* is one of the top-rated shows on the emerging WB Network.

Robert is very generous with his time and was one of the first people whom I reached out to when I started this project. Not surprisingly, he was one of the first people to step up and go on the record.

He was genuinely humbled when I reminded him of a chance meeting we had at one of our favorite restaurants and the lasting impression it had on me as a young writer.

During our three-hour visit, Robert spoke candidly and humorously about the process of getting a career started and the discipline and dedication that it takes to keep it going.

HARRIS: Your television show, *The Parent Hood*, is entering its second season.

TOWNSEND: Yes, we're in our second season.

HARRIS: How many episodes make up a season?

TOWNSEND: Last year was the very beginning, and we did thirteen, because we started in the middle of the year. So, this year we're doing thirteen, but right now we're the number-one show at the WB, and it looks like we're going to do twenty-two. [He knocks on the table]

HARRIS: Knock on Formica. [Laughter] Congratulations.

TOWNSEND: Thank you.

HARRIS: When I was putting this book deal together, you were on the short list of people I wanted to talk to, and I'll tell you why: A few years ago when I was just starting in college, I was having dinner at Chao Praya, in Hollywood.

TOWNSEND: That's where I eat.

HARRIS: I looked over and there you were with Keenen Ivory Wayans. This was right after *The Five Heartbeats* came out. You guys were huddled up in a corner table, and you had your big hat on. [Laughter] I said, "Damn. That's Robert Townsend and Keenen Ivory Wayans." I had just done a national Seven-Up commercial and so I was SAG-eligible and all happy. I went over, introduced myself, and told you I liked your work. I told you that I was in school, that I was thinking about doing some writing, and that I just got in SAG. Do you know what you said to me?

TOWNSEND: What?

HARRIS: You said, "Brother, do it. Do it now, because the time is now." That's exactly what you said. That was it.

You were one of the first people to energize my whole program. It was really helpful. When you're nineteen or twenty years old and you don't know anything or anybody in this business, any positive vibe makes a difference.

TOWNSEND: Thank you.

HARRIS: No. Thank you. I always wanted to thank you for the encouragement, because I got my education and kept my program on track. Now I'm writing.

TOWNSEND: Everything comes full circle.

HARRIS: Indeed. I saw *The Parent Hood* last night. I watched both episodes. You're on for an hour in the pole position. You kick off the Warner Bros. night. [Laughter]

TOWNSEND: I know. I've been totally blessed. In terms of numbers, we've been the number-one show this season for the WB Network.

HARRIS: Do you know why?

TOWNSEND: You never know. But my take is that people are responding to the show on a very positive level because of the images. They see what we're trying to do and we're working to make it happen much more. That's my take on it. What would you say?

HARRIS: The writing. The writing! I found the performances great, but the writing was sharp and fun. You guys are really having a good time with the format. There was a real sense of play there, but also cleverly written scenarios.

TOWNSEND: Thank you. It's funny, because we're in Hollywood, and when people think of Hollywood, they think of movie stars, directors, people like that. In the old days, it was more about the writers. Now Hollywood has gotten away from that, which I think is one of its problems. When you see a movie and say, "Oh my God, that was a horrible movie," it's because of the writing. If it's cleverly written, if the writer has taken the time, if nobody's come in and messed with the concept of the story, then it's good. You know what I mean? I think that in Hollywood's heyday, the writers came up with ingenious scripts that were actor-proof.

HARRIS: I agree. Let's go through your filmography. What was before *The Parent Hood*?

TOWNSEND: *Townsend Television*, a sketch show with a lot of music. My take on a lot of things. It was what I call The Townsend Touch. I created an English detective, Nigel Spyder, who was fighting crime. I did a silent movie, "Pookie Jenkins and the Boys." We did musical numbers, we had musical showdowns. There were dramatic pieces. It was a hodge-podge of things in my head. We had musical guests from Ice Cube to James Brown. We went the gamut.

HARRIS: Before that was *Meteor Man*?

TOWNSEND: *Meteor Man*, my inner-city fairy tale for children. The first African-American Superhero. He could talk to dogs. He was afraid of heights, so he only flew four feet off the ground. I was flipping through the channels on the television today and it was on, and I had to laugh. James Earl Jones is one of my favorite actors. I just love the cast I put together for that film.

HARRIS: That was a great movie for kids. Actually, Julie Dash's daughter, N'zinga, had two questions for you. One: How come you weren't more buffed? And two: How come you flew so low to the ground?

TOWNSEND: [Laughter] I didn't want to buff up for the part because I wanted the character of Jeff Reid to be Everyman. So when you see the character on the screen, you say, "Hey, he's somebody who could live in my neighborhood, somebody on my block." I was thinking about doing it, but I really wanted him to be a regular guy. As a writer, I wanted to do something funny with my take on superheros, because we've seen Superman fly to the highest heights, circle the planet, spin the world around, and do all of that. I said I could never top that as a writer in terms of how high I could go. So I said, Why not keep this character grounded so it is his humanity that we fall in love with? I wanted him to always have a human quality. I sort of grounded him by making him afraid of heights, only flying four feet off of the ground, even though he had these super powers. As a writer, I was trying to be honest and ask, If I really had super powers, would I go to the highest points? No, because you never know when it's going to wear off. [Laughter] It makes me laugh, just the visual, when I see myself flying. It's so silly, but that's what gives it its own special signature.

HARRIS: How did the movie do?

TOWNSEND: It was mixed. I did the movie for children, so a lot of adults didn't understand that. I'm a big fan of Steven Spielberg. The reason I'm a fan is because, as an artist, he walks in different kinds of arenas. He will do *Jurassic Park*, then he will do *Schindler's List*. He will do *E.T.,* then he will do *The Color Purple*. I like that. I believe that being an artist is not about being in a box, it's about taking chances, it's about doing different things. So, in the middle of all of these R-rated 'Hood pictures, Robert Townsend comes in with this PG-13 picture for kids. I don't think the adult audience was ready to see me like that. The kids gobbled it up, but the sad thing about cinema right now is that there are no films geared toward African-American children that all children can experience. We take our kids to see *The Lion King* and *Pochahontas*, but there are no films like *Home Alone* that feature African Americans. So that's why, when I came up this concept, I said, For my kids, for history, I want to create a hero. There's nothing wrong with *Batman*, *Spiderman*, but I wanted *Meteor Man* to be welcome. I think that the audience just wasn't ready for it. I know people who'll take their kids to see *Menace II Society*, but I feel kids should be kids for as long as possible. *Meteor Man* was great because now I have all of these kid fans. I'll be at the mall or in the car, and I'll hear a tiny voice scream, "Meteor Man!" [Laughter] For the adults, it will always be *The Five Heartbeats* and *Hollywood Shuffle*. The thing I was doing with *Meteor Man* was getting back to basic values and morals.

HARRIS: In all of your films, I see a strong family presence and an extreme sense of play. You never seem to take yourself too seriously.

TOWNSEND: [Laughter] I genuinely enjoy what I do. I feel so blessed to do what I do. So when people say, "Is Robert Townsend like that in real life? Is he a bright-eyed kid who can have fun?" I say, "Yes." I grew up in Chicago, on the rough west side, and I remember those days. So when I sit here in Hollywood, in the office, making movies and television shows and what-have-you . . .

HARRIS: And goo-gobs of money. Don't forget the goo-gobs of money.

TOWNSEND: [Laughter] They pay you a little bit here, but I just enjoy what I do. When I write, I try to incorporate layers, so that there's the funny, funny, funny, but at the core there's a message. In *Meteor Man*, the message was, you've got to stand up for what you believe in. I wanted to say that it's not about the powers, it's about what's in your heart. I remember a test screening in Oakland, at the grand Lake Theater. There were a thousand kids there, and when the scene came where Meteor Man lost his powers and the golden lords were calling him out, "Meteor Man!" the kids were so quiet that you could hear a pin drop. Afterward, I talked to the kids and found out that they got it. They'd say, "He really became Meteor Man after he lost his powers. He learned something greater, that he could stand up for himself." For me, as a writer, that's what it's about. Communicating messages, being funny, and telling a story. What's the key to Robert Townsend? I always try to put a little message in my madness.

HARRIS: When I watched *The Five Heartbeats*, I thought the original music was completely authentic to that period. How did you create that sound?

TOWNSEND: I went through so many songs to create a sound that I considered genuine to the sixties. I would talk to cats who were around and into music of that time. They would say, "Well, it was the bass line, we had a real bass. The kids don't use a real bass anymore." I'd say, "Well, what about the drums, did you use a snare?" And we went through this whole thing about why it had that sound. We'd talk about Motown. When they would record at Motown, they had one studio and it was wide open, so each instrument would have a weird echo to it. As I got into the music, I tried to do as much with it—the sound, the arrangements, and our harmonies as a group. I sing, but nobody sang in the movie because I cast the singing voices. I cast the actors, but I also cast the singing voices. I said, I want the lead singer to have that raspy, rough voice. Then you got the bass part, and Choir Boy has that high thing. And I'm a baritone, so I cast that. The actors could sing, but I wanted the music to have that flavor, like Levi Stubbs of The Four Tops, like David Ruffin, like Marvin Junior of The Dells. It was capturing the sound to put you back into the period. In different scenes I would throw in songs like "Oh, What a Night" and "Bernadette" to sort of back up the legend of *The Five Heartbeats*. I did different tricks. I love music, so I was totally into finding the right songs, so that as we went from the sixties to the seventies, we would go for that Parliament thing.

HARRIS: I was thinking of Earth, Wind & Fire when I saw those big Afros. I just fell out laughing. Underneath the music was a solid story. How did the story come to you?

TOWNSEND: The story was co-written by myself and Keenen Ivory Wayans. The story initially came to me because I was a big fan of The Temptations, I was a fan of The Dells and The Spinners. When The Temptations broke up, I kind of took it personally. I wanted to call David Ruffin and say, "Why can't you work it out, man?!" That always stays with me. I'd go to concerts and see groups that sing love songs, but did they have the love in their hearts? When you take a group like The Dells, they've been together forty years. That's a long marriage. Bonded by music, five cats have stuck together. With that, I be-

gan The Heartbeats. As we started to get into it, I found
out that I needed to do more research. So I went on the
road with The Dells. I talked to The Temptations, The
Ojays, I talked to everybody.

HARRIS: That research is critical. How much time did you
spend researching?

TOWNSEND: *Five Heartbeats* was three years of my life. The
initial draft we wrote was very funny, but it didn't have
the heart. I started to do interviews with the guys, and I
would say, "Tell me about the good times, man! Did you
make a lot of money?" They'd say, "We didn't make any
money." I'd say, "But, you know, the songs?" "We didn't
own any of the songs" "What about the cars?" "They owned
the cars." There was this real bitterness coming out, which
I realized that I had to incorporate into the story. Like
The Dells first album, "Oh, What a Night"—their faces
weren't on their own album cover, there was this white
couple walking in a park in Chicago. The Dells were on
the back in a little square. I saw the bitterness in their
faces and I knew I had to deal with this whole thing of
crossing over. They were told that they shouldn't be on
the cover because it would be good for them to cross
over. I asked them how it made them feel. They said that
it made them feel real small. For one thing, they couldn't
go into the barber shop and brag. The barber would say
"Lemmie see y'all album cover! Hey, where y'all at!?" On
the back, bleeding into the print.

HARRIS: There was a scene where the brother confronts Big
Red about his royalties, and ends up taking an ass-kicking and getting hung out the window. I sensed that that
wasn't fiction.

TOWNSEND: That still goes on, and was based on a true
story. I found out that it was standard practice. If someone got out of hand about their money, somebody would
take them and literally dangle them outside of a window.
There were a couple of major artists who they did that to,
to let everybody know that they were expendable. I didn't

really know how many people that had happened to until afterward, when people would come up to me and say, "Why you put me in the movie, man? Why you put what happened to me in there? Huh?" "I didn't know that was you, too, man." I think that the highest compliment was that different groups sent me telegrams, cards, and letters telling me how true to life the film was.

HARRIS: It was a beautiful piece, with some moving performances. Leon was brilliant.

TOWNSEND: Leon was incredible. Good acting all around. As a director, I'll say it was me, but it was really God.

HARRIS: How many drafts did the piece go through?

TOWNSEND: About seven drafts. As we started getting into the lives of the different characters, the music was used to propel us through the different times, and the words meant something different to each person. Like the first song in the movie said something about where they were in their lives. "I got nothing but love. I got nothing but love for you, baby." [Singing] "Don't live the life of a movie star." So, it just said where they were. Later on, it becomes their theme throughout the movie.

HARRIS: Once it was sung to the police to prove that they were musicians. That was interesting.

TOWNSEND: The thing was how they could use that same song of love against them.

HARRIS: Yes, it was all in the subtext.

TOWNSEND: To me, as a writer, subtext is the whole thing in good writing. There's a way of saying something without saying it right on the money. For example, when Eddie is kicked out of the group and he comes back years later, he sings, "Nights like this, I wish raindrops would fall." That was the song we sang when we were on top of the world. It meant something totally different later. It captured something pitiful. It was as if he was trying to audition for us. As a writer, I'm looking for those things to tell the story. I was telling the story through music. When we were at The Apollo, and we jump off the stage to win the contest, and the girl faints, it's telling nine different beats when the song is going on. As a writer, it's like understanding the use of time, as well.

HARRIS: How did that movie do for you?

TOWNSEND: *The Five Heartbeats* is the movie that people love, love, love. It wasn't a box-office hit, but I get tons of fan mail from people who have watched it twenty times. I think that the reaction that affected me most came when I was shooting *Meteor Man* in Baltimore. It was my day off, and I was at the harbor by myself. This guy comes up to me and says, "I need to talk to you, man." I say, "About what?" He says, "I saw that movie of yours over thirty times." I said, "Thirty times? Well, thank you." And I tried to walk away. But he says, "No, man. I gotta thank you." I said, "Why?" He says, "I used to be a junkie, and that movie got me through because you sang that song 'I Feel Like Going On.' And every time I heard that song and saw that movie, I felt like going home. So, I wanted to say thank you." He says, "I know that film didn't make a lot of money, but it helped me to get my life together I hope that's worth something." Then he just walked away.

HARRIS: That really gives you an understanding of the importance of the work. Isn't that what you got into it for?

TOWNSEND: Exactly. That moment was worth a hundred million dollars. Another woman wrote me a letter telling me how her son was considering joining a gang until he saw how the movie portrayed real friendship. She didn't know how to talk to him and all she could think of was taking him to that movie. He didn't join the gang because he realized that the people in the gang weren't his real friends. It blows me away when I get letters like that. I was trying to say something in the film about the nature of real friendship. The story is written in such a way that the character of Dresser's girlfriend comes up pregnant, and Eddie gives him money so that he can raise the kid. Later on, Eddie is responsible for the death of their man-

ager, and Dresser beats him up. He beats him up, but he
starts crying and hugging him. That shows what boys are
really about.

HARRIS: I don't know how films get marketed, but do you
think that that may have had something to do with the
overall lack of success at the box office?

TOWNSEND: The studio didn't know what to do with the
film. I've been looked at, for most of my career, as a stand-
up comedian. *The Five Heartbeats* had a lot of heart, a lot
of soul, and a lot of comedy. When the studio looked at
the film, we tested through the roof. We were one of the
highest test-rated films in Fox's history. They were like,
"Do we put the comedy in the trailer? The music? The
drama?" It tested through the roof because it all worked
together in a stew. When they cut the trailer, it wasn't a
true reflection of the movie.

HARRIS: The whole was greater than the sum of its parts?

TOWNSEND: In that sense, yeah.

HARRIS: *Hollywood Shuffle.*

TOWNSEND: *Hollywood Shuffle*! [Laughter]

HARRIS: Every time I think of that film, I laugh, too. But the
PR on the film was brilliant. The concept of getting it
done on credit, with donated short-ends, captured the
imagination of the press. Was that by design?

TOWNSEND: That was all true. Before that, I had never made
a movie. I had acted. I was in *A Soldier's Story*, I was in
Streets of Fire, I was in *Cooley High*. But, at the time, I
was dying. I was dying.

HARRIS: Creatively?

TOWNSEND: Yes, creatively. I was being offered slaves and
drug dealers and pimps. I started asking myself, "Is this
it?" I felt that there had to be a better way. Making movies didn't look that hard, so that's when I came up with
the idea to make my own movie. I had made money in *A
Soldier's Story* and *Streets of Fire*, and I had that money in
the bank. Being an actor, you learn to bank that check,
because you never know. My friends were asking if I was

going to get a Porsche or a Jag, but I said, "No. I want to make a movie." They told me that I didn't know anything about making a movie. I figured that what I didn't know, I would learn. I took all of my money out of the bank to begin shooting what would be *Hollywood Shuffle*. That money went fast because I didn't know what I was doing. But by then, I was like a strung-out junkie. [Robert begins trembling and panting] "Gotta finish the film . . . gotta shoot some more . . . gotta get raw stock . . . and, and, and . . . " [Laughter]

HARRIS: Were all of the vignettes scripted?

TOWNSEND: They were all scripted. Sam Ace, the detective, was done first, then Sneaking in the Movies. We used the Baldwin Theater for that. Then I acted in another film, *American Flyers*, and put that money into it. But I ran out of money again because I still didn't know what I was doing. That's when the legendary story of the credit cards began. I went to Minnesota doing stand-up comedy for two weeks. And I prayed in the car. I said, "God, if you want me to finish this film, give me a sign. Give me a sign, God. Have I wasted my money? Am I wasting my time?" I came home and there was a stack of mail. There was an application for Preferred Visa and another application for Preferred Master Card, there was a credit card application for The Broadway, another one for Montgomery Wards. So, I started thinking, I could finish the film on credit cards! First, I thought, no, but then I thought, what can't you charge? It totally made sense. Then I started getting credit cards from everywhere. You might say, "How can you do a movie on credit cards?"

HARRIS: Actually, that was my next question. Robert, how can you do a movie on a credit card, man?

TOWNSEND: Sacks Fifth Avenue: wardrobe. Montgomery Wards: paint and supplies. Sears: furniture. Preferred Visa and Preferred Master Card: charge everything. What I couldn't charge, I'd get by way of a cash advance. The only card I didn't use a lot was American Express, because they want their money, in full, at the end of the month. [Laughter]

HARRIS: Or they will come over to your house and cut your card up on your front porch.

TOWNSEND: Exactly. I think that if I hadn't done the film, I would have gone crazy. I love acting too much. And I found myself being put into a box, and the only way to escape that box was to make a funny parody of what was going on in my life at the time. The whole thing of the Black Acting School. People would say, "Hey Robert, act blacker." What do you mean act blacker? I can only act as I am. I knew all of these sophisticated actors, but we were all auditioning for slaves and pimps, so there needed to be a school to teach us how to play these parts, because none of us are from that place. Then, I did that whole thing: [In character] "Welcome to the Black Acting School. Hi, I'm Bobby Taylor. You, too, can be a Black actor . . . "

HARRIS: There's a bit in that film that works perfectly. You are working in the hot-dog stand and Keenen is all over you to let go of your dream. You go into a daydream where you arrive at the hot-dog stand riding in a limo and find them selling Ho Cakes. You get ready to leave and they're holding you by your leg, begging, "Please, please, please." We come back to reality and Keenen is still in your face, saying, "So please, please, please get your shit together!" Those transitions work thematically and dialogue-wise.

TOWNSEND: As a writer you're always looking for seamless transitions. That was one that just flowed. With good writing, you're able to do that and have people say, "Oh, that's what happened there. I was caught up in the moment."

HARRIS: Did you have any mentors or role models growing up?

TOWNSEND: What affected me was reading about Oscar Micheaux. He wrote, produced, directed, and distributed his films. I said, "Wow." He was the numero uno. Then there was Melvin Van Peebles, because he was a smart man, a renegade, a rebel, and he was making movies. I'd have to put Fred Williamson into that equation, too. Fred was acting, writing, and directing his own films.

HARRIS: You have a few hyphens next to the things that you do as well.

TOWNSEND: They make you work, but I love what I do. Like *The Parent Hood*: I'm the executive producer, I created the show, and I star in the show. I was going to direct, but I'm really devoting my time to setting up my next feature.

HARRIS: Do you want to talk about that?

TOWNSEND: Yeah. My next film is called *Justice County*. It's a thriller that takes place in Long Beach. It's about a lawyer who commits a murder and he tells his best friend about it. His best friend tells another friend, and another friend. What comes out of it is some disturbed, upside-down justice. But it's all real, and they all live in a suburb called *Justice County*.

HARRIS: Are you the writer/director/producer/star?

TOWNSEND: [Laughing] Yes, all of the slashes are correct.

HARRIS: Slash gaffer and grip?

TOWNSEND: That, too. I love it all, so my hands are going to be all over it.

HARRIS: I read that Kurosawa was so involved that you would find him painting blood on the fallen warriors in his films. I think his films benefited from his hands-on approach.

TOWNSEND: Wait until you see *Justice County*; it's going to be a ride.

HARRIS: What draft are you on?

TOWNSEND: This is my fourth draft, and we'll be ready to shoot in a few months. I like Hitchcock, so I want to do all kinds of things as an artist.

HARRIS: I wanted to ask some craft questions. What elements make a screenplay great?

TOWNSEND: I think that great writing is finding the simplicity of something, yet making it magical. So when you look at a scene, it's not the obvious. I love foreign films because they always find something beautiful or incredible about a common, everyday-life character. They're magnificent because they're human beings. For me, as a writer, it's finding those little things that make a character special. The enemy is cliché. I always try to throw a curve ball.

HARRIS: When you're starting a new story, say *Justice County*, do you start with a character, or do you start with a plot line?

TOWNSEND: I start with a concept of what I want to talk about. I'm fascinated with the justice system in America. I'm fascinated by the separation of the upper middle-class African Americans and lower middle-class African Americans. So I said, "What if this happened and that happened . . . " Then I started to draft characters based on characters I'd like to see in a situation and characters I know. I gave it a mixture of fantasy and reality.

HARRIS: Structurally, do you work from a paradigm?

TOWNSEND: I tend to follow classic structure, but then I let scenes play. I like to follow classic structure because there is something to be said for pace. I'll spill over one way or another when I begin to create the world. I grew up on classic films, so I'm into classic structure. I want something to happen in the story so that I can go, "Damn . . . What are they going to do now? What's going to happen . . . Is it? . . . Oh no! . . . " I write like that. I want people to be on the edge of their seats, or laughing, or tugging at their hearts.

HARRIS: Do you use scene cards?

TOWNSEND: No, I do an outline. I do a scene-by-scene outline, so that I can see where the story's going, beat by beat. Then I do character bios. They may go something like: These characters met in school. They went to Moorehouse together. This particular character went to Harvard, so they went to Law School together at Harvard.

But they had a fraternity that they were a part of at Moorehouse. So other members went to different schools and, in that time, certain things were lost and gained.

HARRIS: So that's the backstory. Is that backstory spoken in the script? Or is that just for the writer?

TOWNSEND: In *Justice County*, there are different things in each of their homes that say something about their history. I've sprinkled their history throughout. I layer the writing so that verbally there's one thing going on and visually there's something else going on.

HARRIS: Since you know you're going to be directing, do you give yourself more latitude in the writing?

TOWNSEND: No. I try to be as visual as possible. I try to articulate the feeling, the tone, the texture, what the people look like. Especially since I'm directing. It's a guide map for the team, so the DP can say, "Oh, I see what Robert wants here." The wardrobe, the sound designer, the music or whatever, we'll all understand our jobs. Knowing that I'm going to direct it makes it have to jump off the page. If I am not as visual, then I have to work that much harder to describe my vision.

In *The Five Heartbeats* we talked about the hair, we open on Duck. He's in Malibu, aged a little bit. Then we go into a flashback: no mustache, processed hair, goofy hat, lime-green pants, bowling shoes, red jacket. So right away you see that this cat doesn't give a shit about how he's dressed. It's about the art. When I write it, I have a thesaurus on my computer, so I can find the exact words. You don't want to say, "The guy ran into the room." He could have strolled into the room. He could have sauntered into the room. He could have creeped into the room. I get into trying to see something really happening. I like to play with words so that the actors will get as excited as I am.

HARRIS: You wear many hats on the set, but filmmaking is really a team effort. Discuss the collaborative nature of filmmaking as it applies to your work.

TOWNSEND: Filmmaking is totally collaborative. The director has a vision, and the team takes that and builds on it.
If I say that I kind of see them in glittery jackets, the
wardrobe designer may say, "What about jumpsuits with
blue lapels that stick out? And then they can rip the sleeves
off and . . . "

HARRIS: Sort of taking the ball and running with it?

TOWNSEND: Exactly. Then in the scene in *The Five Heartbeats* where I'm singing the song with my little sister, I
said, "I want it to be a warm morning, where she's sleeping and the room has this amber glow to it." I had written
the scene, but the DP suggested that we put a fan on the
curtains to let the curtains blow a little bit. Then the production designer suggested that we go with light silk curtains, with a little pattern in them. The wardrobe person
suggests that the girl should have on a flowing gown so
that she can move around and dance. And my pajamas
should be flannel, because they move a little bit better
and give more than cotton. Suddenly, there's all this energy that comes alive based on other suggestions. As a
writer, I may know the world inside out, but I may miss
things.

HARRIS: When you're writing a first draft, do you aim for
120 pages?

TOWNSEND: It usually paces itself out like that. When I write
a script, I read it, then I leave it alone for a couple of
weeks. Then I read it again. If the same magic works, the
scene usually is left alone. A scene unfolds, and you can
feel when you're long, and you can feel when you're short.
It kind of takes on its own life. If the writing's there, the
characters start to live and breathe. You begin to carve
out what a character will and won't do. Then you also
find out secrets. I like to build secrets into my scripts. It's
like the kisses in *Cinema Paradiso.*

HARRIS: Was that the best movie payoff ever?

TOWNSEND: It was so special. I had completely forgotten
about how the kisses were edited out and saved, so when

it paid off, I sat in the theater in tears. I think I'm going to rent that movie tonight.

HARRIS: What are some of your favorite films?

TOWNSEND: *The Godfather, I* and *II.* I think Francis Ford Coppola is an incredible writer-director. One of my favorite directors is Elia Kazan, and one of my favorite films is *A Face in the Crowd.* It was written by Bud Schulberg, who did *On the Waterfront.*

HARRIS: I love the way that film played as a metaphor for what was going on with the House Committee on Un-American Activities and the Hollywood blacklisting. Kazan gave up some people to the committee.

TOWNSEND: Exactly. He named names. The character of Terry that Marlon Brando played was him, fighting for his beliefs and going up against the machine. I like different movies for different reasons, but the ones I like are all well-written.

HARRIS: Your career started with *Cooley High.* What year was that?

TOWNSEND: That was 1974. Actually, I wanted to be a basketball player, but I wasn't very good. I wasn't fast and I grew up around Isiah Thomas and Mark Aguire. That was the caliber of players who were on the basketball court when I was a kid. I had the ability to do characters and voices when I was a kid. I was the youngest member of a theater company called XBAG, The Experimental Black Actors Guild. When I was in high school, I would go from the south side of Chicago to the west side of Chicago to do plays. They encouraged me to audition for commercials, and I got my first film while I was doing a play. Michael Schultz, who directed *Cooley High,* saw me in a play, liked what I was doing, and gave me a couple of lines.

HARRIS: Was it at that point that you felt that you could go on and, one day, direct?

TOWNSEND: Not then. I was an extra in movies for four years in New York. It was at that point that the process of moviemaking became demystified. I was an extra in *The Wiz*, in *Warriors*, in *Mahogany*. Actually, you see me in *Mahogany*. I'm in a welfare line behind Diana Ross when she goes in to meet Billy Dee Williams. Eddie Murphy makes fun of me when he sees me. [As Eddie] "How old are you? I saw you. I saw you in *Mahogany* and *Cooley High*." [Laughing] But that's when I discovered directing, because I was so close to the camera. It didn't look that hard. As an extra, you sit around and wait for them to use you in a shot, so I just took it upon myself to watch and learn.

HARRIS: So, you didn't go to film school.

TOWNSEND: No.

HARRIS: Would you recommend that young people go to film school?

TOWNSEND: Definitely. It gives you a basic understanding of how movies work. I think that the real beauty of film school is, once you learn the basics, you know how to free-style. I'm still learning my craft. I know the mechanics of it, but the only way to get better is by doing it. I think film school gives you a foundation.

HARRIS: Do you see yourself writing for a specific audience?

TOWNSEND: No. I grew up on movies. All movies. So when I write, I think there's a universal message to all of my films. The thing that I deal with is the human side of people. Anyone who wants to come along for the ride is welcome. The stories that are on my slate run the gamut.

HARRIS: In terms of your work, do you project ahead or do you wait and see what happens?

TOWNSEND: As a writer, I am pregnant with my scripts, and when my water breaks, my water breaks. I'd like to say that by this date, this will happen, but art has its own agenda. I want to rev up and do more, but if the script is not ready, I won't shoot it. Some people may say that that's not the way to do things, because the audience wants product all the time. Movies come and movies go, but I want to make films that people watch again and again. Something that's worth the seven dollars and fifty cents.

HARRIS: Would you direct a film that you didn't write?

TOWNSEND: Yes, but for the most part, the writers don't have a passion for storytelling. A lot of times, it's not well thought-out. Then I have to decide if it's something that I can salvage.

HARRIS: What do you look for when you're reading a screenplay? Does it have to grab you in the first ten pages?

TOWNSEND: I try to give the script a chance. I can tell by the first ten pages where it's going. I look for the writer to catch me off guard. I'm playing mental chess like the audience does. So I want them to throw me some curve balls. I can tell, when I'm reading, if the writer has a knack for storytelling, if the writer has a knack for keeping the reader interested, if the writer visually knows the material.

HARRIS: Your work has always been fresh and unique, and has always had a high level of integrity, but what do you feel about those who dredge up negative images and stereotypes in the name of entertainment?

TOWNSEND: When I did *A Soldier's Story*, I was very proud to be a part of that film. I really applauded Norman Jewison because he just wanted to make a great film. It had nothing to do with color or anything—he just wanted to make a great movie. He cast the characters he thought would bring that great story to life, and we had a great time. I've been on the same path since *Hollywood Shuffle* in terms of creating positive images. Even in *The Parent Hood*, I've created a family with a mother and a father, trying to raise children in the nineties. This year you'll see a lot more of that dealt with. I also want to give values to those out there who may be saying, "Well, what's a father to do?" So, I'm just continuing down the path I started with *Hollywood Shuffle* and I hope people come with me.

HARRIS: Is there any sense of competition between you and the brothers in the black pack?

TOWNSEND: There's more than enough room here. Magic Johnson just opened up his theater. It has twelve screens. There aren't even twelve filmmakers. [Laugher] He's got more screens than there are filmmakers. There's only a handful, man. The cat who's been the most consistent has been Spike.

HARRIS: Why do you think Spike has been so prolific?

TOWNSEND: Spike has an incredible machine. He cranks his movies out. I have to applaud the brother, because I don't know how he does it. Maybe I hold my babies close to my heart, and he lets his babies go to school quickly. I don't know. Spike is a mystery to me, and I have to applaud him. The thing with me is I that have the talent to do a lot of different kinds of things.

HARRIS: Not to mention the creative autonomy.

TOWNSEND: That's what I'm saying. Like *The Parent Hood*—I created it; I based it on my life at home. I'm married with two kids, and I started writing down funny things that would happen around the house. I knew that it wasn't a movie, but it could be funny every week. Then I thought that sitcoms didn't look that hard. I decided to go to Warner Bros. and pitch a sitcom based on my life. I wanted to be the father of the nineties. I love Cosby—he's been an idol and a hero to me on screen and off. He's a smart businessman and role model extraordinaire. So I started looking at television differently. Now is a different time. TV stars are movie stars. Movie stars do television. It's all opening up. I felt that it was something I could do with a good team of writers: I could pitch story ideas, and the writers would go away and write them. I could also do my movies.

HARRIS: How did the network receive your pitch?

TOWNSEND: Right away they said, "You've got thirteen episodes." So I figured the average life of a good television show is five years, so I schedule my films to shoot during the show's hiatus. I still can do a film each year if I want to. It's kind of cool because, at the end of this, I will have a catalogue of television shows, as well as my films.

HARRIS: It's about momentum, and building a body of work.

TOWNSEND: Exactly.

HARRIS: What advice do you have for young writers?

TOWNSEND: It's about the work, at all levels. It's possible to attain your dreams in Hollywood, but you can only reach your dreams by doing the work. This town does not work without scripts. If the script is well-written, everybody wants to be in business. You do the work and you get the results. If you don't do the work, you won't get the results. It's old-school philosophy, but it's real. When I think of up-and-coming writers and filmmakers, I say, attack the work with a passion.

MICHAEL DINWIDDIE

*" . . . do your damnedest, and make
sure the work is really good."*

I first met Michael Dinwiddie at a function at the Writers
Guild called "Karamou," an African feast and celebration of
the arts.

During the reception that followed, Michael told me of a
project he was involved with called the "Small Miracles Workshop" that teaches filmmaking techniques to inner-city children. I was immediately interested in getting involved because, as a child, I had fond memories of a similar project at
Barnsdall Art Park in Hollywood.

In the months that followed, I was to gain a great deal of
respect for the efforts that Michael gives to his craft, as well as
to exposing young people to filmmaking, a process that Spike
Lee calls "the demystification of film."

One incident in particular stands out in my mind. I was
invited to speak at Career Day at Sixth Avenue Elementary
School in Los Angeles. After entertaining a group of fifth and
sixth graders with witty anecdotes of my being a guest star on
an episode of *The Mighty Morphin' Power Rangers*, a popular
children's program, I peeked into another classroom and found
Michael leading a short-story writing exercise. He quizzed the
children on the key elements of creating a short story. As the
children recited "a beginning, middle and end," a wave of
embarrassment consumed me. Though my presentation was
thoughtful and well-meaning, it paled in comparison to the
real skills Michael was trying to impart during his visit. I was
not surprised when I learned that Michael had left Hollywood
to take a teaching position as Playwright in Residence at Florida
A&M University.

In this book, you will meet writers who have enjoyed
more commercial success than Michael, but I doubt that
many can match Michael's generosity, humor, and outspo-
ken honesty.

HARRIS: Let's talk a bit about your background. How long have you been writing professionally?

DINWIDDIE: About eleven or twelve years. My background is as a playwright. I'm from Detroit, and I worked at a theater company there called Satori Theater, which some friends and I founded. Satori is a Zen Buddhist word that means "peace of the inner mind." It also means "sudden enlightenment." We used it as an acronym for Seeking a Theater of Real Involvement. Kathy Ervin, Steven Rambo, and I started the company when we were kids. I was sixteen years old, Kathy was fifteen, and Steve was fourteen. We wanted to do our own plays.

HARRIS: Hey, kids, let's put on a show!

DINWIDDIE: Exactly, and we kind of got carried away. Many of the people who were members of this theater company ended up in the business. A guy named Leigh Donaldson became a writer. He writes for magazines and did a book on the black press. Quite lot of Satorians grew up to become serious people who are involved in the arts.

   I went to New York when I was twenty-one. I went there to be an actor. I started auditioning and I started doing plays, but I didn't like the roles. So I started writing the things I liked.

HARRIS: You know, that is exactly the reason I started writing. I was here on the West Coast, and I was one of the kids who could get work as an actor. I was a little too dark for network television, so the type of shit I was up for was in these top Hollywood movies, playing characters who were always criminals. I was reading for all of the casting agents, but I was always up for the menacing urban types. I had come home from a callback on *Grand Canyon*, Kasdan's film, where I think I had read for the role of Jimmy or Rockstar, or some bullshit like that, which on the credits is probably listed as Thug #3. After the audition I was psyched because I thought that I had nailed it. And I found myself really, really wanting to portray a criminal in this film. Suddenly, I thought, something's wrong with me for wanting this role. There's got to be something else. That's what started me writing. It's really great to hear you saying that as well.

DINWIDDIE: Yeah. Well, I went to New York and everything was pimps. I did a few plays there and then I realized that I should really focus on writing, because that was something in which I could control the images more. I mean, all images should be out there, but there were not any alternative images of black people. So I started writing. And I was very fortunate—I got plays done in New York, I really enjoyed it. Then, in 1990, this Disney program came along, a program where they were trying to get writers from different backgrounds to come out to Los Angeles and experience the film business. I was in the inaugural year of that program.

HARRIS: What was the program called?

DINWIDDIE: It was called the Disney Writer's Fellowship Program. It was started because of a particular Writers Guild report.

HARRIS: I remember that report: The Writers Guild Bielby Report. It said something to the effect that out of the two hundred or so black writers in the Guild, only four percent were working.

DINWIDDIE: Yeah. But, worse than that, Disney was the studio that had not hired a single black writer in the previous year. So former Disney studio head Jeffrey Katzenberg decided that he would do something about it, and he started this writer's program. The idea was to get different people's voices into the film business because, number one, Disney is a smart company. They realize that black people attend more movies per capita, and if we see a movie we like, we'll see it again.

HARRIS: My understanding of this is that we make up only twelve percent of the population, but we account for twenty-five or twenty-eight percent of the box-office receipts.

DINWIDDIE: Right, and it's the same in television. In network television, we are becoming one third of the audience, and it's just good business to represent your audience. So I came to Los Angeles to be a Disney fellow. I spent a year at Touchstone pictures, which was great because I worked with a guy named Adam Leipzig.

HARRIS: They paid you, right? Tell us more about that program.

DINWIDDIE: They paid me $30,000 for the year, and they covered my relocation expenses. You would come in and pitch ideas; they would listen to the ideas, and they would develop the ones they liked. So I spent a half a year working on a screenplay, rewriting it, going through the different steps. My playwriting process was different than screenwriting. We did Robert McKee's seminar, which they paid for, so that we could acquire a language to start to work with. It was fascinating. The main thing I learned was that the people who you're going to work with are the people you go to school with, the people who are in these programs with you. They are the people who will recommend you for jobs, who you'll connect with. They are your peers, and you'd better get to know them. You'd better get a sense of what they're doing and what they're about, because that's the idea of networking. Another thing that I got out of the program was a firm sense of how studios work. I got to see how ideas work, are taken apart, and layered. Disney, at the time, was known for their stories. Their executives really worked at improving stories, getting at the meat of the scripts. Adam Leipzig, who guided me through this process of writing my first screenplay, was out of the L.A. Theater Center, so he was an excellent person, he was a vice president at the time.

HARRIS: So he was one of your mentors?

DINWIDDIE: Oh, yes. He really was. He's at Interscope now.

HARRIS: What did you create at Disney?

DINWIDDIE: I created script called *Finders Keepers*, a love story between African Americans, set in Detroit. It was a romantic trip through the world of an insurance salesman and a woman who doesn't work for a living. She, basically, is able to "get over" in many different ways. [Laughter]

HARRIS: Oh, how Disney!

DINWIDDIE: Sort of *Pretty Woman* in black.

HARRIS: Were you at Disney on a day-to-day basis?

DINWIDDIE: No. It was set up so that you did your orientation, and then you would go in and meet everybody. They gave us all of the books: *Making a Good Script Great*, William Goldman's *Adventures in the Screen Trade*, and they gave us an information packet. The young writer needs to read everything. When I came out here, I was very proud of the fact that I hadn't seen any films in a year. I was busy writing plays. The people around the table were speaking a whole different language. My idea of film was *North by Northwest*. I was really corny because I was turned off by American movies. When I was in film school, I watched a lot of films: things by Jim Jarmusch, Spike's stuff, but as far as mass-appeal film went, I couldn't have cared less.

HARRIS: Movies are very important here.

DINWIDDIE: Movies are the culture here. You people are car-driven and filmdriven. Even the language reflects it. I would hear things like, "It was like the scene in *Taxi Driver* where De Niro . . . " And I would sit there and go, "Wow." I guess you get the same thing in New York around the theater.

HARRIS: Did you feel that you were out of your element?

DINWIDDIE: Actually, I felt good because I really wanted to grasp what the difference was between writing for stage and writing for film. This visual thing.

HARRIS: Could you sum up those differences?

DINWIDDIE: [Laughing] I'm spending my life summing it up. The major difference is that language is very important in the theater, and in film, the image is very important. One of the things I always try to do with a scene is think of it terms of pictures. You know, like you draw cartoon pictures of a scene.

HARRIS: You can call it a storyboard.

DINWIDDIE: You can call it storyboard if you like, whatever language works for you. You should be able to unreel the pictures and tell the whole story. Cartoons do it very well. Think about it: Your first exposure to opera was through cartoons—Bugs Bunny and things like that.

HARRIS: And when you read my work, you see that I love to regress to cartoons from time to time.

DINWIDDIE: [Laughing] You're right. So I spent a year with Disney. After that, I was hooked, and I wanted to work in television.

HARRIS: Why television, specifically?

DINWIDDIE: Well, film seemed like such a long shot. Just the idea of it. I had had all of these different meetings with different development people. You go through the rounds.

HARRIS: What are those development meetings like?

DINWIDDIE: They just want to meet you, see what you're like, and see if your personality connects with theirs. They want to see if there's a project they think you're exactly right for. So it's basically to meet and greet in Hollywood. You have to know people to have a career, and they have to know what you represent, they have to know your work.

HARRIS: How did they receive *Finders Keepers*?

DINWIDDIE: Well, it was really a second-rate rehash. That was how I felt about it. [Laughter]

HARRIS: At least you're being honest.

DINWIDDIE: You know, it was my first script. And what you don't really get coming into the program is that nobody has the time to nurture you and bring you along. That was one of the disappointments of the Disney program. I thought that it was an apprenticeship, but it wasn't. They bring you here and, if you nail it and can deliver it, then you've got it. But if you can't figure it out, then good luck, brother. That's the business, that's cool, but it was news to me. I was glad to learn it. It was a good Hollywood lesson. And I would not have come here if it wasn't for the Disney program. So it was a good thing.

HARRIS: Good to have that access.

DINWIDDIE: Yes! Having that access to a studio lot, dealing with the studio executives, the film library. Adam Leipzig basically said, "If you want to write romantic comedy, here are fifteen films you need to see. If you want to write thrillers, this is what you need to see." I would watch and see how different directors handled things. It was a whole new world. I had gone to film school, but there were things I was ignorant about.

HARRIS: Did you go to NYU?

DINWIDDIE: Yes, I went to NYU, Tisch School of the Arts' dramatic writing program. I was in the graduate program and, although I didn't have to, I took undergraduate film-making classes. I busted my butt taking Sight and Sound and making short films while my friends were hanging out in coffee houses. I wanted to get my hands dirty. I never wanted to be on a set and not know what people were talking about. I felt that was part of what I needed to understand. My undergraduate degree was from NYU, but it was in Liberal Arts, which was really broad.

HARRIS: So it's a year later, one failed screenplay, a world of experience, and thirty K. You're out of the Disney program, loose in the world, and you say, "Television."

DINWIDDIE: Yes, I had friends in television. Ella Joyce, whom I knew from Detroit, was at *Roc*. That was exciting to me, so I thought I'd try and write one episode.

HARRIS: One quick question before we move on: How many people were in the inaugural Disney program with you?

DINWIDDIE: There were about twenty-four. Ten at Touchstone, eleven at Hollywood pictures, and three in television. All three writers in television got jobs right away. I thought that was interesting. I wanted to do television projects when I came into the program, but I was told that television was something looked down upon, and I should just do my time at Touchstone. I never felt that way, and afterward I started looking at and studying television programs. I looked at *Murphy Brown* and other shows and I decided to write for *Murphy Brown*.

HARRIS: You had no representation at this point?

DINWIDDIE: No, I didn't. So I got hold of some scripts and learned the format. I had this friend from New York named Imani who was supportive of my ideas and suggested that I write for *Roc*, since I knew and liked that show. She also knew Ella Joyce. At least we'd get it read there. So I sat down and banged out an episode in two days.

HARRIS: Two days?

DINWIDDIE: Yeah, I came up with an idea and just banged it out. I'm really fast when I want to be. So I showed it to Imani, and she said, "Well, this doesn't really work. I've studied the show and it should go like this and like that, but I'll help you." Now, Imani had been my dramaturge on one of my plays in New York, *The Beautiful LaSalles*. A dramaturge is a person who helps a playwright get his scenes as clear as they should be.

HARRIS: Sort of a script doctor?

DINWIDDIE: That's what they would call it out here. So she sat with me for the next five days, getting it exactly right, nailing the scenes and all that stuff. When we were done, she said, "Now your script is done." I said, "Imani, I can't just put my name on this script—you've done as much on this it as I have." As a playwright, you own your work no matter who contributes, but in film it's totally different. I said that we had to put both our names on the script. And that's how I got my writing partner. Imani then went to talk to Henry Johnson at Warner Bros., and he suggested that she meet with Leisa Henry at the Warner Bros. writing program. At the time, they were accepting applications to their ten-week intensive comedy-writing workshop.

HARRIS: Is that the program that Gus Blackmon was involved with?

DINWIDDIE: Yes. So we got read and were chosen to be in the program.

HARRIS: Excellent! Another victory.

DINWIDDIE: Yes, another small victory. But something else happened at that time. We got in touch with someone at *Roc* who said that we had to get read by Kelly Kulchak to be considered there. We just wanted to write a spec script, get the money, and run, because it paid something like fourteen thousand dollars, which was a lot of money for someone with no agent. So I dropped off the script at nine, and by noon I got a call from Kelly Kulchak. She loved the script and she loved the writing. It was called "Pal Joey," about an older woman seducing Joey, and Roc is, of course, against it. Kelly wanted to set up a meeting for us with the producers, and I immediately panicked because we didn't have an agent and I didn't want to be looked at as an amateur. I called a friend at Disney, Steven Tao, who was partly responsible for my coming out here. Steven said that he would call around and see who was highly recommended and refer us to them. I got the name of an agent who read us, liked us, and signed us.

HARRIS: Another victory.

DINWIDDIE: Yes. So we met the producers. And they loved us, even though we had no credits and were nobodies. But there was all kinds of turmoil going on at the time because Charles Dutton was asserting his authority. What came out of it was that they wanted us on staff, but the powers that be over at HBO wanted another writing team, which was forced down their throats. So they could not hire us, but they promised us an assignment on the show.

HARRIS: What's the difference between an assignment and being a staff writer?

DINWIDDIE: Considerable. An assignment is for one job and a staff writer works thirty or forty weeks out of the year. They're full-time, Monday through Friday. They're involved in the process of the show, they're creating it. Anyway, our assignment never happened.

HARRIS: Why not?

DINWIDDIE: Our agent was new to television and did not know how to follow up and nail the assignment. Those are Hollywood lessons, and those lessons hit us right between the eyes. What people say and what they deliver are often different. But that's life, right?

HARRIS: Life in Hollywood.

DINWIDDIE: But we were going to be in the Warner Bros. writers program based on the *Roc* spec script we had written together. In this program, you would meet once a week with the producers on the studio lot, and you would pitch your story ideas to them. Over the course of the program, you would come up with a story and write it.

HARRIS: Were you paid?

DINWIDDIE: No, they didn't pay you, but they didn't charge, either.

HARRIS: It's good exposure.

DINWIDDIE: It was incredible! We were meeting the producers on the lot and networking with other young writers. And you could write for whatever show you chose.

HARRIS: What show did you choose?

DINWIDDIE: We chose *A Different World*. That's when we learned that it's really difficult for black writers. It's hard to get hired to write for a show that's not specifically about black people. It does happen. Winifred Hervey, for example, who was the show-runner for the *Fresh Prince* and Debbie Allen's new show, her background was *The Golden Girls*, but it doesn't happen often. That was one of the first battles we had with our agent. She wanted us to write for a show that we weren't really interested in, but we wanted to write for *A Different World*. We had this big battle, and our agent, who was black, said that it just wasn't smart.

HARRIS: I've gotten the same comments from people close to me.

DINWIDDIE: My attitude was, "What's the difference? The rhythm of the language?" Well, the rhythm of *Seinfeld* is different from the rhythm of *Frasier*. It's the style of the writer. I was sort of a purist, and I wasn't understanding the mentality of the racial attitudes and the apartheid of where your talent can and cannot take you. You can't give in to that or even acknowledge it, but it's always there. All you have to do is look at the white stars in television versus the black stars. The difference is stunning. Look at the deals that get made and who gets what work.

HARRIS: Yes, we would be naive to pretend there was no bias. The real question is what are we going to do about it?

DINWIDDIE: Well, the way we were raised was to do our damnedest and make sure our work is really good. So, we did our damnedest and we made sure it was really good. After the workshop, we were hired as staff writers on a brand-new show for ABC called *Hangin' With Mr. Cooper*, with Mark Curry.

HARRIS: How did that come about?

DINWIDDIE: Jeff Franklin, the creator of the show, met with me a week before the show was supposed to start. He was basically seeing a writer every twenty minutes. [Laughter] As I came in, someone was leaving, and as I left, someone was arriving. We met and we clicked. He's a wonderful person.

HARRIS: How was the work experience?

DINWIDDIE: Television is long hours. It's hard work and there's something called "table," where all of the writers get together and pitch out ideas. Well, at first we were very excited and enthusiastic, but then a sort of polarization began to occur on the show. Things were taken differently if they were said by a black writer, as opposed to a white writer.

HARRIS: How many writers worked on the show?

DINWIDDIE: There were eleven writers, counting both writers and producers. Seven were white, four were black. It was quite an experience, which sometimes became volatile. During the first week of the show, Mark Curry came in and told us what kind of show he wanted. He wanted to be a role model, he wanted to have something serious say to the kids, he wanted it to be a fun, good show. He wanted to capitalize on his humor, yet be a mentor and a father figure to kids who were in homes without one. He walked out of the room and one of the executives said, "Forget everything that he said. This is television and we ain't buying it." That was the beginning of the show you see on the air.

HARRIS: Is it still running?

DINWIDDIE: Yes. The people at Warner's and Lorimar had very high expectations for this series. They expected it to be a top-ten show, and if you look at the numbers, it debuted very high. People loved the show because they loved Mark Curry, but the writing was working against it.

HARRIS: In what sense?

DINWIDDIE: In the sense that the black audience is very demanding of things like character consistency. They will not let you betray your characters. Here's an example: The show is set in Oakland, California, yet his best friend was written as a white guy, which is cool. But in the script, the white guy has all of the punchlines. We have a star who's a comedian, but a one-week player has all of the funny lines. Now for some reason, Mark Curry begins to shut down and delivers his lines in a way that defeats the comedy in the script. So one of the producers thinks that the problem is racial, that Mark Curry is upset that they had hired a white actor to be his best friend. I went in and talked to the producer and said that that's not what's going on at all. What's going on is that the star is not being taken care of, and it's his show. He feels that people are favoring this other person, based on his tribe. The producer thanked me profusely for coming in. The following week, that same producer took me off his show, which was already on the table. I was never to work with him again during the course of the show.

HARRIS: Were you fired?

DINWIDDIE: No. I just wasn't working on his scripts anymore.

HARRIS: This is like a political gauntlet coming down.

DINWIDDIE: It was totally heavy. It completely alienated me from this producer, who's very successful. It taught me that if you question anything, you're out of line. In black culture, the only way we have survived is by questioning things. So that was hard.

HARRIS: Tell us about the episode you wrote.

DINWIDDIE: It was called "Unforgettable." We had put a lot of our heart into it. But after we turned it in, it was basically thrown out. A producer said that our show was unworkable, and then set out to rewrite it. But the rewrite wasn't done in time, so they had to use our script to audition the actors. When they heard our script in the auditions, they finally got it. They understood that our script had been written for black people. And it worked. So by the time the show went on the air, most of our script had returned.

HARRIS: Another small victory.

DINWIDDIE: Very small. I remember that during the taping, one of the producers came up and said, "You've really got something here. This is really good." But he had already bad-mouthed us to the network by saying that we weren't very good writers and that we had written a show that they had to save. It ended up being one of the top-rated shows that season. But by the end of the first season it was over for us. Our contract was not renewed. Imani decided to go back to New York, and I went back to writing alone.

HARRIS: What are the advantages of having a writing partner, versus writing alone?

DINWIDDIE: The great thing about having a partner, especially in television, is that you have someone to bounce ideas off of before you go into the room. Every writer has strengths and weaknesses, and hopefully you get a partner who has the strengths that you lack. Imani was very much into structure and plotting. I'm more interested in language and gags. So it worked. A partner is also good for moral support. When you're pitching, your partner is in the room, and can sense how it's going. The down side is if your partner sneezes, so do you. If your partner leaves town, you don't exist anymore. So I've had to reinvent myself.

HARRIS: What advice would you give to young writers just starting out?

DINWIDDIE: Save some money, get a degree, and don't move to L.A. without a job. [Laughter] The first thing I would say is that you must write all of the time. Write about things you know about. Write about things you don't know about, just write.

HARRIS: How does your personal regimen go as far as your writing?

DINWIDDIE: Basically, I piss away the whole day and I write all night. [Laughter] Is that honest enough for you?

HARRIS: Whatever works for you, brother.

DINWIDDIE: Seriously, it depends on what I'm working on. I really love to write at night because the phone doesn't ring. Only your close friends will call after twelve. During the day, there's so much of the business—making calls, returning calls. I would also advise young writers to learn the business. Really learn what it's about.

HARRIS: What do you write on?

DINWIDDIE: I write on a computer. I like to move things around. I'm spoiled now.

HARRIS: Do you write scene cards?

DINWIDDIE: Oh yes. I'm very much into historical dramas, and I'm working on a project now that I have broken down onto scene cards and divided into three-act structure.

HARRIS: So you work from the paradigm?

DINWIDDIE: Yes, I have to. I am an Aristotelian, and I really do believe in looking at the work that way. Because I've taught, I really believe in working from a basic structural language.

HARRIS: I wanted to ask you your thoughts on the debate that's raging right now about affirmative action. Clearly your career has benefited from such programs.

DINWIDDIE: I think that the reason they are dismantling these programs is that they are effective. Effective in that they have opened up the society to people other than those who have been traditionally served. For instance, look at the Warner Bros. program. It's closed down now. They can call it budget cuts or whatever they want, but it was very successful at bringing in writers with different voices whom nobody expected to do as well as they've done in the business. So, when it works, it gets into trouble. But if you look at the numbers, you'll see what's really happening.

HARRIS: Not a whole lot.

DINWIDDIE: One problem is that affirmative action is cast in a narrow light. People think it's just for blacks. It really extends to a broader palette: women, Latinos, Arabs, many different tribes, many different voices. One thing that I could never figure out is how five different studios would be developing the same story at the same time. Then it occurred to me that the executives go to the same parties and swim in the same pools. It's got to affect the work.

HARRIS: I read a recent article in *New Republic* entitled "Dumb and Dumber, The Case Against Hollywood." In it, the author launched a scathing indictment of the Hollywood studio system for creating movies that suffer from the malaise of sameness, in spite of boffo box-office receipts.

DINWIDDIE: It's true. Alan Alda wrote an article in the *Writers Guild Journal.* He said that writers are fighting for position in the credits and they should be fighting for copyrights. It should be just like in the theater—you write a movie, you should own it. It would bring the level of integrity up.

HARRIS: What specific aspects of television do you like versus film?

DINWIDDIE: I like the immediacy and accessibility of it. The process is quicker—a story you write today may be on the air in six weeks. And your work is broadcast into millions of homes. The cinema experience is a shared experience, which I also love.

HARRIS: Where do you see yourself in five years?

DINWIDDIE: Living on a farm in Tennessee. Writing and directing films.

HARRIS: Films, not television?

DINWIDDIE: I'd like to believe that I could do both.

LAURENCE ANDRIES

"I'm here to be a storyteller."

I imagine that every young writer dreams of one day being nominated for an Academy Award. Laurence Andries achieved that dream with his very first produced project, *Kangaroo Court.*

I almost expected this successful young writer to be stand-offish or self-absorbed, but I found Mr. Andries to be humble, almost to the point of shyness, yet fiercely passionate about his work. He offers a wonderful perspective on the ups and downs that a career in Hollywood has to offer, as well as some interesting advice on what a newcomer should expect when coming here.

In the car, on the way to photograph him at one of his favorite writing spots, a West Hollywood coffee house called The Abbey, Laurence asked me, "If you could have written any film, what would it have been?" My reply was *Annie Hall;* Laurence said his would have been *Ordinary People.* We sat in silence for the rest of the trip, pondering the meaning of each other's choice.

One of the most exciting parts of writing this book is exposing readers to the dynamic, emerging writers whom they may not have heard of yet. Laurence Andries is one such writer.

HARRIS: Your writing on the short film *Kangaroo Court* helped it earn an Academy Award nomination. What made you decide on a short-feature form, as opposed to full-feature treatment of the story?

ANDRIES: That wasn't my decision. I was brought onto the project by the executive producer, Dan Petrie Jr., and the director, Sean Astin. Sean wanted to prove to Ricardo Mestres that he could be both an actor and a director for Hollywood Pictures. Rather than giving Sean a twenty-million-dollar feature right off the bat, Ricardo agreed to give Sean a thirty-minute short to direct, which was, in a sense, part of his compensation for starring in Hollywood Pictures' *Encino Man.*

HARRIS: At what stage were you brought onto the project?

ANDRIES: Dan Petrie Jr. came up with the initial premise: What would happen if a white cop were kidnapped in South Central L.A.? Sean loved that idea and he wrote a three-page outline of where this might go. Ricardo gulped and said, "If this is what you want to do, then find a writer." Dan, Sean, and co-producers Christine Astin and Nicholas Hassitt read a lot of people within the business. Then, associate producer Chip Catalano had the idea of finding a writer within Disney's New Writers Fellowship Program. I had just finished writing a gang-related action picture that all parties read and loved. Soon after that, Dan Petrie brought me in for the initial meeting.

HARRIS: All of this came from your involvement with the Disney Writers Fellowship Program?

ANDRIES: Right. As of today, this is the only produced project from the Fellowship program.

HARRIS: Excellent. What was your experience in that program like?

ANDRIES: I knew exactly what could happen if I did very well in my year at Disney. I wasn't some naive waif coming in the studio gate for the first time. I knew what the deal was with the studio system, and I was going to exploit the opportunity to its fullest.

HARRIS: You were already based in Los Angeles then?

ANDRIES: I had been living in L.A. for six years. Having grown up in New York and having gone to NYU film school, I had read every single book on filmmaking that there was. If there ever was a documentary on the making of a motion picture, I made sure that I saw it. I got as much exposure to the business as I could, without being in the business. I was ready to apply all of that book knowledge in an actual studio environment. I hit the ground running. I got the call about *Kangaroo Court*— that Dan Petrie Jr. wanted discuss the possibility that I might write a short that would get produced—on the same day that I found out that my fellowship was being renewed for a second year. That was a great day.

HARRIS: Was your fellowship renewed because of *Kangaroo Court*?

ANDRIES: As it turns out, I was being renewed anyway. Out of the eight writers on the Touchstone side, I was the only one to be renewed for a second year.

HARRIS: Did you have an agent at the time?

ANDRIES: No.

HARRIS: Did they pay you scale for the project?

ANDRIES: Within the Writers Guild, there isn't a specific pay scale for half-hour shorts. Because I was under my fellowship contract, my pay scale was predetermined. The fact that it was being produced didn't change how much I was paid. Frankly, it didn't matter. To have a chance to get paid a decent amount to write was great. But there were weeks of executives haggling with each other before I was invited onto the project. *Kangaroo Court* was being produced under the Hollywood Pictures umbrella, but I was working for Touchstone. So, in a sense, Hollywood Pictures had to rent me from Touchstone Pictures. It was all internal bookkeeping.

HARRIS: Fair enough. What was your fellowship salary?

ANDRIES: I was making $50,000 for my second year, which for a first-time writer was great. You're getting paid to write, to get up in the morning and sit around drinking coffee and making things up. What a great opportunity! It's the American Dream.

HARRIS: How much input did Sean Astin or any of the producers have in that first draft of the work?

ANDRIES: Sean and Christine Astin and I sat around in many restaurants and talked character. We talked character for days before the first word was written. Once we knew what the dramatic structure was and had a firm grasp of who the characters were, I was left alone to write the first draft.

HARRIS: Was that process enjoyable to you?

ANDRIES: That's exactly how I work. I want to be left alone because my process is messy. It comes when it comes. It comes at three o'clock in the morning. It comes driving to work. It comes in line in the supermarket. To have a producer or director over my shoulder or in the room with me would drive me batty. I need time to stumble upon what I am doing.

HARRIS: I read the screenplay. And when I watched the film, the first scene was as written, then ten or more pages of dialogue were edited out, then the story picks up again with the entrance of Gregory Hines. How do you feel about the transition from the final draft to the screen?

ANDRIES: I'm very proud of the movie. I've seen it so many times, it's like the *Rocky Horror Show* at this point. Yet when I see the fade out from the riot that begins the movie, I cringe because what's missing is the set-up. What's missing is the context of why all of this is happening. You don't know that Gregory Hines is a former gang leader who's now turned his life around. You don't know that Pee Wee, who is in effect the prosecuting attorney, is forced into it in order to get deeper into the gang. You don't know why the motorist in the first scene is pulled over by the police. Those are editorial and directorial decisions.

HARRIS: So the film was shot as written?

ANDRIES: We shot the entire film as written. Our best running time, in terms of story comprehension and character arcs, was forty-four minutes. However, at forty-four minutes, we're neither fish nor fowl. We're too long for a short and too short for a feature, which would pretty much leave us ineligible for most of the film festivals around the world and the Academy Award nomination. It was a directorial decision to go for the gusto. To go for as much exposure as we could with this project because the purpose of it, for us, was to practice doing a feature and to have people see our work. It was Sean's decision to bring it down to under thirty minutes, and something had to go. There were heated, protracted arguments and discussions and debates about what should go. It was Sean's decision that although the audience would be confused for a few minutes, they would pick up where they were later.

HARRIS: I watched the film with a couple of intelligent and critical friends who decided that, though they were in the dark about that first transition, they were willing to accept it since the Gregory Hines character was blindfolded as well. It also gave more impact to the consequences of the actual kangaroo court. Sometimes audiences don't need as much information as writers want to give them.

ANDRIES: We thought the audience needed the set-up, so we wrote and shot it. We had some very limited test-screenings among people who had no context of the film at all and people who knew the entire story, just to see whether we were right. We wanted to know whether the audience would be confused, were we cutting more than just fat, were we cutting into muscle? It was a leap of faith, and Sean was determined that he was making the right choice to cut it the way he did. There were people who were confused and had questions, but I learned that as long as the credits say a Sean Astin film, or a Quentin Tarantino film, and not a Laurence Andries film, I'm not going to win every battle. As it was, I won an extraordinary number of battles.

HARRIS: If your film was shot as written, you've won more battles than most.

ANDRIES: You bet. I was treated like a playwright on this movie. I was there for the entire shoot. I was there for the location scouting, I was there for the casting. No one rewrote any of the work. Every draft was mine. I was there for a piece of the editing process and all of the screenings. I was treated as an equal player in the creative process. I was also spoiled for the next ten years. It may not happen again for a very long time.

HARRIS: The story felt like a combination of *Twelve Angry Men* and *Man of La Mancha*. [Laughter]

ANDRIES: Now that's a new one! I haven't heard that before.

HARRIS: I know it sounds like a lame studio pitch, but were you influenced by other works when shaping the scenario?

ANDRIES: Let me think . . . The third act of Fritz Lang's *M* is very much like *Kangaroo Court*. *M* deals with a town's search for a child molester. Eventually, he's brought into an underground lair where the whole community is waiting, and they put him on trial for his crime. Someone else said that my story sounded like *M*, so we watched it and said, "Wow, it does." That made me realize that, one, the story was a classic and, two, the story—being in a closed place, with a mock trial—worked in this context. I also watched a lot of courtroom dramas like *Inherit the Wind* and *The Verdict*, to get the lingo and the rhythm of courtroom drama.

HARRIS: The Disney program really gives you access to the film library in order to find parallel works. Did you find that resource advantageous?

ANDRIES: Had I only known it existed. I went to Blockbuster. [Laughter] I didn't take full advantage of all the
little perks until way too late.

HARRIS: I don't know where the readers could find a copy
of this film. Are they packaged with other short films and
distributed that way?

ANDRIES: Sometimes it happens that way. In fact, at the
Academy Awards, Tim Allen, who had once done a short
film at AFI, said something to the same effect. There are
so many films like this out there, and yet there isn't a
forum to show them. Thirty years ago, this would have
been the movie before the main feature or the movie between a double feature. That's gone the way of the dino-
saur. If we're lucky, we'll be packaged with one or two
other films as part of a trilogy. Generally speaking, they
play the festival route, they play on Showtime's Thirty-
Minute Theater, or on PBS. The easiest way for the general public to see a film like this is to check their alternative papers for film festivals in their city.

HARRIS: It's an excellent film, well worthy of a wide audience. This was your première piece. How did you feel
watching it in a theater with an audience?

ANDRIES: We premièred it at the Directors Guild main stage.
One of the best theaters in the country. Six hundred seats,
a full house. We had to show it twice because of the over-
flow. I wanted to sit in the back center to see the full
scope of the audience. I sat there thinking, "Oh my God,
they're going to hate this!" [Laughter] "I drove these people
out of their warm houses to sit through this!" It brings out
every insecurity you ever had in your life. No matter how
many people have said, "This is wonderful," no matter
how many times I've see the dailies, here it comes—it's
do or die. Have I been fooling myself all of these years or
do I have the goods? There is nothing like hearing an
audience laugh at something you thought was funny a
year and a half ago. Or to hear it get so quiet that you
could hear a pin drop at a moment you knew was going

to work. That is as close to being God that I'll get on this planet, and it is an amazing process.

HARRIS: What was your impression of the audience's reaction at the end of the film? Did they give a standing ovation? Did they throw oranges?

ANDRIES: No one left. No one sneaked out. That was part of the reason I wanted to sit in the back. I didn't hear any seat rustling, any talking. When you have a full house, especially with a certain number of black people, there's going to be a certain amount of talking to the screen if things aren't working. I was afraid of it turning into a call- and-response number. People got it. People were so appreciative of what we were trying to do in the whole of the piece. They saw beyond the anger and saw the subtext and the themes and meanings.

HARRIS: You have a character named Gage who really speaks directly to the frustrations of the black man in America and the abuses he's witnessed. He is perceived to be a part of the suspect class by the police. His soliloquy was as passionate as it was inarticulately articulate. It was so honest that it almost seemed ad libbed. Was it?

ANDRIES: Funny that you should mention that. Yes, it was. In fact, his big moment is the only piece of dialogue that was ad libbed. This man, Big Daddy Wayne, lived that life. He's a former gang banger who is now studying with Stella Adler, and he's been in several movies. When he hit that moment, in a particular take, he reverted to what he knew, and he spoke from his own pain. Never have I seen a crew as riveted as ours was that day. No one moved a muscle because they realized that they were in the presence of real human emotions. That moment continues on camera until he breaks down and cries. I'd never seen a crew give an actor a standing ovation when the director yells "cut," but wherever he was in that moment, they were right there with him. We had to take a break because everyone was so moved. If you were to see the movie, you would see two dozen angry, bitter African-

American young men, but in between takes, these guys were hilarious, just wonderful. What did you think about Gregory?

HARRIS: I thought he was fantastic. He ad-libbed some profanity. "I've seen this kind of repression everyday of my fucking life!" You could see by the response from the other actors that it energized that whole scene. He connected with the gang as one of them. Though the exposition that explained the fact that Gregory's character used to be in the thug life was cut, I felt his rage came through in that moment. I'll tell you a secret: I auditioned for Rick Milikan for the role of Pee Wee.

ANDRIES: Did you?

HARRIS: Yeah. I told my agent that I couldn't do it.

ANDRIES: You don't do gang bangers.

HARRIS: No, I don't. If you read my interview with Michael Dinwiddie, you'll understand why. Let it suffice to say that I prefer not to be portrayed in that light.

ANDRIES: I truly do not blame you. A lot of these actors said that they were choosing not to do any more of these roles but they would do mine.

HARRIS: I read the sides to the piece, then I read the script. I wanted to do the film after I saw how sharp the writing was. Had the audition process progressed further, I would have been faced with a difficult choice. Luckily, that choice was made for me.

ANDRIES: You'll learn as a writer, just as you learned as an actor, there will come a time when you'll have to make the choice about taking those roles on a writing assignment. It is so easy for executives to say, "Let's go ethnic, let's go tough, let's go gang." Then they go through the Rolodex looking for a black writer who can give them the "true black experience." Do you take a writing assignment that has people wearing clichéd do-rags when the landlord's calling? Or do you hold to your guns and say, "I do not do this," and take your chances?

HARRIS: I've given that a certain amount of thought. I never looked at acting as anything more than what it is: a job. I realize that the luxury of choice that I had at age twenty may be tougher at age thirty, and youthful idealism often fades in the face of poverty. When I was twenty-one, it was easy to stomp my foot and say, "No! I'm not going to do this gang shit!" and stand on my principles, because I was living at home. [Laughter]

ANDRIES: It was very easy when somebody was making dinner for you.

HARRIS: Exactly. But, of course, it's different now; I'm in the real world, but I regret nothing. An agent by the name of Guy Chateau once told me, "This is called show business, not show art." He was right and I had to face certain realities of this business.

ANDRIES: Right. Now, if you reach a point where you have enough "screw you" money, and you don't have to take a demeaning gang-banger role, yet you do, then that's my definition of selling out. If it's a part of a process, a means to an end, and it's going to get you to a point where you can dictate your own terms, then you go out there and do the best multi-layered depiction that you can.

HARRIS: Everyone's choices are their own: artistically, business-wise, or otherwise. Ultimately, your own reflection is the only face you have to see in the mirror in the morning when you're combing your nappy hair. All a man really has in this world is his own integrity, and if you can look into your eyes and say I did this for these reasons, and you can live with that choice, then you've said enough.

ANDRIES: Put on that do-rag and go to work. [Laughter]

HARRIS: Tell us about the day that the Academy Award nominations came out.

ANDRIES: I was clued-in that that branch of the Academy had narrowed their choices down from 124 films to ten, and that we were one of those ten. I considered that in itself an honor. If the nomination happens, it happens. So I was asleep that Tuesday morning, February 14, 1995.

HARRIS: Is that Valentine's Day?

ANDRIES: You bet. So, at seven o'clock, I got a call from a friend of mine at Disney who simply said, "Good Morning, Larry, congratulations on your nomination." I said, "Don't kid me, this is not funny!" After I realized that he wasn't joking, I got off of the phone, got out of bed, and screamed, "Yes! Yes!" I was pacing in my apartment like a rat in a cage. Then I called Sean Astin and asked him if it was true. He called the Academy just to hear it officially from someone there. Then he lost his shit. I'll tell you a true story. I found out at seven in the morning about the nomination. At nine that morning I had an appointment at London Temps to take a typing test because I had no money. So, I went. I had to get paid. [Laughter]

HARRIS: You can't eat the nomination letter. A nomination letter and a dollar fifty will get you on the bus down to London Temps.

ANDRIES: I filled out the application and sat down for the test. I'm typing "A S D F J K L" when suddenly I look up at the tester and say, "I can't do this today. I just got nominated for an Oscar." She said, "Listen, go home, get drunk, get out of here; you don't belong here. If you need us, call us."

HARRIS: The award in your category was given at the big show, not the one taped two days earlier, right?

ANDRIES: Oh yeah. We were in the big show. This town goes completely dysfunctional for six weeks. I got no writing done. I got invited to so many parties. I got taken to lunch very often. All of these agents wanted to woo me away from my agency. It was fun. It didn't become real for me until the Academy luncheon where all of the nominees were invited and introduced to one another. I was bumping into, literally bumping into, people I dreamed about and idolized. Samuel Jackson here, Tom Hanks there, John Travolta over there. Then Arthur Hiller said something I will take with me to my grave. He said, "Welcome to the inner circle. You have arrived. You have been chosen by your peers as the best in the business. Welcome to the class of 1995." Then it hit me: I have crossed a certain barrier. I have crossed the Rubicon of this business. It doesn't mean that it's going to be sweetness and light, but I have gone from being an aspiring screenwriter to being there. I stood up straighter and I felt the responsibility of that. This means something, and people are watching—I can't slack off, and I cannot do my second best. I've got to trust myself that I got here for a reason. This wasn't a lottery. This was the end result of a lot of years of risk and work.

The day of the awards, I was completely out-of-body. Dan Petrie had gotten us a stretch limo. I felt like Don King. We were sitting in the back wolfing down gin-and-tonics and watching the award pre-show on TV. I will never forget stepping out of the limousine and hearing the sound of the helicopters filling the sky like in *Apocalypse Now* and the roar of the crowd, the red carpet, and, once again, Tom Arnold is over here, Oprah is behind me, and Quincy is over there. I'm in a sweet-looking tux, walking down the red carpet past the three-story statues framing the entrance to the Shrine. Here I am. I have been dreaming about this moment since I was a little boy. Year after year, watching the show. And Goddamn, I am here. No matter what happens with the award and who gets it, they can't take this moment away from me. I hope it happens again in my lifetime, but at least, for one golden moment, it happened.

So, we're sitting in the ninth row. We're across from Quentin Tarantino, Gary Sinese, and Oliver Stone. We're the ninth award of the night and I'm sitting there with Sean and Christine Astin and Nicholas Hasset, our other co-producer. I'm trying to play it cool, like I've been there before, but we're all going, "This is great!" We're sitting behind Jo Beth Williams, who's also nominated for her short film. She turned to me, smiling and trying to be cordial, and I had on my game face, like Mike Tyson before a fight, as if the whole thing would be decided by arm wrestling. [Laughter] If I ever see her again, I will have to apologize for being an ass.

HARRIS: Did you write a speech?

ANDRIES: No. After a lot of discussion, we decided that, should we win, Sean and Christine would go up and accept the award, because in the short-film category, the Academy only allows two people to represent the film. But I made a deal with Sean that he would have to mention my name in a fashion that would make every producer in town want to call me the next day. Tim Allen opens the envelope and says, "It's a tie!" Only the fifth time in Oscar history, and it wasn't us. It was a tie between *Trevor* and *Franz Kafka's It's a Wonderful Life*. It's what the press had predicted, so I wasn't shocked that we didn't win.

HARRIS: Did you get to see the other nominated films?

ANDRIES: No, I didn't go to any of the screenings, so I didn't know what we were up against. But from reading the trades, I knew where the Oscar pools were heading. There were four gentle, accessible, crowd-pleasing movies, and our very dark, grim, political drama in the year of *Forrest Gump*. Listen, once you get down to the actual nominations, it's a crap shoot, it's a roll of the dice. Paul Newman didn't get one that night. Sally Field didn't get one, Robert Redford didn't get one. I was in very good company.

HARRIS: You were in excellent company, just being there.

ANDRIES: Exactly. The cliché says it's an honor just to be nominated, and it really is.

HARRIS: How are you received around town these days? I'm sure your nomination is on the top of your résumé now.

ANDRIES: Yeah, it is. I certainly bring it into the conversation when I am looking for work. But I don't bring it into conversation socially because it changes the dynamics of the interaction. I become something else beyond Larry Andries. I want people to meet me, not my résumé. But in terms of the town, I've thrown that sucker out anywhere I can. I'm shameless in that regard because it does mean something in this business.

HARRIS: Did the nomination bring any new money to your table?

ANDRIES: It certainly got me a lot more meetings for projects that normally I wouldn't be considered for. A producer came to me to develop a project for Sydney Poitier. Matty Rich asked me to collaborate on his next project. For several months, he and I worked on structure so that he could make his next movie the best that he could.

HARRIS: How was the Matty Rich experience?

ANDRIES: From meeting Matty Rich, I'm a stronger person. I've grown in ways that only war gives to a person. "The horror, the horror." [Laughter]

HARRIS: What's the project called?

ANDRIES: *War Zone*, though that may change by the time it comes out.

HARRIS: Good luck with that. People feel that he's a young talent with a lot of room to grow. What else is on your slate? Anything you want to talk about?

ANDRIES: Yes. there's an adaptation of a French film called *Le Trou,* meaning *The Hole* in English. It's the story of a middle-class man thrown into a jail with four hardened criminals, and how he changes them and they change him as they all attempt to tunnel out.

HARRIS: I like it. A character drama set against a prison escape. How is the adaptation process different from creating something from scratch?

ANDRIES: It's a different kind of challenge from doing a spec on your own. It's not easier because, if you believe in the source material at all, you want to remain true to it. Yet you have to make it your own, and adapt it to the market that is eventually going to see it, which is as difficult as starting from a blank sheet of paper. If you screw up a spec, no one's going to blame you for getting it wrong, but, in this case, there's another successful film to compare it to.

HARRIS: Other writers have expressed a certain sense of claustrophobia in the adaptation process, in staying within the scope of the source material. Do you feel that way?

ANDRIES: Not at all. This film is very French, so there's a lot of down time. American audiences want a jolt every scene. I'm going to amp up the tension, the suspense, and the excitement. There's a history of success with adaptations of French films: *Three Men and a Baby* was a French film. *Nine Months* was a French film. This is not new. I hope I do it nearly as well as Steven Zaillian, who's a brilliant adaptation specialist— everything from *Schindler's List* to *The Falcon and the Snowman* and *Awakenings.*

HARRIS: Do you work from the classic three-act paradigm?

ANDRIES: I do. It's worked for two thousand years; it will work for another two thousand years. I grow weary of people who try to recreate the wheel. When it works, like in Quentin Tarantino's *Pulp Fiction*, fine. But most of the time it doesn't work. I think that before you start breaking rules or creating new rules, you've got to learn the old rules. Learn the scales before you start improvising. I see a lot of new writers not wanting to learn the scales— not learning what three-act structure is. They think that their vision is so unique to the universe that it can't fit into three-act structure. Or that it is so conflicting or so confining or so Hollywood that they won't lower themselves to get their hands dirty with three-act structure. Arrogance and extremism. Just roll up your sleeves and learn how to do it. After that, if you want to do something else, go for it. If you want it to get made, you've got to know what an inciting incident is, what a mid-point and a second-act plot point is.

HARRIS: What other advice would you give to young writers?

ANDRIES: I've thought about this. Five things, all equally important: Number one, you've got to read. I have seen so many scripts that are based on comic books and TV shows and music videos. In this country, we've lost the passion for reading. Art, history, science, philosophy informs and gives texture to what you write. I tell people to read books with hard covers, read the newspaper every day. Inform yourself about the world, bring it into your life. It will make everything that you write that much more resonant.

Two, write everyday, even if it's lousy. It's very much like weight-lifting. If you do it every day, your brain will be trained to think creatively. If you wait for inspiration to write a first draft, you may write one every seven years, if you're lucky.

Three, meet people, especially people who are not like you, because that's what writers write about—people. If you only write about people who are in your neighborhood or people on your block or people in your school, unless you're Woody Allen, you're closing yourself off to an amazing universe of stories.

Four, learn about the business. Do not become a sheep among wolves. Know how to protect yourself.

Five, be prepared to struggle. It is hard to write a good anything. It is hard to write a good science-fiction movie, it is hard to write a good drama, it is hard to write a good comedy.

HARRIS: How long did it take to write *Kangaroo Court*?

ANDRIES: Paradoxically, sometimes the Gods smile upon you. I wrote that first draft in four days. I'd spent two and a half weeks researching it, thinking about it constantly. Then in four maddening days, I pumped it out of my system. The first draft is twice as long as the final draft. On my other scripts I've done as many as six drafts.

HARRIS: How many drafts did *Kangaroo Court* go through?

ANDRIES: About five. When I read it now, there are pages where I smile, and then there are pages where I say, "I know how to fix that now." It's ongoing.

HARRIS: An artist's work is never finished, merely abandoned. Do you work with scene cards and outlines?

ANDRIES: Oh yes. Staples is my friend. I'm fascinated by all of that cool stuff. I have a huge cork board in my office. I paste up cards so I can see the movie. I graphically watch the entire movie on my wall. I generally write free-hand.

HARRIS: You don't use a computer?

ANDRIES: I do eventually. I feel more comfortable writing on one of these. [Out comes a yellow legal pad] This pencil is an amazing word processor. You can erase, you can underscore, you can bold. It's amazing how this thing works, and for under a quarter. I take what I write free-hand to the Macintosh and input there. I also prefer to write outdoors away from my house because there have been days when I have gotten up at seven in the morning, with my "to do" list all printed out, my pencils all sharpened, and my pad in hand, and I sit there and I say to myself, "My God, that refrigerator is filthy." I could perform surgery in my apartment, it's so clean from the procrastination.

HARRIS: What are some of your favorite books on the screenwriting experience?

ANDRIES: Goldman's book is really good—*Adventures in the Screen Trade*. It still holds up. It is so practical and so readable. "Nobody knows anything."

HARRIS: That's his adage.

ANDRIES: That's the one people know. The one people forget is "Screenplays are structure." Get the structure right. Sure, sparkling dialogue is lovely. Sure, beautiful scenes are important . . .

HARRIS: Your work sings with great dialogue. I'm surprised you're poo-pooing it.

ANDRIES: I'm not poo-pooing it, and thank you, but it's not the engine. The engine is the dramatic structure. If the structure is off, the dialogue won't help you. It's very much like building a house: You can have beautiful drapes, but if the foundation is off, then the house will fall down.

HARRIS: What should young writers just getting out of film school realistically expect when they come to Hollywood?

ANDRIES: Nothing. They should expect nothing. I think they expect to be treated like the flavor of the month. Or, if they have had any success at all, they will be treated like the conquering hero. They should expect nothing. They should expect not to get their phone calls returned. They should expect to spend a lot of their own money copying scripts that won't get read. They should expect not to be the only one in town who's ever written a movie, but just another guy off the plane who's written a movie. They should expect nothing, which is not unfair—it is simply realistic. Now, given that you're expecting nothing, you can build a base with what you have to bring to this town. It's not enough just to be good. This town is filled with writers who are good and competent and workman-like and almost machine-like in their mediocrity. Before you're allowed to be a hack, you have to prove that you're extraordinary, and that's done by getting someone's attention, getting above the pile of scripts on someone's desk. If you're not there yet, expect nothing. It sounds harsh, and it is. If it were easy, everyone would be doing it.

HARRIS: How long have you been at it?

ANDRIES: It depends on when you consider me starting. In terms of being in Los Angeles, this is my eighth year. In terms of how long it took me before I got into Disney, five years. I was a semi-finalist for the Nichols Fellowship the year before that. The Nichols is run through the Academy Award foundation. They offer five screenwriting fellowships of twenty-five-thousand dollars to emerging screenwriters. They pay you to work on your next screenplay under the guidance of noted screenwriters and other people in the business. It is a very competitive, prestigious program. About four to five thousand people apply every year for the five spots that are open, but it's a great launching pad. I didn't get it that time, but I stayed in the game and the next year I got Disney.

HARRIS: So you encourage young writers to enter competitions?

ANDRIES: Right. Because you can enter fellowships and competitions from anywhere, whether you're in New York or

Milwaukee. People will find the good script. It may take a while before someone recognizes how good it is, but no one ever throws away a good script. The problem is that there are a lot that are almost good, or pretty lousy. It is a mistake for black screenwriters to automatically assume that the reason that they have not been successful or have not been recognized is because they are black. It may be because they can't write a tight second act yet. When you're at a point when your work is brilliant and you're still getting rejected, then it's time to look at the dynamics of race and class and gender and sexual orientation. But first, get your own stuff stored.

HARRIS: That comes from having a body of work. Can you tell from someone's first script what their potential is?

ANDRIES: Well, if it's really bad, yes. If this person doesn't know what a screenplay looks like, then it's a marker. But the way to get better is to keep writing. I'm not discouraging anyone's first script because it is a very tough form to master. In the number of rules and regulations one must adhere to, it is as difficult as haiku. It's a very narrow form to write in. It's not like writing a novel. A novelist can spend a half page describing a chair. A screenwriter has got to describe the Death Star in fifteen words.

HARRIS: Do you see yourself writing for a specific audience or does it change from project to project?

ANDRIES: The reason my agent is great is that he understands that I want to be a utility player and not a specialist. My work has gone from drama to farce to romantic comedy. I don't want to be pigeon-holed. I want to be considered for *New Jack City*, as well as *Four Weddings and a Funeral*. That makes me hard to market because I'm not the action guy, I'm not the comedy guy, I'm not the black homeboy writer in Hollywood. Yet, that's how this town receives me because it's easy to do. He's black, he's from New York, he must have killed someone. Call him in for a meeting.

HARRIS: Well, we don't have to talk about that. I'm sure the statute of limitations has not run out on murder. We can talk about anything just short of murder.

ANDRIES: I swear it was self-defense. [Laughing]

HARRIS: We hear the story of Eszterhas making three million for writing *Basic Instinct* and we hear the story of Singleton's *Boyz N the Hood* grossing one hundred million dollars worldwide, but what can we as black screenwriters realistically look forward to making?

ANDRIES: Good question, and you phrased it exactly. We are not making the long green because we are narrowing ourselves to a small niche of a huge marketplace. As long as we keep doing variations of turf battles in movies, or tiny domestic dramas, then we are going to generate budgets that are very small, which will generate writing fees that are very small, which will generate audiences that are very small, which will feed upon itself. In order to make Eszterhas money, we need to write films that will reach a worldwide audience with themes that a worldwide audience can relate to, and not be defined exclusively by skin color.

HARRIS: That's an excellent point.

ANDRIES: If a black person wrote *Jurassic Park*, it would change the face of the industry and the types of role models blacks have to follow. But we're not writing *Jurassic Park*, we're writing *Juice*. Nothing against the writer of *Juice*, but that market is saturated. How many more specs about the Tuskegee Airmen do we need?

HARRIS: Who were some of your heroes, mentors, and role models?

ANDRIES: My NYU film teacher Charles Milne was the North Star of my career. He believed in me before I believed in myself. I was lucky to blessed with parents who understood my bizarre career choice. This is a leap of faith not only for the writer, but the parents of the writer. Look at it from the parents' point of view: You've raised a young ambitious black person, who certainly has a mind and an imagination, wanting to get into an endeavor where most people end up starving. "How are you going to make money doing that? Why not go to business school, or law school, or something sensible?" But I had parents who said, "If you want to do that, all right. Go. Let's see what you've got. We're behind you 100 percent. We don't know a thing about this business, but if that's what you want, you have our support."

HARRIS: Who are some of your favorite writers and film-makers?

ANDRIES: As I said before, Steven Zaillian hasn't written a bad film in his career, he's astonishing. Sidney Lumet can direct anything. Sidney Poitier doesn't get anywhere near the recognition that he deserves for being a pioneer. Spike Lee made the current renaissance possible. Robert Redford is a filmmaker of remarkable dedication and focus. Oliver Stone is fearless. Although I don't always agree with him, the man has a point of view and knows how to articulate it. What is really heartening for me are the new writers. People like Spike Lee and John Singleton, blessed as they are with talent and opportunity, have had the court pretty much to themselves to define what "black filmmaking" is. Now there are an awful lot of different voices coming up through the ranks.

HARRIS: That's part of the reason I chose to do this project. It has been ten years since *She's Gotta Have It*. What direction do you see black cinema moving in?

ANDRIES: Black cinema is very much like Asian cinema or Latino cinema or gay cinema. We are basically freshman in this school. We're learning our way, and we are telling fairly predictable stories, by and large, right now. The more we become savvy in this business, and the more we get beyond the fact that a black person made a movie, we'll hear more voices and different voices, beyond just a young male urban voice. There are so many stories to be told within our culture and without. We can tell them. We, as black people, are, by default, bi-cultural. A white person can reach the highest success of his career without having any significant contact with a black person. But for a black person to succeed in this business, he is required to walk in all kinds of waters, with all kinds of peoples. That multi-cultural life experience is invaluable.

HARRIS: Do you feel a responsibility to dismantle these stereotypical images of our people? I'm speaking of the images that cause white women to clutch their purses when they are in the elevator with a black man.

ANDRIES: I mostly am responsible for what I put out there as entertainment. I don't feel so much a responsibility as an opportunity. I don't feel like I have a debt to pay, but an opportunity to exploit. My first job as a screenwriter is to draw a crowd, to bring people into the tent with a damn good story. Once they're involved in my story, what I do with my characters and how they interact with each other will form how I see the world, which is beyond the stereotypes of menacing black men. What I'm saying is that I'm not here to be a political cheerleader, I'm here to be a storyteller.

HARRIS: I'd like to thank you and conclude this interview, but before I do, is there anything you'd like to add?

ANDRIES: Yes. Don't trust your friends and family with your first drafts, because they love you. They don't want to hurt you. Especially your parents. If you were to write it in crayon, they would think it's wonderful. "You typed this all by yourself? It's wonderful!" That won't get you far at CAA. You need someone who loves you enough to say, "My God, this sucks!" That person will make your work better.

HARRIS: You spoke of agencies. You're not at CAA or one of the big boys?

ANDRIES: I made a choice not to get lost at one of the big boys. I'm at a very good boutique agency called Paradigm. I get the attention I need. It's terrible to be at a prestigious agency and be just another name on a phone list. If you can't get your own agent on the phone for a week, what good is that? You need someone to be your champion, and to be your ambassador in town. You need someone who believes in you as a writer, who doesn't just believe in a single spec script you have, but believes in you in the long term because you're going to have years when it's dry.

HARRIS: Do you project ahead in your career, or do you go where it takes you?

ANDRIES: I project all the time. I've projected since I was twelve years old. I think that within the next two years, I'll have a feature in theaters. Within the next four years, I'll be directing. I do not want to direct now. I want to make sure my screenwriting craft is so sharp that when I direct, I know what I'm doing story-wise. Anybody can direct a lousy movie. It takes no talent whatsoever. But if I'm only going to get one shot at the basket, I had better be prepared. A lot of directors get a shot too early and are never heard from again. I don't want that to happen to me.

TIM
REID

"I've never allowed 'don't' and 'can't' to interfere with my dreams."

Tim Reid is probably best know for his many acting roles. In his long and successful acting career, his credits include *WKRP in Cincinnati, Frank's Place,* and most recently, *Sister, Sister,* which presently airs on the WB network.

Mr. Reid has always viewed himself as more than just an actor. In 1993 he created United Image Entertainment, a production company dedicated to presenting a dynamic range of the African-American experience on film. In under two years, United Image Entertainment has produced four feature films, with several more in development. Tim smiles wryly and says, "It's quite an achievement for a company that nobody knows anything about."

Tim wears many hats as the head of his own production company. On the day we spoke, he and his editor were hard at work getting a rough cut of his latest feature ready to show to investors. We spoke at length about writing, commitment, and what it means to be an independent filmmaker in a studio town.

HARRIS: People say that you are the modern-day Oscar Micheaux.

REID: He is my icon. We all have to judge this business from our own backgrounds, based on our limited exposure and knowledge. I come from a totally black environment. I grew up in a small town in Virginia that was basically all black. I didn't speak socially to a white person, or work for one, until I went to college. Growing up, all the jobs I had and all the shops I went into were all black, except for the occasional Saturdays when we went uptown, into the white world, and we dealt with the racism and segregation. By and large, I was protected, nurtured, and educated in an entirely black environment. I graduated from a black university. I went to all-black schools with all-black teachers. The community in which I grew up was a self-sufficient, self-motivated community. We had black cab companies, black newspapers, and black-managed or -owned movies theaters. It was this little community that no longer exists. That's part of the reason that I made my directing debut with *Once Upon a Time...When We Were Colored*. When I read the book, it spoke to me about my past and what it was like growing up in a little town like that. My view of movie and television writing comes from a very proud and diverse black culture. When I think of writing, when I think of ideas and concepts, that background comes out. My work is always built around that. When I look at my heroes, I think of Oscar Micheaux because he was someone I admire, and did what I need to do. He wasn't a great filmmaker, by the way. [Laughter] I hope to be a better filmmaker.

HARRIS: What initially attracts you to a project?

REID: What drives me is to tell our stories. To tell our stories in the broader spectrum. We are a diverse people, but the material about us, written and performed, has been very narrow. Myopic in a sense. It goes through periods. It used to be musicals, and right now we're in our rage period. It's an interesting rage: it's past rage, it's urban rage. It is rage that is very difficult to solve, sort of a "drive-by rage," if I may coin that term. So I'm trying to break that cycle. I'm not interested in rage movies, I'm interested in love stories and thrillers and eroticism and family. The whole broad spectrum. And I'm not the only one— I think we all are. But I've bet my career on it. I've decided to make the movies that the town won't make. I don't have a "mainstream movie." What I hope to do is build a mainstream.

HARRIS: You're building an audience.

REID: Right. I don't think the studios would do the movies that I'm making now. So, to go boldly and say that I'm going to take a shot like that is financially very difficult. It's certainly easier to make mainstream movies.

HARRIS: I agree, but if this is your passion or your higher purpose, doesn't it transcend the desire to just make that dollar?

REID: Well, it's a funny thing about show business. Yes and no. Yes, it certainly should from a creative point of view, but the ultimate goal is to combine the two words. It shouldn't be all show and it shouldn't be all business; it should be a combination of the two. I think that show business is now only one word: business. My constant struggle is how to make my investors and partners comfortable in backing me from year to year in our quest and our mandate to tell our story. But, also, I've got to give them a hit, and it's obviously very difficult to do. If it was easy, this town would be a totally different place, we'd all be driving Rolls-Royces and Mercedes-Benzes. I look for the work to be technically true to the cultural aspira-

tions of the character. I don't see the need to cliché the
things that the town has set up to be the standard occupations and standard aspects of buddy movies. No matter
who you are, or if you're in a big-budget action movie,
very rarely do you get the girl. You're the buddy guy. I
want my leading man to get the girl, no matter what. That's
what leading men do. It's very difficult to sell that to a
town that's resistant to those themes on a broad base.

HARRIS: You've had some success circumnavigating those
obstacles, haven't you?

REID: It's not so much circumnavigation as going boldly, or
bully, and ignoring the people who say, "don't" and "you
can't." I've never allowed "don't" and "can't" to interfere
with my dreams. A lot of people do. I have made a lot of
enemies on both sides of the racial coin because of my
bullheadedness. I feel that I'm at risk out there, I'm taking the slings and arrows, so I should have the freedom
to make some choices. It hurts sometimes, but I know
that if Oscar Micheaux had not gone against the people
who didn't want him to do what he wanted to do, on
both sides of the racial coin, he wouldn't have had the
forty or fifty films on his shelf.

HARRIS: Absolutely. I think people forget that Micheaux did
most everything on his shows. Right down to bicycling
the prints over to the theater and coming back later to
pick up his receipts. How many hats are you wearing?

REID: Too many. Far too many. We've done four movies.
One that we co-produced out of Canada is called *Race to
Freedom*. I think it took eight years to get that movie made.
We did it for two million dollars, and it got nominated for
best picture at the ACE Awards. We were also nominated
for writing and cinematography. I really take that to heart.
I had a lot to do with directing the focus of the story, so I
take a personal pride in that story. Of the three movies
that we've done solely on our own, two have been developed from stories that I have written or conceived, and
one was based on a book. It's been a difficult process

because I've noticed that no one wants to apprentice. They want to go from "I want" to "master." The thing that's tragic is that you'll never be a master if you don't apprentice. Apprenticeship is the learning process. You may call yourself a master, you may be paid like a master, you may do the work required of a master, but you'll never be a master if you don't pay those years of apprenticeship.

HARRIS: Learning your craft.

REID: Learning your craft, applying your craft and failing and succeeding, and all of those things that you do over a period of time. I think that people don't want to do that. I've been writing and producing for quite some time. I think my first thing was around 1980. I've written and co-written television pilots, and now I'm in the film side. I've been at it for fifteen years, yet I feel like I'm a neophyte because I'm learning so much. My first directing assignment was one of the most frightening experiences that I've ever had as a creative person. I've learned so much and I feel so confident in my ability to learn that I look forward to the next opportunity. But I didn't come out of that saying, "I AM A DIRECTOR!" What I am is a creative person who chose to direct, and learned an awful lot. But in a few films, I will be a director. I know that it's going to take other films to get me ready.

HARRIS: People probably remember you most from your career in front of the camera. At what point did you decide that you wanted more and set your career in that direction?

REID: When I got fired from a show in 1977. I got fired because I "wasn't black enough." That was the quote they used at the time. The movies and sitcoms had an edge of buffoonery in them at the time, even the leading shows, which I won't name because I don't want to insult my peers. That was the trend, and if you worked, that's what you did. It's not as if anyone had a choice or could say, "I want to do Sidney Poitier's role." So, I got a role that I just wasn't able to do. It had too much buffoonery. I got into a hassle with the director, and two days before the shoot, I was fired. The good news was that three days later, I got hired on *WKRP in Cincinnati.* Had I not been fired, I would not have been able to do *WKRP in Cincinnati.* What I learned from that firing was that it was all about power, and I had no power. My career and my future rested in the hands of someone who knows nothing about me culturally, nothing about me in spirit. I decided that, from that day on, I would look for ways to have a creative input into what I did. I started writing screenplays first, then television scripts. I have written a minimum of four scripts for every show that I've ever been on.

HARRIS: Was it a struggle to get the producers to allow you to have more of a creative input?

REID: My mentors are people whom I respect. Hugh Wilson was the first person to give me a chance as a writer and a producer. I have always respected and admired his ability to go against the system and give a guy a shot. He's given a lot of people a shot, and many are still working. I learned a lot from him. He is a master craftsman as a writer. Other people then gave me a shot. Then it was a matter of me taking a shot with the opportunities that I was offered. Whenever I do something in television, I make a point of saying that if you want me, then I have to have some creative input. If not, then good-bye. I've always felt that I could survive with "no." You must be willing to lose, you must be willing to sacrifice something before you can get something. I realized that if I don't do this, then my fate will rest with someone else.

HARRIS: That's a good point, and one that many would identify with. At some point, somebody's got to take responsibility for the images. Why not you? Why not me?

REID: That's the key. In the five years since I started this company, we've gotten a lot of scripts. We have an open-door policy. Legally, it's nuts, but we have to do it because that's the way we mandated the company.

HARRIS: Expand on that a little. I haven't really heard of that. I usually get asked if I have all of the key personnel in place before I can get read. "Agent?" Check. "Lawyer?" Check. "Signed releases?" Check. "Okay, the executive assistant's assistant might give you a read in a few weeks."

REID: That's for good reason. Everyone thinks the idea is the thing. I used to think that if you came up with the idea or a treatment, you had something. That's not the case. The case is execution. You have to have a script, from the first page to the last page, with the ideas fully materialized and with your signature on it. Then you have something that you can legally stand on. In this town, there are a lot of ideas—we get them out of the ether. Many times I've been working on something that I thought was completely unique, and I later find out that there are two or three similar projects in the works elsewhere. It's the nature of creativity. So our lawyers told us not to take blanket submissions. But I said that other writers have the same problem that I have. I'm not going to get Spike to read my script either. And I must treat them like I want to be treated. So we drew up a very simple release form. We'll take submissions from anyone. Of course, they have to be registered or copyrighted or we won't read them. It's very difficult, and we open ourselves up to some degree, but that's the nature of the beast. It's very difficult to get something out and into circulation in this town.

HARRIS: Yet there are a lot of things being made, right at this moment. I live in South Central L.A. near Baldwin Hills. And on my way to the bank today, I literally passed three productions: Martin Lawrence's *Thin Line Between Love & Hate*, a music video, and what looked to be a low-budget, 16mm film starring the guy who played the lead in *South Central*. All in the Limert Park area of L.A. today. I thought that it was dynamite to see all this work going on.

REID: Well, it's good and bad. What's good is that people get a chance to apprentice. What's bad is that there is so much out there that lacks the purpose of growth. The purpose is money, or some other purpose. I have problems with a film we're doing now because the focus was not the film. The focus was on what the film could bring.

HARRIS: To your table?

REID: To anybody's table. To the director's table, the producer's table. Everybody had a focus that was away from the project. They were focused on the goal, not the film. What you end up with is a film that doesn't work. It's frustrating because you see all of this stuff being made, and you know, point blank, that you'd be lucky if five percent is any good. We simply have to get those percentages higher within the material about our culture.

HARRIS: Are you afraid that we are in jeopardy to kill off this renaissance, if you will, by deluging the market with inferior work?

REID: First of all, I don't think we're in a renaissance. We're in the beginnings of a potential renaissance. The word renaissance usually denotes mastery. When I think of renaissance, I think of people like Rembrandt. [Laughter]

HARRIS: Point taken. I stand corrected.

REID: What I think we have is a tremendous opportunity. I hope more people of color get involved in the filmmaking process. I hope that, as a group, as we move toward the work, we re-focus on our goals. We should not think of it as an end in itself, but relative to the growth of the creative persons involved in it. We are being driven by the town. It's like the chicken and the egg. The town says only certain kinds of films will sell to the black audience, and none of them will sell foreign. So, if you don't have a script that fits that pipeline, you can't get the movie bought or distributed by a major studio. So, if that's true, why not create a market by designing your product for the foreign market? That not a big secret. What you do is look at your target audience, and you design your properties for your target, rather than design them for a studio. And that takes courage.

HARRIS: Is there a conflict between what's commercial and what's uplifting to the race?

REID: It doesn't have to be uplifting, it just has to be about the truth of the culture. Not all films have to be noble. I'm not trying to make *Sounder* every time I make a movie. What I'm trying to do is be true to the cultural aspects of the character. We are many peoples, many different occupations, races. We are but a small percentage of the worldwide population. One of the reasons our films don't go worldwide is that we are myopic in our racial tones. We think that black is America. We are very small. We are what, thirty-three or thirty-four million? There are seventy million Brazilians. There are almost 100 million Nigerians. There are twenty-five million South Africans, another thirteen or fourteen million Europeans who are black. We haven't talked about the Caribbean, we haven't talked about many other places in Africa, for that matter. We force them to accept our material, but we don't include their culture, or even the contemporary aspects of their world in ours. I think that if we want to be more international, then we need to begin to think internationally. Why not have one of the characters be African? Or why not have one of the sisters be a Brazilian transplant? There are ways to do that in our culture and the culture of our films. But we don't do that because we think Hollywood. If you don't have the names of whoever the town says are the première black actors on the front part of your pitch, then you don't get it made. And that's a problem. What's got to be set up is a Miramax style for cultural types of films. You get one *She's Gotta Have It*, one *Daughters of the Dust*, one *When We Were Colored*, and the rest are mainstream product. And you don't have enough products coming down the pipeline to support a black art-house film. Not every film is for mass appeal. We have to have niche films, we have to be able to say that certain films shouldn't be expected to be released in any more than twenty theaters. If it looks good, fine, build up. Let's keep the budget down, the story rich, and make the film. In the life of the film, it will make money. Every film is not going to make ten to thirty million dollars.

HARRIS: For some Hollywood films, fifty million is a disappointment.

REID: That's why a company like mine tries to hit singles, as opposed to going for the wall. If we can make movies that make a profit of two and three million dollars, I am a king, my investors are happy. With four films, that's eight million dollars profit. We can keep going. The problem you run into is that when you bring the creative people together to make these films, you find people who have other purposes. Everybody tells you they want to be a producer, everybody says they want to direct. You tell them how much money you have in the budget and they say, "I can do that!" The first day on the set they want meal penalties, they want this, they want that. They want to go into overtime. We can't go overtime, it's not in the budget. We all say we want it, but in the reality of what the job takes, very few people are willing to make the sacrifice.

HARRIS: Very few people outside of the business understand the level of commitment that it takes. How do you begin to explain what your body feels like after forty sixteen-hour days?

REID: One of the most difficult things to do is make a low-budget movie. It's more difficult than just about anything. If someone ever gave me ten million dollars to make a movie, I'd think that I'd have died and gone to heaven. I made a movie, a period piece from 1946 to 1963, with eighty-three speaking parts, hundreds of extras, cars, and a clan march for 2.6 million.

HARRIS: Which film?

REID: *Once Upon a Time...When We Were Colored*. We shot it on location in twenty-eight days. It was a very tough show, yet we pulled it off. Most people don't want to work that hard. I don't think the reality of the job sets in until you get there. But they should do what they want: If they want a studio picture, if they want a commitment from New Line, that's where they should focus their material. They should leave little guys like me alone.

HARRIS: Do you think that without big credits, or a body of work, the big studios will be interested in getting involved with them on any level?

REID: There are ways to get to them. They all have their minority executive who filters in the material. There is now a look in our direction, to see if we can have another period of profitability on the black-hand side, like we did in the sixties and the seventies, movies like *Fridays* and *Low Down Dirty Shame* and all of those pictures that have made a lot of money at a very low negative cost. There are opportunities now, more so than there were in the past. I think that there are a lot of people who can break in. You have to know that that's what you want, and you have to focus on the work. You can't have it both ways, you can't say that you're going to make low-budget movies and focus on the work, and then say to yourself, "By making this, I'm going to show it to Warner Bros., and they're going to give me a contract." Two different purposes. You've got to focus on the work and not even think about the outcome.

HARRIS: What is the status of your *Spirit Lost* project?

REID: It's a movie that we've postponed the post-production process on until my investors and I can evaluate the work and see what we have. After that, we will know what can be salvaged, what needs to be re-shot, and all of those things. This is the nature of the beast. Not every film, at any given stage, turns out to be what you wanted it to be. It's like having ugly children—you have to love them just the same. [Laughter]

HARRIS: What was the genesis of this project?

REID: The story is based on a book. Of course, the characters in the book were white. The story was brought to my attention seven years ago as a producing and acting vehicle for myself and my wife. They couldn't get the movie made with white actors. Some producer said, "Why don't we recast this? I have never seen a movie like this in the black genre." So they came to me, I bought into it, and we shared the option. I tried to get it made as a TV movie with myself, Daphine, and Jasmine Guy. NBC was interested in it, but they got a little nervous because it has a certain eroticism about it, whether or not you choose to show it. It has a certain feel, it's an erotic thriller. Not sexual, but sensual. The story is about a guy who works in an art house, but decides to leave to pursue his dream of becoming an artist. He and his wife move to a house out on Nantucket. The house is haunted by the ghost of a mulatto slave, who was brought to the house by a slave-ship captain who promised to marry her, but sailed back to England and married a proper English woman. She was left in the house and died of a broken heart, but her spirit remains. This couple moves into the house, and both women battle for the man's soul. It's sort of *Fatal Attraction* meets *Ghost*. A wonderful concept, the script is wonderful, the actors are wonderful, we had a wonderful house, but it just didn't gel.

HARRIS: You saw a rough cut. What didn't work?

REID: There is no spirit in *Spirit Lost* [Laughter] to put it mildly. It's there, but it just doesn't work yet. My job, at this point, is to find out what the investors want to do. I am wearing the business hat now. I am totally on the business side, which is the most distasteful part for me. It's not even about judging, because some of my people may look at it and say, "It works for me." The problem here is that my investors looked at it and said, "It doesn't work for me." I have to satisfy my investors. They are the ones who will ultimately put it out theatrically or on video. What I have to do, which is very unpleasant, is just say stop. So that's where the project is right now.

HARRIS: How much creative control do you have over this project?

REID: In this particular project, I have final cut, which is a real bone of contention with most directors. I am the one who ultimately has to take the responsibility. A lot of people say they want control, but if you ask who wants the responsibility, hands don't go up as fast. Those are two words there that mean two entirely different things. What I am saying is that I take full responsibility, which means the good and the bad. If it goes wrong, I made the mistake, I hired the wrong director, I hired the wrong screenwriter, I hired the wrong producer. That's responsibility. I'm willing to take that. Most people aren't.

HARRIS: Who wrote *Spirit Lost*?

REID: The original piece was written by Nancy Thayers; I don't know much about her. This is the only thing that I have read by her. The screenplay was written Shirley Pierce, a friend and budding screenwriter who has written two wonderful screenplays for us: this one and one that I'm going to direct called *Hoochie-Coochie Man*. I think she's an undiscovered gem. Then a young lady named Joyce Lewis came in and did a rewrite.

HARRIS: I was wondering where all of the women screenwriters were. Apparently they're in your camp.

REID: Yes, we use quite a few. I've worked with Shirley, and I've worked with a woman named Tina Andrews on something called *The Power of No*. It's one of those things that everybody loves but won't make. I wrote the original treatment based on *Lysistrata*. It's gone through several drafts, but I am no closer to getting it made than the day I took it to Disney and Dawn Steel four years ago. Yet everybody loves it. This is just the nature of the beast. Everybody has a different vision of the piece.

HARRIS: Is this part of the reason that you started your own company?

REID: It's more than a part of the reason, it's the answer to those kinds of problems. I know that this film is going to

be made, and it's going to make a lot of money. It's probably one of the most commercial projects that I have in
house right now. It's come back to us in turnaround. I
just hope it doesn't take eight years.

HARRIS: Isn't this just part of your plan to build that body of
work? You have already made three films in eighteen
months or so, and you're starting another.

REID: But it's quiet. What I'm doing is quiet. I don't put myself in a league with Carl Franklin and Spike Lee because
I'm not at their level. I'm just starting to do what they've
been doing for years. These guys are masters and I am at
the journeyman level. We haven't had a hit yet, in terms
of this town's definition of it. None of our films have made
big money, so we're just at the learning journeyman stage.
They have made the kinds of films that have sparked the
reputations that they deserve. I am learning a lot from
people like Carl. We have similar backgrounds. Carl came
out of television, and he went into film, writing, and directing for the same reasons I did—for control. He was
not going to be dictated to, he was going to have some
say about things. He also went out and he journeyed.

HARRIS: He told me how it was working for people like
Roger Corman.

REID: And he learned his craft. I respect that. Corman will
work you to death, but you'll learn your craft. What an-
gers me is that when you go to work for Corman, people
know and accept the fact that you're going to have to
work. Like Carl, he made more than one film with him.
But when you're black, and a company like ours, people
don't come in with the same work ethic. For some reason, people feel like I'm taking something from them. I
heard producers say the tragedy of what I'm doing is paying name talent scale plus ten and I'm taking them out of
the talent pool, where people with serious money can't
use them. If Al Freeman works for me, I am hurting him
somehow. But at Roger Corman's, you'll find Jack
Nicholson, everybody will work for Corman.

HARRIS: I heard everybody in *Pulp Fiction* worked for scale. They shot that movie for eight million. Most of the people in Altman's films as well. They see it as a privilege of some sort.

REID: I have a reputation. They say I work people for no money. But I never promised anything. All I promised was a chance to work at their craft. I tell all of these people that if you've got nothing to do for the next twenty-eight days, come do it with me, and this is what I'll pay you. Quite frankly, they come and they bitch and moan and call me a black Roger Corman. I say that I'm an Oscar Micheaux. Corman does what he does, but they would work for him. Yet they expect me to pull rabbits out of a hat and start paying what the studios pay, which I can't.

HARRIS: Isn't the nature of independent low-budget films to get it done by any means necessary? Sometimes that means sacrifice.

REID: And people will do it. I've gotten very high-quality people at much lower rates. What I always give is an opportunity to move up. I gave a camera operator his first job as a DP, Johnny Simmons, and he is excellent. He is one of the future giants in cinematography. There were more first-time people working for me than anywhere else in town. I give you an opportunity to learn your craft the way you wouldn't get it anywhere else in town. My philosophy is, if I'm making a film and John Frankenheimer is available, I will ask him what he's doing and if he'll come work on this film. I think you go to the best first, and you say, "Be a part of this." If they don't, they don't. But don't get angry with me for asking. I'm going to ask.

HARRIS: This isn't a studio system anymore; people aren't working under contracts.

REID: Right, but I get a lot of heat. Where there's responsibility, there's heat. It's not a pleasurable experience, but I'm not going to let it change my passion and focus.

HARRIS: What's the most difficult problem that you've encountered on a production?

REID: The most difficult problems I've encountered are lack of focus and a disillusionment with process. As I say, everybody's a wannabe, but very few want to pay the price to be. That's a generalized view of a very specific problem that blankets the movie industry. At these prices, you don't have time to stop and focus people. You've got to hit the ground running. Another problem is getting stories. It all starts with the written word. And you just don't have the money to get the kind of script and the kind of time that you have to put into the script, the rehearsal, and the pre-production process sometimes. That's the most frustrating part of it for me. Some of these stories are excellent stories, and we go into production way ahead of when we should and try and play catch-up. Because when the money comes, you have to make the movie. You may not get the chance again. I think that we went into this movie under-produced. Some movies catch up. *When We Were Colored* caught up, but it was a race to the finish. There was more passion and commitment on that movie. The script and the story were about something that we all, in our hearts, wanted to make. The first one we did was *Out of Sync*, and the major problems were script problems.

HARRIS: *Out of Sync?* Was that directed by Debbie Allen?

REID: Yes. Debbie Allen directed and it starred L.L. Cool J and Victoria Dillard. I have to say that I didn't give her the kind of script that she deserved. Ultimately, we could have made a much better movie. Sometimes you get rushed into things. It was our first project and they said that we had to get something into production. We just had to do it. This was the closest we had, but the script just wasn't there and the work suffered. This one was just the opposite. We had a great script, and everyone who read it wanted to be a part of it. But somehow the commitment and the participation never gelled and it never got off to a good start, so the work suffered.

HARRIS: Bill Duke says that black filmmakers should be allowed to fail.

REID: I don't know if you should be allowed to fail as much as accept failure as a part of success. You shouldn't focus on it. It is the nature of being a journeyman. I think that when you go into it, you must realize that what you have to do ultimately is to complete the project. Just make the film. We made three films in just under eighteen months. That is a tremendous accomplishment for a company that nobody knows anything about. We've used all kinds of actors, producers, and journeymen. We've given jobs to people who normally may not be working. That is an accomplishment. Then you have to look at the work creatively. Getting a movie made is an incredible task. I take my hat off to anyone who can complete a movie. I don't care what it's about, you get my respect. Since we're talking about screenwriting, I must say, words first. What it all boils down to is what you have to shoot. The word, the written word is key. Develop your stories. Most writers don't want to take the time. I'll never forget this story: A young writer brought me a screenplay that was poorly structured, with misspelled words and disjointed scenes, but I loved the characters. She had a knack for character development, but her characters weren't saying anything. I said to her, "I really like the characters and the premise of what you're writing so much that I will pay your way to take McKee's writing class, to learn structure. Because if you learn structure and how to connect scenes and transitions and all of those things, you'll have a hell of a story here." The young lady was insulted, but she ultimately took me up on it, and I haven't heard from her since. Whenever I get off track, I go back to the beginning. The beginning is the word. I use it as a process to keep centered.

HARRIS: Give us a window into your process. How do you write?

REID: A lot of the stories come out of what I call the food-of-the-mind time. I busy myself with the less mental things:

gardening, driving. I have to be in a place where I have time to do that. My farm is where I do it best. So I'll be there in the garden planting something, and at the same time, I'll be writing movies in my head. After a period of days, maybe weeks, I will literally have run the movie from beginning to end in my head. I think from scene to scene, but what I've really done is outline it in my head with pictures. Sometimes I wake up in the middle of the night and write a scene. I dream in continuation of these stories. I'll sit down at the farm in central Virginia and I'll start structuring this thing and I'll get the end, then the beginning, and sort of work it out like a puzzle. I outline it, then I start writing scenes.

HARRIS: Do you write longhand?

REID: Sometimes, if I get writer's block on the computer, I'll get the legal pad, and when I go back to transpose it, it will cause me to rewrite. Sometimes, if I'm on a legal pad and the structure is too blah, I'll get onto the computer. In the end, it all ends up on the computer. Then I print it out and my wife and I will look at it. Before I let anybody else see it, it has gone through a few drafts.

HARRIS: Yeah, I'm very self-conscious of my work. It usually goes through three drafts before I let my mother see it, and that's just so I can hear an enthusiastic "I love it!" before I send it to less-nurturing eyes. How difficult is it for you to find objective readers?

REID: Well, I have a disadvantage and, in many ways, an advantage. The advantage I have is that I don't write anything that I don't think, as a producer, I can't get made. A lot of people write to sell; I write to produce.

HARRIS: What do you think about people who write to sell?

REID: I think it's a good living. [Laughter] I should think more about it myself, but right now, my chosen field is producing the things that I write. I primarily make my living as an actor. At night, I'm Producer Man, but in the daytime I'm an actor. A lot of people tell me not to give up my day job. Well, I'm willing to give up my day job; in fact, I plan to when this series ends. Anyway, I have the advantage of saying that I've got to see this materialize visually, not to sell. That's also the disadvantage, because I don't have the objectivity that I should have. When you're writing to sell, you're forced to shape your product to the commercial marketplace. When you're writing to produce, you take what people say with a grain of salt, because you know that you're going to make this somehow. It's hard to say whether it's a good or bad thing—I only know that it's different.

HARRIS: Do you have a circle of trusted ones who will give you script notes without pulling any punches?

REID: I don't think there's any such person on this planet. I don't think your wife or your family can give you what you ultimately need. You have creatively taken the passion of your spirit and put it on paper. No one can say you've done that but yourself. What you can do is get someone to assist you and infuriate you and force you to write, or inspire you to keep writing, but the bottom line is that nobody can say "you've done it" but yourself. I don't think that anyone says to Steven King, who must write a hundred pages a day, "Good job, Steven." Steven King doesn't need that.

HARRIS: Do you work with the three-act paradigm?

REID: I know what my forté is as a writer. I am not a "practicing screenwriter." I don't think that I could ever make a living as a full-time screenwriter. There are people who are and can, but I am someone who can put ideas to paper. What I am good at are characters. I am a good storyteller, that's all I am. No matter what the medium is—pencil, computer, film, camera, or standing on stage—I am a storyteller. That's all I've ever been able to do well and to the satisfaction of my spirit, even when I was a little boy. When I was in Africa, they called me a raconteur. I had to look it up in the dictionary, then I said, "Yeah, that's what I am." Structurally, I am not journeyed enough to call myself efficient as a screenwriter. But I'll put my story development and my ability to tell a story up against anyone.

HARRIS: Knowing your limitations is a strength. Ideally, how long do you like to spend developing a story?

REID: It depends. As you know, some stuff comes out rather quickly and some takes a while. My life's work is entitled *The Don, an Equal Opportunity Employer*. I've been working on it since 1973, since I sat down in Chicago and started writing. I'm still writing it. There are other things that I've put together in months, sometimes weeks. I've got a story in me right now that I haven't had time to write. But when I sit down to write it, I will probably have a finished form of the story in just a few weeks, because I've already worked it out in my head.

HARRIS: Waldo Salt used to infuriate producers because they would call him daily for a page count, and he would tell them that it was almost finished and then point to his head and say, "It's all in here." He'd work out the story completely in his head, but producers want to see those five pages every day.

REID: I think that's a real good discipline. If I were going to pursue screenwriting full-time, I would have to discipline myself. A writer writes. Period. That's all a writer does. If you don't have the discipline to sit down and put out those pages every day, then you're not a writer. You're someone who wants to write. Maybe an apprentice, but you're not a writer. Paddy Chayefsky was a writer, Steven King is a writer. If I had the discipline, I would probably turn out a screenplay a quarter, and would have been doing that for years. I give a lot of stories to other writers, because I just have the nucleus. Sometimes I take story credit, sometimes I don't, because I know that I'm going to produce it or attempt to produce it. That's how Shirley Pierce did *Hoochie-Coochie Man*, that's how she got *Spirit Lost*. Tina Andrews got *The Power of No*. Robert Dorn did *Out of Sync*. These are stories that came out of my head. I ultimately knew that I could not write them, so I gave them to professionals.

HARRIS: What issues that elude mainstream cinema do you try to capture in your work?

REID: The truth about who we are as a people. No one really knows who we are as a people. They have no general feeling. If you say Jewish, you'll have a real good feeling of triumph and of pain. Images come to your mind. If you say Italian, you get a good feeling and images come to your mind. But if you say black, by and large, people will think slavery and disenfranchisement, because they don't know. I spend a lot of time in Brazil. They love American blacks, and they laugh at us in a warm, wonderful way because they say that our problem is that we don't know our history. The Brazilian know more about us Americans and our history than we ever stopped to take the time to learn. If you want to know where we come from, go to Brazil and Bahia. It is one of the shortest points on the main line between Africa and this hemisphere. Most of the slave trade came through Bahia. When they came through Bahia, most of the families were separated. Some came on to America, some stayed there. So, my gene pool, your gene pool, more than likely came through there. When I went there, I saw so many people who I thought I knew. I was amazed. I had never seen that many people and been so comfortable in my life. There are seventy million Afro-Brazilians. We don't even think about it here. We lost our history. They have their history, they know where they came from; we don't. So when you tell stories about us, you get a symmetry of story that's really not our own. You get a version of what we are based on the written propaganda or the written modicum of the time. Whatever Hollywood accepts as the image of who we are, are the stories that we write. What's missing are stories about courage. Of course, we get the stories of icons who have fought through the darkness. They can't be ignored. But what's the story of the last slave in America?

Do you know that story? I once got a story out of Ripley's "Believe It or Not!" I picked up the paper and it said, "Bombs have only been dropped on United States soil once." Everyone thinks of Pearl Harbor, but it was in Oklahoma in 1921. A black community was bombed from the air. People were killed. A group of people attacked this black town because they controlled the town and owned the land and the oil rights. They were the wealthiest people west of the Mississippi. So I came up with this story: *The Day They Bombed the Promised Land.* I took it around, and people thought I was nuts. They had never heard of it. Those are the stories I want to tell.

HARRIS: How has the trend of big-budgeted films affected the work that you do?

REID: It hasn't. I am not a member of this community as a filmmaker. Nothing that they do affects me. Good or bad. I cannot say that my career or the way I run my company or anything that I do is affected by what they do, because I am not a part of this town. If I had a studio deal it may be different.

HARRIS: How do you feel about the work of the new black pack?

REID: I think we are all soldiers in the battle. I look at them as young people who are trying to tell a story. I have a lot of admiration for anyone who attempts to do that, and is successful in getting a movie made. I also have a personal distaste for a lot of the work that is being done by these young filmmakers. But to take them to task in print, or verbally, is not my goal. Personally, there are a lot of films that are being made where I wish they would have taken more pride in culture, and more pride in their goal to tell a story.

HARRIS: There's an audience that wants it. Otherwise they wouldn't keep getting financing.

REID: In the land of the blind, the one-eyed man is king.

HARRIS: What audience do you see yourself making films for?

REID: I make the kind of movies that I want to see. I'm a storyteller and I hope that there's somebody who wants to see the story that I want to tell. I don't make films for a particular audience. I do, however, feel that the audience that has been ignored for the last thirty years has been the adult black audience. The mature, hard-working, average black American doesn't really have a lot of movies to see. Everything is aimed at what I call the five-percentile group, who get seventy percent of all the action. Young black urban teenagers get all the action in this town. It's not only unfair, it's absurd. When you break down the demographics and look at the actual hard figures, it is absurd that we are making so much product aimed at this market. They are not the major consumer. In fact, most of the money comes from the parent. The twenty-two- to forty-year-old doesn't have a lot to see, and I think that it"s a real sleeping giant. That's Oscar Micheaux's audience, that's *Sounder*'s audience, that's *Driving Miss Daisy*'s audience. There aren't a lot films for that audience. So they go see *Forrest Gump*, they go see all these other movies, but they don't go see themselves. I've talked to a lot of these people, and they aren't interested in these young urban movies. If they want to see young unruly kids, they can see that at home, or in their front yard. Who wants to see a bunch of young kids running around with bandannas on their heads, shooting Uzis?

HARRIS: I don't know, but last year when I was in Paris, the lines for *Menace* were around the block.

REID: It's not surprising. There's so little of it for one thing. Secondly, it is the image being sold to the world by CNN and other global conglomerates. Nike, Reebok: What image of us do they sell? The urban, hip, arrogant, dangerous figure. That's what they sell. That's what they know. But you send over a story about a composer or an astronaut, then it suddenly becomes fiction.

HARRIS: So, where do you see your company in five years?

REID: Making one to two pictures a year, based on stories

that I want to tell. Hopefully, the company will have gone public by then and have made everybody a lot of money so that people will get off of my back about this money situation. I will go into semi-retirement and build an editing facility out at my farm, where I will plan a movie and make sure it's well-written. Then I'll shoot it, take it back to my farm for the post, and then bring it out here and deliver it and go back and make another one. Some will be commercial, some will be art films. There are great stories that I want to tell.

HARRIS: Do you think that you can actually make movies from a farm in Virginia?

REID: Definitely. I've made one in Virginia and one in North Carolina. You do not have to be in Hollywood to make movies. It certainly helps, because you're in a community that's geared for it, but you don't have to be. The only thing it takes to make movies is money and a script.

HARRIS: That's a great notion. I think that there are a lot of people who are ideologically in alignment with you, but practically, functionally you just don't see it much in the work. So, I'm wondering if we are just paying lip-service to this mission.

REID: No. I'm going to do it. I'm arrogant and bullheaded enough to see it through. There also is no fear in me that life will not work if I don't accomplish this task. I'm doing this because I like it and believe in it, and I am totally committed to taking the responsibility one must take to do it. I don't need a pat on the head by some studio executive for a job well done. I don't need to be called up to Sundance and to be given my kudos. I don't need to be in the *Hollywood Reporter* Pic packing a deal. All I have to do is tell my stories with pictures. That's the best that can happen to me. Everything else is gravy. I got nine Emmy nominations for *Frank's Place.* It was critics' choice for best show of the year. I was nominated for two: one for acting, one for producing. My producing partner, Hugh Wilson, won one for screenwriting. The show was canceled. So all of the kudos mean squat. What was important was that the show was on the air. And all of the nominations and good work couldn't keep it on the air. Now I can't be flippant and say awards don't mean anything, but the work is the most important thing.

HARRIS: How long did *Frank's Place* run?

REID: Twenty-two episodes. Seems like twenty-two years, but it was twenty-two episodes.

HARRIS: Everyone who has seen those shows would agree that you were tackling issues with a great deal of integrity. I recall a show dealing with a brown-paper bag. What were you saying with that episode?

REID: Basically, it was about racism within the black community. About people who have clubs, and if you're blacker than the tone of a brown-paper bag, you couldn't be a member. That's nothing earth-shattering—it happened in my community, it happens in a lot of black communities. Of course, the "system" didn't know about it. It's a part of our culture that people don't talk about, so it was a revelation when it was done on television. That's what the show offered me. Sometimes I become a little incensed because people assume that I didn't have any input into the show other than as an actor. But that's really not true. Hugh Wilson wrote the majority of the scripts and oversaw the production, but there were many story ideas that came from our collaboration. He and I both wanted to do something different on television. He wanted to do stories about the south, and I wanted to tell stories about my culture. I knew those people at *Frank's Place*. They lived in my community. I knew those kind of people and we put those images out there. That was our commitment. I think *When We Were Colored* is very close to *Frank's Place* in its feel, and in its exploration of our culture and our community.

HARRIS: In television, is there usually much collaboration between writers and producers and actors?

REID: No, there isn't. There is very little collaboration whatsoever in television. It's between the network and producer. That's why power is very important in television.
In film, there is more collaboration, because you've got
your writer, you've got your producer, you've got your
director, you've got your production designer all coming
together to make the whole. In television, there's the producer and the network. That's it. Actors are told what to
say and what to do. There is no ad-libbing on television.
There is no "let's work this scene out." It doesn't happen.

HARRIS: What advice would you give to young people who
aspire to write?

REID: Write. Write consistently, every day. And read. Read
history. Read fictionalized history, like Michener and
Wallace. Read books like *Sarum*. Read books that mix
fact with fiction, because they teach you to tell stories.
They teach you to take facts and play with them. If you
don't, you may be able to put the pen to the paper, but
you will always have a weakness in character development and story structure. That's it. Read the masters. If
you're going to become a dentist, you don't ad lib, you
study the masters. Read the works of the greats, read
Emerson, read Baldwin, read Langston.

HARRIS: Is there work available for new black writers?

REID: There's always work available for good writers. It depends on what you expect it to be. I think that well-written work will ultimately find an outlet. It's like a spiritual
quest. A good idea will find a mind that's capable of shaping it.

HARRIS: In your work, we see that you've made a real effort
to dismantle certain negative stereotypes and replace them
with a more dynamic representation of African-American
culture. Why don't we see more of that?

REID: Because it's dangerous. When you go against the status quo, you take on a certain amount of risk. It could
mean career, sometimes it's life-threatening. I don't mean
that people will kill you, I just mean that due to the stress,

you may put your health in jeopardy. It's a risk, and people sometimes don't want to pay the ultimate price. I believe that every time you take on a image, you expose a certain part of your soul. If you expose your soul, you damn well better protect it, because it's the only one you've got. So every time I get involved with a character, I fight. My father told me to always check my heart. If it's about the truth, then it's pure. It may not be right, but if it's true, then your soul will be protected.

YVETTE LEE-BOWSER

"Each one should teach one, or more if possible."

My interview with Yvette Lee-Bowser at the production offices of the hit series *Living Single* was brief but informative. The apparent quiet of her pre-production offices was only an illusion.

Inside Yvette Lee-Bowser's office, a storm of last-minute contract negotiations, production scheduling, and script approvals were threatening to postpone our interview. I quietly waited outside and enjoyed the general good will and family atmosphere of her multi-cultural staff.

Once inside, I was greeted by the congenial smile and firm handshake of one of the few female African-American show-runners in the business. She took off her telephone headset, lit a vanilla-scented candle on her desk, and gave me her total attention.

HARRIS: We've spent a bit of time talking about mentors and role models in this book, and I understand that Bill Cosby was very important in the beginning of your career. Do you want to talk about that experience a little?

LEE-BOWSER: Cosby was someone who gave me an opportunity. He was a role model more than a mentor. He was an African American who had made it in television, and there were only a handful of us who had done it at that time. And there are about two handfuls of us who are continuing along that path. I knew someone who knew someone who knew him, and I was introduced to Cosby on a movie set. I just went up to him and said, "I have this creative energy that has to be tapped. I'll get coffee, I'll get lunches, I'll do whatever it takes, but I want to get some exposure to this business, and I have a desire to be a writer." I showed him some short stories that I had written in high school and college that made him chuckle a bit, then he basically set me up as a writer's apprentice, working for free.

HARRIS: It's excellent to hear that you were willing to apprentice.

LEE-BOWSER: Oh, definitely. So I arrived at *A Different World,* and I started contributing ideas for different characters and different storylines that people on staff were actually turning into scripts that were becoming produced episodes. So, I thought, "I should call Mr. Cosby and see if I should be getting paid for this." I ended up calling him and letting him know what my contributions were. Other writers and producers verified that I was contributing, so I ended up getting a salary of about $200 a week. [Laughter]

HARRIS: Just enough for gas money to get to work.

LEE-BOWSER: Right. It was nowhere near what the other people were getting, but I was happy to be in that environment and feel like my contributions were being acknowledged. That was all that I really needed at that time. It was a sign that I was headed in the right direction. The fact that my ideas were worthy of being used was a very good indication that this was something that I should stick with.

HARRIS: How did you feel the very first time you heard the actors saying your words?

LEE-BOWSER: I got a rush. I really did. It's the best part of writing. On *Living Single* in particular, when I come up with something and see the actors perform it, it is just that much richer, seeing it come alive. And because I created that show, it means that much more to me when it works. We all have what we think are these great ideas, but sometimes they are not as great as we think they are. So, you are forced to rework them and rework them and rework them. To then see them work and to see people appreciate what you have done is incredibly rewarding.

HARRIS: What were your primary goals when you created the show?

LEE-BOWSER: To produce a positive, hilarious show about young African Americans trying to make it. That was my primary goal. It's important to me that the show came from a positive place, and that it depicts us loving each other in our way. It must also be honest to who we are. That it's funny is also critical. [Laughter] After all, we are doing a situation comedy.

HARRIS: The characters whom you have created are all progressive, intelligent, educated people. Speak to the importance of projecting those values.

LEE-BOWSER: The characters are basically people whom I have plucked from my world, and those people tend to be pretty educated and pretty progressive. But that doesn't mean that everything that I create will have that flavor to it. That was just the flavor that I chose for this show. The women are, basically, the four sides of Yvette, sprinkled with a little bit of Queen Latifah, and a little bit of Kim Coles, who were involved at the inception of the show. The show was created as a vehicle for them. I cast the rest of the actors, but Queen Latifah and Kim Coles were involved from the beginning.

HARRIS: The show was an immediate success.

LEE-BOWSER: It blew my mind. [Laughter]

HARRIS: Did it surprise you?

LEE-BOWSER: Yes. I did about seven drafts of this show before the network gave a green light to the pilot. I just reworked and reworked and reworked. I thought that I could not write it again without hearing the actors read the words. I just couldn't do it again. There was a tremendous battle getting the show to the point where it was actually produced. They were able to read the script and kind of feel the characters, but not really, because the show is different. The show feels different, and I think it reads differently from a lot of other shows. They wanted a show about black women, but I think they were looking for more hands-on-hips, finger-popping, gum-snapping women, and that wasn't quite what they got. I think that, to some degree, they were a little intimidated by some of the characters and how strong they were. They actually asked me to get rid of one of the characters, and I really had to stand my ground. Having gone through all of those battles to get the pilot produced, the show's immediate success was just that much sweeter. I felt it in my heart. It was important enough to me that I felt that the camaraderie these people have was worth putting on paper. I thought there must be someone else out there who feels the way I do about their friends. And apparently there are a lot of people who feel that way, because there are a lot of copycat shows. People have referred to *Friends* as the original, but we all know that *Living Single* was here first.

HARRIS: Do you think that has anything to do with the fact that *Friends* is an NBC show?

LEE-BOWSER: I think the network does have something to do with it. Fox clearly had a lot of faith in the show, by putting it on Thursday night, and strengthening their line-up. They put a lot of money into the show. *Living Single* is number one among African Americans. But, as African Americans, we have fewer Nielsen boxes. It's like number sixty overall. There are about 140 shows, so we're somewhere in the middle of the pack. Again, it's a wonderful thing to have a gift and be able to have voices in your head and be able to translate that into a script. It's another thing for other writers or peers to praise that. And it's another thing to have America watch it, and to have created a show that people write letters to you about. That is so far beyond what I dreamed I would be capable of doing. I have created something that makes other people feel so good about themselves that they make an appointment to watch. There are people who call this their favorite show. I never knew that I would be responsible for something that great.

HARRIS: How much do the ratings actually affect what you do?

LEE-BOWSER: At this point, only to a small degree. It's not so much about ratings, but about what the network temperature is. How the network feels about the show. At the beginning, they really wanted it to be about women and their boyfriends. It was heavily pushed in the direction of a show about dating. I always wanted it to be about more than that. The premise was sisterhood, for me.

HARRIS: Interpersonal dynamics?

LEE-BOWSER: Yes, exactly.

HARRIS: How much of the character and scenario arc is decided in the pre-season?

LEE-BOWSER: A lot of what we do each season is decided at the beginning of each year, and some of the storylines were storylines that I came up with when I created the show three years ago. We are doing those shows when they are appropriate in the character's evolution. Each pre-season we sit down and talk about what the evolution of character is going to be. We try to come up with a theme for the season that will give us some story ideas along the way. This season is about reaching for our dreams. Last season was about self-empowerment. The first season was about getting to the second season. [Laughter]

HARRIS: The first show this season is a show that you've written. We should talk about that since the first show sets the tone for the whole season.

LEE-BOWSER: Right. The first episode kind of reaffirms and restates the series' premise. It's an episode about sisterhood and what we mean to each other; how even though we could make it on our own, we really need each other. This episode focuses on two childhood friends, Khadijah and Rajine, who have had some miscommunication along the way that led to Rajine moving out. It deals with them missing each other, wanting each other, and reconciling in the end.

HARRIS: Let's talk about the work.

LEE-BOWSER: The most important thing, because it is work.

HARRIS: It absolutely is. I think that we've spent a lot of time over the course of this book reinforcing that fact. What would you say is the biggest problem that you've encountered in the material submitted to you?

LEE-BOWSER: A lack of depth. People often set out to tell a story, but don't end up telling it because they skim over the heart of the story. Another thing I find is that storytelling skills are essential. I think that a lot of people have good ideas, but don't know how to lay out a story properly. You can always make something funnier, but if you don't have a story, you really don't have a script.

HARRIS: The structure of a situation-comedy script is a bit different than the three-act structure that you typically find in film scripts. Could you address that?

LEE-BOWSER: There are some sitcoms that are in three acts, but most of them are in two. Each show has its own tempo and flavor and its own storytelling mode. Like *Seinfeld* doesn't really have that much structure to it.

HARRIS: Yes, it's very loose.

LEE-BOWSER: Right. By reading a *Seinfeld* spec, it's hard to assess whether someone has the story skills they need for a show that is story- and character-driven, like *Living Single*. *Seinfeld* is more situation driven, and our show is more character driven.

HARRIS: How many writers do you have on staff?

LEE-BOWSER: Eleven.

HARRIS: Is your season thirteen episodes?

LEE-BOWSER: No, its twenty-seven.

HARRIS: So, each writer gets a couple of episodes?

LEE-BOWSER: Oh yes, and we have a couple of freelance writers who come in and do a couple of scripts here and there.

HARRIS: When you're evaluating new writers at the beginning of the season, what criteria do you use? Is it based on past relationships, referrals? How often do new writers break through?

LEE-BOWSER: It's very tough to break in. I wouldn't want to discourage people from trying. Persistence does pay. Often, people will break in the sitcom business as a writer's assistant or production assistant and get exposure to how a comedy-writing room works. A sitcom is a very collaborative effort. You write your script and you may do a second draft, but eventually it hits that table and five other people will massage it into what you see on television. For me, there's a lot of angst that goes into being the creator or the executive producer or show-runner. I don't want the staff to have to massage mine too much. [Laughter] But to answer your question, writers do break in. I look for people who are funny, and people who are hardworking, because I'm hardworking. I look for people who are like myself, or people who bring something so different to the table that they are going to round out the show. I make that judgment based on scripts I've read and personal interaction.

HARRIS: In the climate of the table, there's a way of critiquing the script that's constructive, and you have to foster that in order to develop the stories. Do you find that writers are protective of their work to the point of being too sensitive to criticism?

LEE-BOWSER: All writers are protective of their work, but you need to learn over time that the people providing criticism of your work are really there to help you and make you look better by improving your work. I have never perceived notes as a negative thing. The worst feedback is no feedback or just positive feedback. We do it with love here. There are some places that are brutal, but here at *Living Single*, we find a way. You also find a way to give notes differently to each person. I know what each person needs. Some people need more strokes before you say, "Now, this didn't work!" [Laughter] And others can take it straight, no chaser.

HARRIS: Do you find that the discipline between each writer varies?

LEE-BOWSER: Very much so. Every writer has their own level of discipline, their own level of dedication, and their own wacky means of getting it done. I have personally never approached any two scripts exactly the same way, which is probably insane on my part, but there's just a whole different set of circumstances each time I sit down to write something. There's a whole other vibe in my life, there's a whole other set of distractions. So far, whatever energy I take into it tends to work out in the script.

HARRIS: I've noticed in putting this book together that most of the writers are men. The balance is way off. How can we get more women involved in the writing process and into this business? How can we foster their creativity in a safe space?

LEE-BOWSER: I think one thing we have to do is acknowledge that it is not a safe space, and we as women need to just jump into it face-first. This world of writing is just like the world at large—it's a man's world. We have to go in and grab what we're going to get, because people are not necessarily going to pull us into it. I have found that a lot of women who are in the business tend to be very protective of the little space that they have been able to grab. I have made a conscious effort to try and mentor other women. We have three other female writers on the show. That's really the best that we can try to do. Each one should teach one, or more if possible.

HARRIS: Do you have writing interns?

LEE-BOWSER: No, we do not. We have staff writers and writing assistants, who are basically in training to become writers. You have to have experienced writers on your staff if your show is to succeed. I definitely keep an eye open for new talent, but I haven't met anyone whose work so impressed me that I had to fire someone on my staff to hire them. [Laughter]

HARRIS: I'm sure it doesn't work like that.

LEE-BOWSER: No, but spaces become available. People will move on, as they eventually do. This business is a grind. It's very tough to write the same show. I spent five years on *A Different World,* and when I left, I felt that I had written all that I could write through those characters and those situations.

HARRIS: How many episodes did you write for that show?

LEE-BOWSER: About twenty-five.

HARRIS: I would think that around the third or fourth season it might get tough to find fresh storylines for your characters. What challenges are you facing in that regard?

LEE-BOWSER: It just keeps getting better, actually. I think that on this show in particular, the characters are so well defined that you take any situation that you may have seen or may have happened to you, or someone who you know, and ask, "What would these characters do in this situation?" Then you have a story. We really have had no problem coming up with stories because the characters really work well. There are certain series that have been on for nine, ten, eleven years. So it can be done without having to repeat yourself. I think that for two years people have been asking, "What's going to happen between Max and Kyle?" Well guess what, Max and Kyle are going to be dating now. Is it going to last? Who knows! [Laughter]

HARRIS: Tune in next week and find out.

LEE-BOWSER: You have to shake up the status quo so that you've got something totally new with characters that you already have an attachment to.

HARRIS: What impressions do you get when you look over the landscape of shows produced about the African-American experience?

LEE-BOWSER: I think that there's room in the world, and in television in particular, for all different kinds of work. Everyone's experience is different. I can't say that *Living Single* captures the quintessential African-American experience. I can say that it captures this African American's experience. I can say that, with no doubt in my mind, what does work about this show is that it has a universal appeal, it deals with humans. Because they are African Americans, they have a very specific take on things, they have life experiences that contribute to who they are and make the show a little different than some of the other shows. *Living Single* also has a goal to portray African-American life, whereas many shows with African-American cast members do not have that goal.

HARRIS: Could you illustrate that point for me?

LEE-BOWSER: I don't think that shows like *Family Matters* really set out to depict African-American life. It is a situation comedy about a family who happens to be black. Which is different from what we do. Which is very different from what Martin Lawrence is doing. Which is very different from what Mark Curry and Will Smith are doing. I think that there's a reason why *Living Single* is number one with African Americans. There are all different types of people, and just because there are other African Americans on other shows doesn't mean that we have the same agenda, or that we all have the same sensibility. *Living Single* was created to be a companion piece for *Martin*.

HARRIS: Those two shows seem completely different to me.

LEE-BOWSER: I personally cannot see the similarities at all.

HARRIS: Your show is up against some stiff competition this season.

LEE-BOWSER: We're now up against one of the most popular shows on TV, but my job is the same. I have to produce the same quality show that I would produce if I were up against the world's worst show.

HARRIS: When *Cosby* was up against *The Simpsons*, *Cosby* seemed unfazed.

LEE-BOWSER: It did have an effect. It did have an impact. Who knows, maybe the show would have lasted longer. But every show has its shelf life, and hopefully we're going to be on for a little while.

HARRIS: In you fantasies, where do you see *Living Single* going in, say, five years?

LEE-BOWSER: It could go on forever. How long I'll be here is unknown. I plan to go on and create other shows. This show is at least around for four years, and I would bet on five.

HARRIS: Is it too soon to talk about syndication?

LEE-BOWSER: Not really. On page five of today's *Variety*, you can read about it yourself. "*Living Single* Rolling Out In Syndication."

HARRIS: Well, I'm lucky to be here on a banner day! Congratulations! [Laughter and handshakes]

LEE-BOWSER: Thank you.

HARRIS: This changes everything. Now the show will become a part of the American psyche for future generations.

LEE-BOWSER: Yes, this will be one of them. They call it a hit. I'm amazed.

HARRIS: You're a showbiz family now that you're married to Kyle Bowser. Does your work influence his and vice versa?

LEE-BOWSER: I do believe that we influence each other. We consult with each other all the time, and we have plans to do something together in the future. But right now, I'm doing my thing and he's doing his.

HARRIS: The amount of dedication that this work takes is amazing. The forty-hour week is a myth.

LEE-BOWSER: Truly. If we only put in eighty hours, we're doing okay. But we try to keep it reasonable. As the series gets more mature, the hours become more reasonable.

HARRIS: How do you keep the level of writing so high on your show?

LEE-BOWSER: Focus and desire. I think the same thing any individual has to have within himself in order to write quality scripts, the whole staff needs to have to produce a quality show. I have high standards and demand them of others.

HARRIS: What's your proudest moment associated with the show?

LEE-BOWSER: There are so many moments. Being picked up. It got better from that point. But the show being picked up for a series was really a proud moment for me. I had hushed all of the nay-sayers. Also the ratings from the first night until now. Each week brings another moment of pride. [Laughter]

HARRIS: Let's say a new writer comes on staff. What can he or she expect in terms of the day-to-day scheduling? Walk us through a week in the life of *Living Single*.

LEE-BOWSER: A production week on *Living Single* is a little different, because we have scripts that work and actors who are quick studies and very much into their characters. We have a four-day schedule now. On Thursday morning we will read a script. On Thursday afternoon we see a run-through. We do rewrites on that script based on what did or didn't work on its feet. On Friday we see the same show again on stage. The network and the studios give us their notes and we do a rewrite based on that. On Monday, the staff is basically polishing a script that is coming up in the future. We also look at the camera work that's been done on stage, performance direction, lighting, and every last detail. On Tuesday we shoot the show twice.

HARRIS: Why twice?

LEE-BOWSER: Just because we do it in front of two audiences. One is more or less a dress rehearsal.

HARRIS: Have you any parting words for the readers at home?

LEE-BOWSER: You have to be willing to do the work. If you're not willing to do the work, if you're just in it to get paid, I don't think you'll last, whether you're good or bad at it. You can get better. I mean, if you're truly not talented, I think you'll come to that realization before too long, but you have to be in it for more than just the money, or else it will wear you down before you get out of it what you'd hoped.

CARL
FRANKLIN

Photo courtesy of Monarch Pictures

"If you're creative, you are going to create your own stories."

Carl Franklin is a filmmaker whom the other filmmakers I have spoken to name as one of their favorites. I found it quite a strange phenomenon, since he has only two films that he is known for directing: *One False Move* and the recent smash hit *Devil in a Blue Dress*. At the time when we had this conversation, *Devil* was not yet in theaters, but the buzz screenings at TriStar were eliciting the kind of vibration that had people speculating on Oscar nominations for Carl.

Sitting down and having a drink with Carl Franklin is an experience like none other. It is easy to be intimidated by Carl's enigmatic, yet strong, no-nonsense demeanor. But beneath that you will find a acutely sensitive and caring individual with a world-view that is as unique as it is profound.

This is more a conversation than an interview because I hadn't yet seen his new film, and he wasn't familiar with my work. Instead of probing into his approach to adapting Walter Moseley's novel to the screen, we raised our glasses, toasted to success, and enjoyed the unparalleled beauty of the women in the bar at Gagnier's restaurant in Baldwin Hills as we discussed the world we live in and life in general. At one point, I asked if I could turn on the recorder, provided that, at any point, he could tell me to shut that little fucker off. He smiled and said, "Okay."

I found Carl open to talking about anything but his new

film. Perhaps this was because *Devil in a Blue Dress*, which was getting raves from the industry insiders, hadn't yet been put before the public. Or maybe he was just exhausted from the filmmaking process. Either way, it was the first and only time that I had a chance to talk to him at any length. By the time I was allowed to screen the film, three weeks had passed and the enigmatic Carl Franklin was again unreachable for comment. Here is our short—but interesting—conversation.

HARRIS: We were talking about missteps and their availabil-
ity. There's the fact that when your desires exceed your
means to attain them, the opportunity to go into crime
becomes more attractive. I know this kid, about eighteen,
who was having some trouble finding a summer job. We're
on the phone when the call waiting clicks in and he says,
"Yo, E, I gotta go. I'll call you later." A couple of hours
pass, and I get a call from the kid. "Where you been?" He
says, "Oh, I had to talk to a homie about possibly slangin'."
I say, "I know I'm not hearing any of this from you." Then
there was this long pause.

FRANKLIN: Don't even think about it.

HARRIS: I just said, "Dude, you're all wrong. It's not even
the answer. I can't know you if you make that decision. I
can only pray for you."

FRANKLIN: Right, right.

HARRIS: I was amazed and saddened that my young homey
felt his only options were to go to work at McDonald's or
sell drugs.

FRANKLIN: In some instances, there's a compounded thing
that happens with brothers. There's this whole culture that
seems to discourage them from doing well, especially in
school. I understand what it is. Walter [Moseley] and Trey
Ellis were saying in a conversation that, in some instances,
a black student may raise their hand in class and people
will say, "Stop acting like a white person." Just because
they answer questions in the classroom.

HARRIS: Really?

FRANKLIN: Yeah. There's a little of that pressure, and I think
there's a strong resentment, too. The whole educational

system is rife with lies and half truths and information that's not very useful. A lot of black people feel they've been excluded from the traditional, conventional history of this country. It comes down to a male trip, really.

HARRIS: I would agree that it's true more for the brothers than the sisters. You see the class clowns being rewarded in school. But at the college level, they can't excel. You may see a lot of brothers at the beginning of the term, but they've disappeared by the end. The ratio of black female graduates to male is something like four to one.

FRANKLIN: It's a manifold thing. There are a lot of reasons for it. One of the reasons is that, oftentimes, there's a pressure on young men to get out and get a job earlier. I especially hear it from these young dudes who want to make it yesterday. There's also the fact that men are built externally, and women are built internally. So those symbols of what we are also are indicative of psychological predispositions. If you notice children playing in a stream, little girls will be out there splashing each other and having a good time, getting their feet wet, enjoying the water. But boys have to damn it up and divert it and send it somewhere else. Boys are reaching and exploring. Women have a tendency to be more accepting. Their whole trip seems to be to listen and hear the knowledge that's around them. They're wiser than us because of that, because they stop and listen. We're out of balance, however. Man has a tendency to want to forge forward, and that balance between gaining wisdom and forging forward is a very strong thing. But we're chauvinistic. The whole society is. The whole western civilization has been. Since Judaism, really. I mean, everything has become more patriarchal since those indigenous religions of Africa stopped being prominent.

HARRIS: Weren't those religions matriarchal?

FRANKLIN: Yeah, or androgynous. So, you have brothers who are in school with the male trait working. They don't want to hear a whole lot that doesn't necessarily deal with them. I think that young white males don't have that problem, because it all glorifies them. The whole educational system is for them. The television symbolism, all of that stuff, the mythology that we see and all of the basic input that we get from this society fosters them a lot more than it does black people. Because if you are creative, you are going to create your own stories. That's just the way it is. I don't know that it is necessarily racist.

HARRIS: Well, thank you for taking us from the existential and bringing it into an urban-contemporary context, because that's right on. But my take on racism today, from the point of view of a young black man who's getting older, thank God, is that I see it more as economics. If I'm applying for the same job that some producer could give to his white fraternity brothers, then why not? The economic ramifications of that are incredible.

FRANKLIN: That's right, and you would do the same.

HARRIS: Probably. If a brother could do the job.

FRANKLIN: I've been under criticism for not following that principle.

HARRIS: In what way?

FRANKLIN: For hiring white people at different times for jobs that I have canvassed and tried to get black people for. I haven't found qualified people, so I'm hiring white folk.

HARRIS: It's important first and foremost to get the job done.

FRANKLIN: I think so, too. On *Devil in a Blue Dress*, it was a multi-ethnic experience. My cinematographer was Japanese, my operator was Japanese, my first AC was a brother, second AC was a white woman, my producer was a white woman, my first AD was white woman, my prop master was a brother. My wardrobe mistress was a sister. My casting director was a black woman. My location manager was a black man. We had an array of different kinds of folks on the show.

HARRIS: A rainbow coalition.

FRANKLIN: Totally, and there were black people who were pissed at me for hiring the first AD that I hired. I was glad that I got this lady. I would work with her every time I could—she was wonderful. There were a couple of brothers I wanted who were busy because they're always in demand.

HARRIS: A good AD can make the work move like a hot knife through butter.

FRANKLIN: Exactly. They also represent the signature of the show in some sense, because they are the ones who communicate with the crew, with extras, cast, etc.: all of the cats whom you deal with on a daily basis. They communicate your desires to them and organize them within your formation.

HARRIS: The days of the director shouting through the megaphone are long over.

FRANKLIN: Thank God. She was great. I'd go in places and they figured that she was directing. I loved it. I'd sit back and do what I had to do.

HARRIS: That leaves you to set up the shots at hand and get the performances that you need. The rest of the moviemaking machine is incredible. How many people were on your crew?

FRANKLIN: I couldn't tell you. It was a good-sized crew. The art department alone was huge. The art department must have been twenty people or more.

HARRIS: I just worked as a PA on a film entitled *The Truth About Cats & Dogs* over at Fox and the caterer fed over 100 lunches every day. Cast and crew.

FRANKLIN: We must have served that, when you break it down like that, teamsters and all.

HARRIS: How long have you been directing? Was *One False Move* your first picture?

FRANKLIN: No. I directed some [Roger] Corman films, three of them.

HARRIS: Really? You came up through the Corman school?

FRANKLIN: I have no shame. [Laughter]

HARRIS: We laugh because he's machining those bad boys out. But the thing is that Roger Corman will hire young directors and see what they can do. And you will get a limited, limited budget, but it's a budget. And you will be able to learn your craft.

FRANKLIN: Yes, he will. You know, what he does most importantly for a young director is demystify the process. It ain't no big deal.

HARRIS: Isn't that Spike's mission as well?

FRANKLIN: I don't know. Did he say that?

HARRIS: At some point he did.

FRANKLIN: It's a good mission, if that is his mission. That's one of the major things that separates us from a lot of successes that we could have, business-wise and otherwise. You go into a little liquor store, you see the Korean grocer, and he's got his little boy behind the register with him. That child has grown up around commerce, he sees himself as someone who's a capitalist, on the selling end of the relationship early on.

HARRIS: From counting change to loading eggs into the cooler.

FRANKLIN: Not only is that an exception in reference to the black American, it is an exception in reference to white Americans as well. We're all in the United States, so we all live in a capitalistic society. Still, we seem to somehow prefer the good job over the small business. People would much rather dress up in a suit, have business cards, a little expense account, and drive back and forth to work in a flashy car, maybe pulling down seventy-five a year, than work hard, wear work clothes, get their hands dirty for their own business that may net them one hundred fifty or two a year, where they're the boss.

HARRIS: Do you think that's because of the twenty-four/ seven, three-sixty-five nature of owning your own small business?

FRANKLIN: I think it's that, but I also think that we live in a society that puts a high premium on perception and image. We live in a society that heavily values image. The advertising industry spends billions of dollars a year to try to make you dissatisfied with everything you have, so you'll continue to be a consumer and always want more, when what you have is perfectly cool. Your car may be two years old, but you need a new car when, mechanically, it's sound. You have a house, the furniture is cool, maybe five or six years old, but you have to have new furniture. Clothes every year, a change in fashion, even though the clothes still fit you. That's strictly a psychological trip. That's what makes the society go around—commerce. Any muscle that you exercise becomes stronger, and if you exercise a muscle that makes you reach out instead of reaching in, then that's where you're going to go. We're much more an externally oriented society than we are an internally oriented society, I think.

HARRIS: I'd agree. How does that psyche manifest itself in the work ethic of the kids you see today?

FRANKLIN: The work ethic, or the work?

HARRIS: Both.

FRANKLIN: One is more result-oriented than process-oriented, or purpose-oriented. Within that whole result there is the need to cut corners, to not fully go the distance with things, to not fully mine all of the emotions, to go with the flashy elements—the things that will get the quick response.

HARRIS: Perhaps to stop writing the script at the third draft instead of doing another painful draft?

FRANKLIN: I don't think so much in terms of the work you put into the work as much as the intent of the work itself. What I am saying is that people don't aspire to anything that is designed to appeal beyond a first showing.

HARRIS: Aspiring to the mediocre?

FRANKLIN: Yeah, aspiring to the current appetite of the time, without thinking about anything universal, or in terms of anything that will resonate on any kind of an extended basis.

HARRIS: Do you see that in the films of the new black pack?

FRANKLIN: I see that in most American films. Especially with young people. I'm actually surprised by someone like John Singleton.

HARRIS: In what way?

FRANKLIN: In something like *Boyz N the Hood*, he strived for some principles. He went down pretty deep in some ways with what he was trying to do. I feel the same way about the Hughes brothers. A lot of people knock that movie *Menace II Society*.

HARRIS: I loved it.

FRANKLIN: I did, too. A lot of people had problems with it because it was an inner-city piece. So what? It raised questions about morality and living in an environment where morality gets muddled or muddied by necessity.

HARRIS: Are we speaking to the same issue of deviating to a life of crime as a means of reaching desires?

FRANKLIN: It goes even deeper. Oftentimes, young men find themselves in a situation where they have to respond, just in order to defend themselves.

HARRIS: I don't follow you.

FRANKLIN: There's a thing in prison known as moral self-defense. I go to prison, you're already there. You know the ropes. The first day, I've got my little issued pack of cigarettes. You say, "Can I borrow a cigarette?" I loan it to you. A little later in the evening, I look up and you've got a cigarette, another one of mine. You didn't ask me this time. The next morning, you want to use my shoes, so you're wearing them. Later on that evening, you've got my shirt. A few days later, I wake up in the middle of the night and you're on me. I don't do anything. A couple of days later you say, "Go down the hall and take care of him." In prison, because you live in society that's so compressed, you cannot let it get that far. Because there are no real fights in prison. You don't John Wayne somebody: they hit you, you hit them back and do that shit. You've got to live with that person, or with these people, for years. So whatever you do has to be decisive, and you have to do it in such a way that nobody knows you did it and you can get away with it, so that you don't suffer repercussions. Otherwise, you may have to deal with people who are supporting your enemy. So, you have to make a determination to be aggressive when you peep the shit, before it ever really happens. And according to Jack Henry Abbott's *In the Belly of the Beast*, the first time you decide to kill somebody for doing that, it has to be capital, in has to be the ultimate act. It can't be nothing half-assed, because he's going to be living with your ass. You've got to do it the first time he takes a cigarette.

HARRIS: He is dead.

FRANKLIN: Yeah. It is the same thing in a diluted sense for some of these kids on the streets. To live in certain neighborhoods, you have to put up a certain kind of persona in order to keep people from fucking with you. Like Cabrini Green, for instance. I was back there doing some research. Certain brothers in the family would have to go out and sacrifice themselves, become part of the gang, to protect the rest of the family. See, there was some representation. You dig what I'm saying?

HARRIS: I hear you.

FRANKLIN: That's what I'm talking about. I don't know how many kids have gotten into situations where they're carrying guns to school because they're scared, because other people have guns, and because people are threatening them. The whole little macho dance that these kid have gotten into now has gotten so strong.

HARRIS: It's gotten lethal. It used to be an ass-kicking or a straight razor, maybe a bicycle chain. Now it's guns.

FRANKLIN: It's gotten complicated.

HARRIS: Do you really think that Tyger really covered that dynamic in *Menace*?

FRANKLIN: I felt a hint of a sense of being trapped, because he kept talking about "getting out." You got the sense that he was a product of his environment, that he was aware of what was happening to him. The character played by Larenz Tate didn't seem to be aware. He didn't seem to give a shit. He was totally involved in it. He seemed to have a consciousness that suggests that he had been reared a certain way by his environment, not necessarily by his parents. One of the things they did show was neglectful parents, which is another thing that has become a real problem in the black community nowadays. We've been getting a lot of flak about black men not being in the family. Now, there ain't nobody there. Grandmother is raising the kids. In fact, that's been going on a while.

HARRIS: It's always been going on.

FRANKLIN: We've just caught a whole lot of crap. Some of it deservedly, some of it bullshit.

HARRIS: I think most of it is bullshit. This may be a weak analogy, but when it came time to approach the brothers for this project, I didn't have to ask twice for brothers to come on the record. The response was immediate and overwhelming. If there was no sense of responsibility, or a feeling of mentorism, I would have had real problems putting this book together. Now, when young brothers and sisters read this, they can see that this life is viable. If the pen is mightier than the sword, a word processor can do more than an AK-47.

FRANKLIN: I just look at my life. I've always had trouble trying to identify with the stereotypes of black men. Maybe because my old man, who did not live for me to see, was an exception. A lot of men who I saw when I was grow-ing up were in the home. Southern brothers from Texas. That's where my family's from.

HARRIS: Really? My people come from Houston.

FRANKLIN: We're from a little old town. You wouldn't know it—Austine—in Sherman, Texas, which is up about sixty miles from Fort Worth, which is about fifty miles from Dallas. Them folk were regular family folk. I think that black people have grown accustomed to going to the movies and watching television and not expecting to see anything up there that resembles them. Even black folks like Jimmy Walker in *Good Times*. I never knew anybody like that, ever, in life.

HARRIS: Marlon Riggs did a documentary called *Color Adjustment*. In it, he explored the origins of some of stereotypes of black people in media images. By using slow-motion clips of J.J. and archival footage, he drew a parallel between the J.J. character and some of the coons from the minstrel shows from the days of reconstruction. It was a disturbing visual analogy.

FRANKLIN: It's interesting. You know, you spoke of the real issue with racism being economic. That's really always been the case. What black people need to become aware of, and realize, is that we are a conquered people. We are a people whose history was rewritten. Within the last 160 years, black people's history has been rewritten. Around 1830, you began to see the rewriting of African history in Europe, because there had been a fairly healthy relationship between Europe and Africa up until that time. You will also see it played out in Spain. The Moors had conquered Spain and there was a lot of resentment that took on racial connotations, even though that wasn't the basis of it. It was, here were foreigners who took over the country, even though they brought Europe out of the Dark Ages and into the Renaissance. Spain did not go through the Middle Ages. The Moors came into Spain around 800 and lifted them up. They did not experience what England, France, and some of the other countries went through in terms of the loss of the arts and sciences. I don't think that it is a coincidence that the Moors and the Jews were kicked out of Spain in 1492, and that was the same year that Columbus went to the New World, which we now know was not new.

HARRIS: That's a point that most modern scholars are only now conceding. It's funny how there comes a point where any thinking black man must acknowledge that almost everything we've been taught in regard to world history is, to a large degree, false. Usually, you're around college age when you do.

FRANKLIN: I did not. Part of it, for me, was because I benefited from having succeeded in college education, and being that person who was considered "the exception." It was always myself and three sisters in college prep classes. Never any other brothers.

HARRIS: Did you benefit from affirmative-action programs?

FRANKLIN: I benefited from the first affirmative-action programs they designed. I went to a program called the SOS program: the Special Opportunity Scholarship program. It was not just for black people. It was a program oriented toward getting economically disadvantaged people into college. My grades were pretty good. Most people in the program had good grades, they just didn't have any money. I benefited from that program, as did poor whites, Asians, and Latinos. Everybody has benefited from affirmative action. Dan Quayle was one of those people, incidentally. It's an emotional issue that the Republican party is using as a flash-point issue, as opposed to dealing with real issues.

JEANNE WILLIAMS

The two most-asked questions in Hollywood are "Who is your agent?" and "How do you get an agent?"

Jeanne Williams represents talent for International Creative Management, one of the most powerful agencies in Hollywood. She is one of the few African-American talent agents. Her client list reads like a virtual who's who in Hollywood. She will not give the exact number of her clients, but will say that most of them are not black, and describes her duties as more of a team effort. Jeanne recommends that other young people who are considering a career in the business give agenting some thought.

On the subject of screenwriting, she concluded, "Most of the great directors were great writers first. Spike Lee, Oliver Stone, and Coppola have amazing storytelling skills."

Jeanne Williams has been at her job long enough to give some excellent insights to the business aspects of this creative industry.

HARRIS: What drew you to becoming an agent?

WILLIAMS: I don't think that I planned on being an agent. I was an attorney, practicing law in Washington D.C., but I always wanted to work in the movie business. I thought I wanted to be a producer or a director. I was fascinated by the creative process. I had studied history of literature in college and I was much more interested in the artistic side, as opposed to the business side of it. I thought about moving out here, but being sort of a risk-averse person, I decided to be more strategic about it. I started reading about agencies, in particular, CAA. Then there were the newer agencies: Intertalent, UTA, and other smaller agencies that were coming into the forefront. The spec market was taking off, and it seemed like the role of the agent was pretty interesting. It seemed like it was at the center of things. It was an interesting liaison between the creative community and the business community. Since I've always believed that knowledge is power, I thought it wouldn't be a bad place to start off. So, I sent out résumés, and because of my background (I went to Harvard Law, which opens a lot of doors), there were a lot of people who took an immediate interest in me and asked me if I wanted to go into their training program. I didn't know what a training program was. I didn't realize that it meant you were pushing a cart in the mailroom. But I'm not afraid of a little bit of hard work, so I interviewed and I was going to go to New York, but at the last minute CAA called and offered me a job out here. So I moved and started. I was delivering packages and buying groceries at six A.M. and, for some reason, I really took to it. I thought it was fascinating. Training at a big agency is almost like being a fly on the wall—you get to see everything going on around you. There's a certain process of osmosis that takes place: You start to hear things and pick up things. I was always a voracious reader—I read trades, and newspapers, and scripts—so it was great for me. I still didn't know if I would survive, because it's pretty grueling, emotionally, but I knew early on that it was for me. My only concern was that I was too genteel for this profession. Coming out of the legal world, there is so much emphasis put on being tough, but it's a quiet kind of toughness. Lawyers were the quiet ones—you didn't brag. There wasn't this relentless self-promotion.

HARRIS: Which is pretty much its own commodity in Hollywood.

WILLIAMS: It's a huge commodity. That was the hardest thing to learn, and at the same time, the most liberating thing. I think that women are not raised to be that ruthlessly aggressive about their own agenda.

HARRIS: How many clients do you represent?

WILLIAMS: It's hard to say, because I work in a lot of different areas. I think that's true of most agents. I started as a literary agent—my roots are in representing writers. I also represent directors and production companies because I've become very involved in packaging projects, which I love doing. Unfortunately, it's almost the only way to get anything sold. I'm always nervous about saying how many clients I have, because it sounds like it's more than it really is. At ICM, we don't believe in having just a single agent involved in a client's life. The business is far too complex and sophisticated for that.

HARRIS: So, it's more of a team approach?

WILLIAMS: It's a team approach. I don't feel that I can adequately represent a client, being the sole person in their life. There are too many projects. And the distinctions blur between television and features and low-budget features and cable. One person can't possibly know everything that's happening, so it's nice to assemble a team: somebody in television, somebody in features, somebody in interactive. Depending on what the client's interests are, we try to have at least two, sometimes more, people whom he or she can access for information.

HARRIS: I want to ask a seemingly naive question. Why do I need an agent? Why can't I just do everything for myself?

WILLIAMS: There are a lot of reasons for that. A big reason is that the studios and producers are very concerned about liability. I'll give you and example. Say you submit your script to any big producer or studio. They read it, they say they don't really like your script, and they return it to you. Say six months later someone pitches them an idea very similar to what you did, but not based on your project, and they buy that project and develop it. There's nothing to protect them from you suing them, unless there's an agent who is your representative, who is franchised by the state, who has the authority to represent your interests, who has a fiduciary duty to you as a writer, serving as an intermediary and protecting them from any potential liability. It's sort of a way for them to hedge their bets on you. Agents also serve as a screening process. If the agent has decided to represent you, you have to be a certain caliber of writer. The assumption is if you've found somebody who believes in you and is going to be out there selling you, then someone has given you the stamp of approval. You have to realize that there is so much material. You've just been siting in my office, you see the quantity of things that come across my desk. You have to find some way of establishing some boundaries or else you'll drown.

HARRIS: How do you personally choose your clients?

WILLIAMS: I feel like I am a very picky agent. I read everything. It's exhausting and it takes a lot of time, but I think my clients are very happy with me because they know that I will read every draft of their script, and I will give them notes. I love material—that's what drew me to this business and that will always be where I come from. So, for me, it's all on the page. I don't care what your personality is like, although it certainly helps to have a great personality. I look for an interesting voice. I don't necessarily like regurgitated movies that I've seen a million times. I like someone who's not afraid to take certain creative risks. I like people who are truly committed to their craft, that take writing very seriously, and are constantly trying to improve their writing. I like writers who have at least done enough research that they are presenting me the script in the proper format, with the proper page length.

HARRIS: You don't still find work like that, do you?

WILLIAMS: You find that a lot of people submit material that's not in acceptable form. It's shocking.

HARRIS: Doesn't that hamper the read?

WILLIAMS: Quite honestly, if someone sends me a script that's 200 pages long, I won't even read it, because no studio's going to read it. Unless you're Kevin Costner or Mel Gibson, who can get a three-hour movie made, no producer, executive, or agent is going to read a 200-page screenplay. It's got to be between 100 and 120 pages. I'm not going to read a seventy-page script, either. I don't care how brilliant it is, it's just not there. Typos? Fundamental things really make a difference. It shows whether you're someone who is taking this very seriously.

HARRIS: Everything counts.

WILLIAMS: Yes. I like writers who are thoughtful. I love great characters. I love action. I have a real broad range of tastes. There's no genre of script that you can send me that I wouldn't like. There are some areas that I think I have better gut instincts with. For example, I think that I am terrible with comedy. I think very little is funny. There are things that go on to sell for a tremendous amount of money that I would have passed on because they seemed too silly or too broad to me, but nevertheless they sell. Obviously, sometimes those scripts need a major piece of casting in order to make them work. But on a gut level, I love action, I love dramatic pieces. I don't respond well to pieces that are too precious, really sentimental, sweet family pieces. I like a little bit of edge. I like crime, I like murder, I like mayhem, all that kind of stuff.

HARRIS: How does someone get read by an agent?

WILLIAMS: A lot of times, someone will call me or send me a letter asking if they can submit material. They will often give me a synopsis of their script. If that seems interesting, often I will read the script. Normally, that's not how I get clients. There are two ways we normally get clients. One is by recommendation. Recommendations mean a lot. You can be recommended by another writer who's represented here or by an executive out there in the community. Someone who's read you and likes you. That means so much. Once again, it's that screening process. Somebody sees something in your work, and because I respect their judgment, I am willing to give you a chance. Sometimes, I will go to a play, love the play, and call the writer and ask him if he wants to get into the movie business or into television. It all goes back to responding on a real gut level to the work. There are a lot of talented writers who will send me their material and I'll say, "It's well-written, but I can't represent you, because I don't have a passion for what you do. I don't get it. I don't feel strongly enough about it. I don't think that I can sell you." It may hurt the writer's feelings, but it is truly in the writer's best interest to be with an agent who loves their work, who really believes in them. An agent who's going to be not just a representative, but an advocate, who's going to go out there and fight as much as they would. It's interesting, there are certain clients whom I am very loyal to. They may send me something and I'll believe in it and I will send it out and it may not get the reaction that I think it deserves. I will argue with executives and say, "You know, you missed it. This is what this piece is really about." I will argue for the writer and explain the writer's work to an executive. I can only do that if I understand the writer's work. Or I will encourage the executive. I'll say, "Sit down with this writer and you will get a better sense of their work by meeting them." Whatever it takes to help make a personal connection. This is a business about relationships, it truly is. It's all about whether I connect with you in terms of your writing, whether an executive connects with you in a meeting. It's that personal connection.

HARRIS: What about talent?

WILLIAMS: Talent I do believe wins out. If you're talented, if you hang in there, eventually you will find that person who is passionate about your work. Talent always rises to the surface, it's too rare.

HARRIS: Most of the people who will read this will probably be diffused around the country. Do you recommend that writers come to New York or Los Angeles?

WILLIAMS: Well, it depends on what you want to do. If you're interested in the television business, you need to be in L.A. because that's where the shows are. Once in a while, they will staff out of New York, but it's mostly in Los Angeles. You need to be here, meeting the executive producers who run these shows, going to tapings. You need to be out and about and having a sense of what's going on out here. If you're interested in theater, obviously on a certain level, you would need to be in New York. But be where you are. If you're in Baltimore, pursue every opportunity there. If the work you're doing is good, we will hear about it. We track these things. They're all reviewed in the trades. If something is exceptional, an agent will know about it, and the next thing you know, someone will be flying out to Baltimore to meet with you. I discourage people from giving up everything and coming out here when they have a thriving creative base. If you're in television, you have to do that. If you're in features, it depends. If you're in a small town and you shoot a short film, it could do just as much for you if not more than being out here with every Tom, Dick, and Harry who's got a screenplay in their chest of drawers. You would do just as well to stay where you are, make an interesting short film, and submit it to the festivals and get attention that way. You do not have to be in L.A. You really don't. If you look at a lot of these people who have succeeded in this business, they weren't in L.A. when they were noticed. They came to L.A. eventually, but when they got their first bit of attention they were somewhere else.

HARRIS: I read somewhere that the average budget on a feature film is around thirty million dollars now.

WILLIAMS: I would say between twenty-five and thirty-five million.

HARRIS: How does that affect black projects?

WILLIAMS: I think that it really makes things difficult for black projects. I make distinctions between television and the film world, because different rules apply. When a movie costs that much, I think that there are very few black projects that are going to make that kind of money back. When you look at the budget, there is the perception that black films aren't going to have any foreign revenues, so there's no real afterlife after the domestic box office. That's the perception. It may not be the reality, but I've heard it used so many times by executives as an excuse for not financing black projects.

HARRIS: When I was in Paris last year, there were lines around the block for *Menace II Society*.

WILLIAMS: That was *Menace II Society*. Certain types of black films will do fairly well. There's a difference between having a cult following and making real overseas dollars. Black projects and black culture has always been something of interest in Europe, but whether those movies make a tremendous amount of money is another thing. A Sylvester Stallone movie, while it is not great art, has a wide base of appeal overseas.

HARRIS: Anyone can understand explosions and car chases.

WILLIAMS: Exactly. They get it. *New Jack City* and *Boyz N the Hood* have probably done the best overseas. They're pretty much action movies that people can relate to in that way. Take *Menace II Society*. While the Hughes brothers are terrifically talented, and I would imagine that the critical community in France would recognize their achievement, do you think that the average French citizen will go out and see that movie? I don't know. All of the numbers seem to indicate that they wouldn't. You think that there's some conspiracy?

HARRIS: No, I have no conspiracy theories.

WILLIAMS: I've heard theories that these movies are actually making more money than is being reported. I think that kind of thinking destroys the spirit. I don't believe in conspiracy theories, because you can't prove them.

HARRIS: That's their beauty.

WILLIAMS: I think that if you get wrapped up in that kind of thinking, it's disempowering, and it will prevent you from doing anything.

HARRIS: I believe they foster cynicism, which is probably the flip side of romantic idealism. In light of everything, I still have a cautious optimism about Hollywood.

WILLIAMS: I would agree with you. I think it's a great time for black filmmakers. Listen, it's still tough, but I think it's better than it's ever been. It truly is. If an African-American writer sends me a script that I believe in, I can call any studio in town, any executive, any production company and say, "I've got a terrific project, read this person." And you know what? They will read them more quickly than the average white writer. They really will. There's a tremendous openness. Of course, a lot of these things don't get made, and we need more black stars who are perceived as being able to open a movie.

HARRIS: Explain "open" to the readers.

WILLIAMS: I'll tell you what it means to me. An actor who can "open" a movie is a star who, because of their stature in the community and their ability to get bodies into the seats, can ensure that any movie they're in is going to make back its money. With white actors, it's people like Tom Cruise and Tom Hanks and Jim Carey. In the African-American community, it's people like Whoopi Goldberg and Denzel Washington. They are stars, and they make tens of millions of dollars because people will go see their movies without really knowing what the movie is about.

HARRIS: Let's talk about packaging. How important is it to bring more than one creative element to a project to make it more attractive to a studio? How often does it happen?

WILLIAMS: It happens fairly often. The idea of packaging isn't necessarily more than one element, it's whatever it takes to make sure that the movie is going to get made. Sometimes it's just a star. There are some movies that you don't need to package with anything else other than the sincere interest of a major movie star. For other projects, because they're difficult or controversial, you may need to add more than one element. Sometimes a star will only get you part of the way there. Sometimes you need a director to commit. Sometimes you need a couple of stars and a director. Packaging usually happens when the project is a little more difficult. If something is a high-concept picture, you may not need a star, because it's so strong conceptually that you will get an actor to do it. The studios tend to make big comedies and big action pictures, so if something is a drama, you may have to package it to make it more appealing. I have tended to package something if it's a little unusual or a little more special. For a smaller, more unique picture, or something more artistic, you're going to need an actor to help the picture raise money.

HARRIS: Do you enjoy packaging a picture, or would you rather not have to?

WILLIAMS: I like it. It's like putting together the pieces of a puzzle. It's always nice to have a slam dunk—a piece that is so high-concept that people are going to want it right away. But there is a certain kind of joy of getting a project to an actor who read it and just responded knowing that it's not set up. Then maybe you'll find another star and maybe a director. It's difficult, but there's a certain pleasure, especially if it's a really good piece of material that deserves to be made.

HARRIS: I've been told that you encourage your black clients not to limit themselves and to write for white shows.

WILLIAMS: It's a complicated issue. In the television business, there is still a fair amount of racism. That's just the reality. I have been in many meetings at studios, with television production companies and executive producers, and the second they find out that a writer is black, they don't take them seriously for their show if their show is not an African-American show.

HARRIS: Really?

WILLIAMS: Absolutely. I can honestly tell you, and I don't think that I am saying anything out of school, that you will find confirmation from anyone in town. For certain shows that are perceived as being sophisticated white shows, be it *Seinfeld,* or *Mad About You,* they're not going to respond to a *Roc* spec. They are not going to respond to a *Hangin' with Mr. Cooper* or a *Martin.* Part of that is because those shows don't have the same sensibility. But another part of it is because people are very narrow-minded—they don't think that black writers can write their shows. It is certainly true that most black writers write on black shows. I don't think that it's just because they want to write on those shows. I think it's because it's easier to lump them into that category. I've heard it. I've fought for too many writers. I've stood on that soap box and said, "This person is a very talented writer and they would be right for that show. Yes, they're black. Yes, their samples are for black shows, but read them—their stuff is really good." And I've been told, "You know what, I don't think that they have the right sensibility." It will be phrased in a way that's polite, but at the end of the day, unless you have that *Seinfeld* spec, unless you have that *Larry Sanders* spec, it's going to be very hard for you to get in those doors. I'm just giving you the cold, hard realities. You have got to have samples that reflect the tone of their show. I'm not saying that it's exclusively about race, but a lot of times, black shows are not taken as seriously. So it's not about telling people to write white for approval, it's about giving you as many options as you can possibly have. If you don't have any desire to write on one of those shows, then write whatever you want to write. I'm just telling you the realities of the business. I think that sometimes people get angry with agents because they don't want to hear the truth. Our business is about being rejected. People are very honest about a piece of material. People will call me and say, "I hated this, this is a piece of shit!" Now when I talk to my writer, I don't repeat that to the writer, but I will tell him that they didn't like his work, they didn't respond to it, they didn't feel that he did X, Y, and Z. I try to be constructive about it. But I think that I would be doing a disservice to the writer if I didn't give them the realities of the business. You need to know what's really going on. Hopefully I addressed that particular situation.

HARRIS: I think you did.

WILLIAMS: I tell people to write whatever they want to write. The television example is sort of a unique example. If you're talking about features, you can write whatever you want to write. The rules for features are a lot more fluid. You can write black projects as the day is long that may or may not get done. In television, the process is much more collaborative. You are there with a team of people whom you work with day in and day out. As a result, a certain kind of conformity is expected. You can be much more of an individual in the feature world. The other reason I tell a writer to write whatever they want is because I have some African-American clients who don't want to be limited to writing black projects. If there's a terrific book out there, a fabulous project set up at a studio, they don't want to be perceived as only the black writer. They want to have the option of writing whatever they want. And they want me to go out there and say, "Read this person. They are the right person for this project. It may be about a forty-year-old white woman who lives in Texas, but this writer is the perfect person for this job. She knows how to tell this story." So it's not that I tell people to write white or black, you have to write to your experience.

HARRIS: How much work is out there for a new writer? Isn't television pretty much closed to new writers?

WILLIAMS: I actually think that television is a great place for new writers. I think that there are opportunities everywhere. It's not closed. You need to write a sample, meaning you would write a sample for whatever show you like, say *Friends* or *Martin* or whatever. I would then expose that script to executive producers, the networks, and production companies that produce those shows. You try to find fans and supporters who will think about you for episodes and put you on staff during staffing season. There are certainly opportunities. If you're funny, if you've got a great script, people will read you.

HARRIS: Most people who approach you for representation presumably want to work in features.

WILLIAMS: It depends. Some people come to me wanting to work only in television. I represent plenty of television writers. I encourage my writers to be flexible. I represent writers who work in television and in features. When times are lean in one area, you've got the other area to fall back on.

HARRIS: The realities of getting a feature made are pretty daunting.

WILLIAMS: Exactly. And a lot of feature writers that come to work in television love it. Whether it's a television movie or a cable project, you write it and six weeks later it's being shot. It gives them such a feeling of elation. They love that. They have a sense of control. Television is a writer's medium. The features world is a director's medium. Since the writer is God in television, it's not a bad place to be. The quality of TV is growing in leaps and bounds.

HARRIS: Do you try to steer certain writers in that direction?

WILLIAMS: No. It's all about what you want to do. I try to respect what people want to do, and all I can do is make sure they're prepared. If you want to work in television, it's my job to prepare you. You have to know what kind of samples you need and what you need to do. If you want to work in features, you've got to write a spec. That's what will open doors for you. I don't try to guide anyone one way or another. I see where their interest is and make them aware of opportunities wherever they may be. But my biggest job is to prepare them. I try to prepare them for meetings so that they will know who they're meeting with and why and how to handle that situation.

HARRIS: Is one's demeanor in a meeting important?

WILLIAMS: I don't think that there's a particular demeanor that's appropriate or not appropriate. People respond to honesty and you being who you are. I have one client who's a madwoman. She's very funny and very confrontational. She loves to stir it up. She will come in and say the most outrageous things. But you know what? She's being who she is, and people love her for it. You can't deny the force of someone's personality. I would never dream of telling her to tone it down or to not say what she thinks, because that's not who she is. That's what works. Now, I know that there are certain personality types who are going to connect better. Often, I will tell a client if the producer is quiet or hard to read or doesn't give a lot of feedback. Just that little bit of information will put them more at ease. I don't believe in general meetings just to sit and talk about where you're from and how many kids are in your family. It's a waste of time. The producers don't like those meetings, and the writers hate them as well. If you have ideas, save them up. Keep a list of books that you have always been passionate about, or movies that you have loved and would like to see re-made, so that when you go into that meeting, you've got something concrete to talk about. Often, people find that they have tremendously similar likes and dislikes. Often, projects develop full-blown from that kind of encounter.

HARRIS: As an agent, you've got your finger on the pulse of Hollywood, as it were. What's hot right now in black cinema? What types of films are we going to see in the future?

WILLIAMS: I don't know if there are any trends per se. I haven't noticed any particular genre that I'm seeing more now than before. The bulk of black projects are still action-themed pieces. The gritty, urban, real pieces. The *Boyz N the Hood* movies, I call them. The young black male coming-of-age stories. Sometimes they'll put a twist in them by making them female. You also see a lot of black historical material. There's a wealth of black history that still hasn't been tapped. There is a trend lately toward a lot of black romantic comedies. People trying to find the black *Sleepless in Seattle*, finding something that reflects the experience of twenty-something, sophisticated, black urban people. I think there's also a real push to find movies that try to capture the black middle-class experience, which a lot of people feel that we haven't seen in movies yet. People want to show the diversity of the black experience, and that it is not a monolithic experience, that not everything that happens to one black person happens to us all. We all have very rich histories and come from different parts of the country. I think that there's a real attempt to expand the definition of what a black movie is. That's exciting. I think those are all good things.

HARRIS: Do you think there's a need for writers to go to film school?

WILLIAMS: I think it depends on where you are in your life when you decide to do this as a career. Certainly there was a time when there was a feeding frenzy over these

film-school graduates. But I think that with the proliferation of film schools around the country now it's harder to
get attention out of film school. I know tons of people
who graduated from film schools, and nothing has really
happened for them. They work in the business, but they're
not doing what they want to do, they're not filmmakers. I
think that if you go to film school, you should take full
advantage of it. Get your stuff out there, be hustling, be
aggressive. Establish contacts, take advantage of everything that school has to offer. Because once you're out,
it's much harder to do. Try to get as much attention as
you possibly can. Now, you don't have to go to film school.
There are plenty of people who get together with friends,
scrape together some money and make a film. Though
often, technically, the work from the people coming out
of film school is better, because they have the training
and techniques. They know how to make a movie. It's a
little less raw, a little more polished, a bit more Holly-
wood-looking, something the people in Hollywood can
relate to because it looks like the movies that they see all
the time. But if you have a fresh, interesting vision, if it's
good, you will get attention. People will take a look at it.
Now there are so many outlets. The Black Filmmakers
Foundation always has screenings of all sorts of films.
The key is to network, establish relationships, get anybody and everybody to look at your work. Send it to anyone who is vaguely connected, who may have an idea or
give you some input, or who may know somebody who
knows somebody. Don't worry about anybody stealing
your ideas.

HARRIS: That doesn't really happen much, does it?

WILLIAMS: It doesn't really happen. It's very funny; I always have to reassure people. People are terrified of that.
They somehow think that they are going to write something, send it out, and then see their movie right there on
the screen, word for word, stolen from them. It really
doesn't happen like that. Once in a while, sure, things

have happened, but I can't think of a time that that's happened to anyone I've known.

HARRIS: Shouldn't the work be registered with the Guild as some measure of protection?

WILLIAMS: Yes, it should. It costs about ten bucks—it's worth it, do it, protect yourself. Copyright it if you want to.

HARRIS: You, of course, require submission release forms. Explain that.

WILLIAMS: Yes, we do. Submission release forms absolve the agency of any liability and basically say that you have given us permission to read your work, and that we are not using this for any commercial purposes, that we are not going to exploit it without your permission. It just protects us: it's a standard form used by basically every agency. Most people sign them, we take a look at their scripts, and we proceed with them if we're interested. But if someone wants to read your work, let them read it.

HARRIS: I know that plenty of black-themed scripts have sold on spec, but have you seen any that have gone to auction and had bidding wars?

WILLIAMS: Not that I'm aware of. I think black cinema is very filmmaker-driven, very director-driven. If Spike Lee wants to make it, if the Hudlin brothers or John Singleton or Mario Van Peebles want to make it, then it's more than likely going to be made. But I haven't seen too many black-themed specs optioned. Often, there's a spec that was written white, but by the time they cast it, they put a black actor in. Something like *Virtuosity*. That wasn't written for a black man, but Denzel Washington has transcended all of those boundaries. He wanted to do it, and they wanted him to do it. Sure, specs have sold, but are they getting a million dollars? I'm not aware of it happening at that level.

HARRIS: Let's talk about money. What ballpark are feature specs going for now?

WILLIAMS: There's a huge range. Often, the numbers in the papers are completely inflated. A lot of times, the trades will say that the script sold for a "six-figure sum." Which is a fine spec. Is it a huge spec? No. Was there a big bidding war on it? Probably not, because the numbers probably would have been driven up. But it gave a writer a chance and it got the writer some money, which is a good thing.

HARRIS: A spec that sells for a hundred thousand dollars doesn't guarantee a career—it's simply a break.

WILLIAMS: It's a break. It could open doors. Hopefully, that writer is still going to be attached to do rewrites on it. And the heat associated with the sale of that spec will get that writer a lot of meetings that may turn into other assignments. So, it's a good thing.

HARRIS: Invariably, it seems, a writer will be rewritten. How do they usually react?

WILLIAMS: It's a painful process. Being rewritten is probably the most painful and difficult thing for a writer to go through. As their agent, going through that process with them is really hard.

HARRIS: The usual deal a writer gets includes a couple of revisions.

WILLIAMS: They will give them a couple of steps, usually a revision and a polish. Of course, the higher your stature as a writer, the greater the guaranteed amount of money, and the fewer writing steps you'll have to do. The problem with the business is that, no matter how great you are, no matter how talented you are, it's very likely that you are going to be rewritten. I tell my clients to get ready for it. It is not personal. It does not mean that you aren't a good writer, that you aren't talented. People are rewritten for all sorts of reasons. Sometimes the person just isn't capturing what they were looking for. Often, the studio changes their mind about what they want, or there's some other element that's brought in that alters it, and they need a different type of writer. Maybe they want somebody who has a particular style, who's going to give it a different spin for a star that might be attached. No matter how talented you are, being rewritten is part of the process. It's painful when you've done a lot of work and you've given your heart and soul and they come in and say, "Well, this just didn't work out." It's very easy for them to say that and very hard for a writer to go through that experience, then see someone else come in and rip apart everything you've done and start over. It is especially painful when you are the original writer on something and another writing team comes in and changes it so much that you don't even get screen credit.

HARRIS: Not even in arbitration?

WILLIAMS: This particular instance happened to a client of mine on a very high-profile project. It went into arbitration and my client lost. That's very unusual, because traditionally it was very difficult for the original writer not to get some type of credit. If you were the first writer, you had a very good shot of at least getting a co-writing credit. This is changing now, because the people who are rewriting are coming in and completely starting over and making a tremendous amount of changes, and they lobbied to make sure that they were getting credit for their contribution. So there's a constant battle to find out what's fair. I encourage every client to arbitrate. This is what will happen. Say you write the project and you're replaced by another writer. The project moves ahead and is green-lit by the studio. The studio goes ahead and shoots the script, and when it's time to determine credit, they submit all the versions of the draft to the Guild, and they come up with a proposed writing credit. The Guild looks at everyone's work and makes a determination. Now it's up to the writer whether they want to challenge the studio's proposed writing credit. Some writers feel like they shouldn't challenge the studio, for fear of repercussions. My feeling is, always arbitrate.

HARRIS: It's your legacy.

WILLIAMS: Absolutely. And not just that, but usually the way the deals are structured, if the film is produced, the writer is going to get some kind of writing bonus. If you don't fight for your credit, you're not going to see that money. If you've done the work, you should get every penny you're entitled to. That's an example of what an agent may have to do for a client. Agents may have to be aggressive and push the client to do something that the client may not want to do. My feeling is that it's my job to be the bad guy, to be the tough guy, to fight for you. I don't care if people don't like me. I'm the one who should take a lot of the heat and hostility, instead of it being directed at you. Let the producers and the studio get angry with me.

HARRIS: Fair enough. Let's talk about the development process. How are stories usually developed at the studios?

WILLIAMS: What it usually means is that a script will be optioned for a small amount of money. Even big spec scripts get developed. But usually when you talk about development, we mean either something that's in another form—for example, a play or a book that will be adapted for the screen. Or it could mean a script that may not sell for a tremendous amount of money, but they see promise in it, and they will option it for a relatively small amount of money and work with the writer to try to refine and develop it into something that has some viability, that can get a green light and a production order.

HARRIS: How often do you see that?

WILLIAMS: Most of the market is development. You hear about the big spec projects, but that's not most of what gets made out there. The bulk of what gets developed are plays, or books, or interesting articles, or interesting screenplays that may be flawed, but show a lot of promise. And most black projects come up through development. An August Wilson or Toni Morrison project, things like that.

HARRIS: Do you see many films that come out of pitch meetings, or has that gone the way of disco?

WILLIAMS: Only occasionally. Some writers just have the knack for that and know how to do it. But that's a tough way to go. People just aren't buying pitches. Most times, there's just not enough there. If the pitch is really that good, I always encourage the writer to go off and spec it. At least you'll have something as an asset. I always tell a client that even if you don't sell a big spec, any script is an asset. It has value. You may not be able to get it set up now, but maybe a couple of scripts down the road, after you've improved your craft, maybe written a couple of other things, somebody will come back and want to buy the very first thing you wrote. That happens all the time. Everything is an asset, and the market changes. One year they want comedies, the next year drama. You just have to wait. It's a very cyclical business.

HARRIS: Do you have any final words of advice?

WILLIAMS: I like what you said about cautious optimism. I would agree with that. I think that's the best way to be. I came into this business with no contacts. I don't come from a family in the business. Certainly, those things may open doors, but they don't keep you here. Perseverance, talent, and cautious optimism may be the keys to sustaining a career in this business.